Fundamentals of International Business Management

Fundamentals of International Business Management

Mitlesh Dhumna

CYBER TECH PUBLICATIONS
4264/3, Ansari Road, Daryaganj, New Delhi-110002 (India)
Ph.: 011-23244078, 011-43559448 Fax: 011-23280028
E-Mail: cyberpublicationsdelhi@yahoo.com
Website: www.cybertechpublications.com

FUNDAMENTALS OF INTERNATIONAL BUSINESS MANAGEMENT

Mitlesh Dhunna

First Edition 2011

Published by :

G.S. Rawat for **Cyber Tech Publications**
4264/3, Ansari Road, Daryaganj, New Delhi-110002 (India)
Ph.: 011-23244078, 011-43559448 Fax: 011-23280028
E-Mail: cyberpublicationsdelhi@yahoo.com
Website: www.cybertechpublications.com

CONTENTS

Preface

This book interweaves the concepts of the guidance on globalization, international management, and the intricacies of international business that many books on the market treat independently. It clarifies and explains culture, cultural misunderstandings, and cross-cultural interactions. It is for managers seeking to thrive in the global economy. This book focuses on managing global organizations, providing a basis for understanding the influence of culture on international management, and the key roles that international managers play. It clearly shows how to develop the cross-cultural expertise essential to succeed in a world of rapid and profound economic, political and cultural changes.

Designed for instructors who want to go beyond the facts and figures in standard textbooks, this affordable paperback is a unique teaching resource that adds a "real life" dimension to courses in international business. It can be used to supplement any basic textbook on International Business or International Management.

— *Author*

1

Globalization

INTRODUCTION

Whether a business student is studying marketing, finance, accounting, strategy, human relations, or operations management, the differences between countries in which a firm does business will affect decisions that must be made.

A fundamental shift is occurring in the world economy. The world is getting closer in terms of cross border trade and investment, by distance, time zones, languages and by national differences in government regulation, culture and business systems and toward a world in which national economies are merging into one huge interdependent global economic system. Globalization is affecting firms that previously operated in a nice, easy, protected national market. It also illustrates the increasing importance of thinking globally.

What is Globalization?

Definition: globalization is the trend toward a more integrated global economic system. The rate at which this shift is occurring has been accelerated recently.

Globalization has two faces:

- Globalization of markets
- Globalization of production
- Globalization of markets.

Globalization of markets refers to the fact that in many industries historically distinct and separate national markets are merging into one huge global marketplace.

There is a movement towards a globalization of markets, as the tastes and preferences of consumers in different nations are beginning to converge upon some global norm. The global acceptance of Coca-Cola, Levi's jeans, Sony Walkmans, and McDonald's hamburgers are all examples. By offering a standard product worldwide, they are helping to create a global market. Even smaller companies can get the benefits from the globalization of markets.

Despite the global prevalence of global brands such as Levis, City Bank, Pepsi etc, national markets are not disappearing. There are still significant differences - Germany still leads in per capita beer consumption, with a local pub on almost every corner and in some cities, women selling beer out of their front windows to passers by on the street. The French lead in wine consumption, and the consumption of wine is a natural part of life anywhere in France. Italians lead in pasta eaten, and these differences are unlikely to be eliminated any time soon. Hence, often there is still a need for marketing strategies and product features to be customized to local conditions.

Globalization of Production

The globalization of production refers to the tendency among many firms to source goods and services from different locations around the globe in an attempt to take advantage of national differences in the cost and quality of factors of production. (labor, energy, land and capital)

Through this companies hope to lower their overall cost structure and or improve the quality or functionality of their product, thereby allowing them to compete more effectively against their rivals. The examples of Boeing and Swan Optical illustrate how production is dispersed.

Boeing company's commercial jet airliner, Boeing 777 contains 132,500 major components parts that are produced around the world by 545 different suppliers. Eight Japanese suppliers make parts of fuselage, doors and wings, a supplier in Singapore make the doors for the nose landing gear, three suppliers in Italy manufacture wing flaps etc.

The result of having a global web of suppliers is a better final product, which enhances the chances of Boeing wining a greater share of aircraft orders than its global rival Airbus. While part of the rationale is based on costs and finding the best suppliers in the world, there are also other factors. In Boeing's case, if it wishes to sell airliners to countries like China, these countries often demand that domestic firms be contracted to supply portions of the plane - otherwise they will find another supplier (Airbus) who is willing to support local industry.

DRIVERS OF GLOBALIZATION

Two key factors seem to underlie the trend towards the increasing globalization of markets and production:

- The decline of barriers to trade and investment and
- Technological change.
- The decline of barriers to trade and investment.

Decline in Trade Barriers

Definition: International trade occurs when a firm exports goods or services to consumers in another country.

Many of the barriers to international trade took the form of high tariffs on imports of manufactured goods. However, this depressed world demand and contributed to the great depression of the 1930's.

After World War II, the industrialized countries of the West started a process of removing barriers to the free flow of goods, services, and capital between nations. Under GATT, over 140 nations negotiated even further to decrease tariffs and made significant progress on a number of non-tariff issues (e.g. intellectual property, trade in services). The most recent round of negotiations known as Uruguay round was competed in December 1993. The Uruguay round further reduced trade barriers, covering services as well as manufactured goods provided enhanced protection for patents, trade marks and copyrights and established WTO to police the international trading system. With the establishment of the WTO, a mechanism now exists for dispute resolution and the enforcement of trade laws.

Average tariff rates have fallen significantly since 1950's, and under the Uruguay agreement, they have approached 3.9 percent by 2000.

This removal of barriers to trade has taken place in conjunction with increased trade, world output, and foreign direct investment.

Decline in Investment Barriers

Definition: The Foreign direct Investment: FDI occurs when a firm invests to international trade activities outside its home country. The growth of foreign direct investment is a direct result of nations liberalizing their regulations to allow foreign firms to invest in facilities and acquire local companies. With their investments, these foreign firms often also bring expertise and global connections that allow local operations to have a much broader reach than would have been possible for a purely domestic company. The evidences also suggests that FDI is playing an increasing role in the global economy as firms increase their cross border investments. Between 1985 and 1995 the total annual flow of FDI from all countries increased nearly six fold to $135 billion, a growth rate in the world trade The major investors has been U.S, Japanese, and Western European Companies investing in Europe, Asia, (particularly in China, and India). For example, Japanese auto companies have been investing rapidly in Asian, European, and U.S auto assembly operations.

This also shows that firms around the globe are finding their home markets under attack from Foreign competitors. For example, in Japan, Kodak has taken market share from Fuji recent years. In the United States, Japanese firms have taken away market share from General motors, and Chrysler and in Western Europe where the once –dominant Dutch company Philips has seen its market share taken by Japan's JVC, Matsushita and Sony. The growing integration into a single huge market place is increasing the intensity of competition in a wide range of manufacturing and service industries.

These trends facilitate both the globalization of markets and globalization of production. The lowering trade and investment barriers also allows firms to base individual production activities at the optimal location for that activity, and serving the world market from that location. Thus, a firm might design a product in one country, produce component parts in two another country, assemble the product in yet another country, and then export the finished product around the world.

The Role Technological Change

While lowering trade barriers has made the globalization of markets and production a possibility, technological changes have made it a reality. "Telecommunications is creating a global audience. Transport is creating a global village. From Buenos Aires to Boston to Beijing, ordinary people are watching MTV, they are wearing Levi's jeans, and they are listening to Sony Walkman as they commute to work." — *Renato Ruggiero, Director General of World trade Organization.*

Improved information processing and communication allow firms to have better information about distant markets and coordinate activities worldwide. The explosive growth of the World Wide Web and the Internet provide a means to rapid communication of information and the ability of firms and individuals to find out about what is going on worldwide for a fraction of the cost and hassle as was required only a couple of years ago.

Microprocessor and Telecommunications

The single most important innovation has been the development of the microprocessor, which enabled the explosive growth of high power, low cost computing, increasing the amount of information that can be processed by individuals and firms. Over the past 30 years, global communications have been revolutionized by the developments in satellites, optical fiber, and wireless technology, and internet and World Wide Web. All these technologies rely on the microprocessor to encode, transmit and decode the vast amount of information that flows along these electronic highways.

A phenomenon known as Moore's law, which predicts that the power of microprocessor technology doubles and its cost of production falls in half of every 18 months. That means the cost of coordinating and controlling a global organization will reduce phenomenally.

The Internet and World Wide Web

This is the latest expression of this development. There are more than 150 million users of the Internet. This will develop into the information backbone of tomorrow's global economy. Real time video conferencing and commercial transactions can be transmitted through WWW. WWW will reduce the costs of global communications and it will create a truly global electronic market place of all kinds of goods and services. Such as the soft wares and bulldozers, and this will make it easier for firms of all sizes to enter the global marketplace.

Transportation Technology

Improvements in transportation technology, including jet transport, temperature controlled containerized shipping, and coordinated ship-rail-truck systems have made firms better able to respond to international customer demands.

As a consequence of these trends, a manager in today's firm operates in an environment that offers more opportunities, but is also more complex and competitive than that faced a generation ago. People now work with individuals and companies from many countries, and while communications technology, with the universality of English as the language of business, has decreased the absolute level of cultural difficulties individuals face, the frequency with which they face inter-cultural and international challenges has increased.

The Changing Demographics of the Global Economy:

In 1960's there were four facts described in the demographics of the global economy.

- The U.S dominance in the worlds economy and world trade.
- U.S dominance in the world Foreign Direct Investment picture.
- The dominance of large multinational U.S firms in the international business scene.
- Roughly half of the globe (communist world), was unavailable to Western International Business.

All these four facts either have changed or now changing rapidly. The changing demographics has four facets.

- The changing world output and world trade picture
- A changing world Foreign Direct Investment picture
- The changing nature of the Multinational Enterprise
- The changing world order
- The changing world output and world trade picture:

The U.S. share of world output has declined dramatically in the past 30 years and a much more balanced picture is now developing among industrialized countries. Looking ahead into the next century, the share of world output of what are now referred to as "developing countries" is expected to greatly surpass that of the current "industrialized countries."

For example, Japan's share of world manufacturing output increased their share of world output included China, South Korea, and Taiwan.

The changing pattern of World output and trade

Country	Share of world output 1963 (%)	Share of world output 1985 (%)	Share of world output 1995 (%)
United States	40.3	21.9	12.2
Japan	5.5	8.2	9.4
Germany	9.7	4.3	10.1
France	6.3	3.5	5.6
United kingdom	6.5	3.4	4.9
Italy	3.4	3.2	4.5
Canada	3.0	2.1	3.9

By the end of 1980s, the U.S position as the world's leading exporter was threatened. Over the last 30 years, U.S dominance in export markets has reduced as Japan, Germany and a large number of newly industrialized countries such as South Korea, and Taiwan has taken a large share of the world exports. During the 1960s, the U.S accounted for 20% of world exports of manufactured goods. However, this reduced to 12.2% by 1995. Despite the fall the United States remain the world's largest exporter, flowed closely b Germany and Japan.

Rapid economic growth rates now being experienced by countries such as, China, Thailand and Indonesia, further relative decline in the U.S share of world output and world exports. The World Bank predicts more future growth by developing nations in East and South East Asia, which includes China, India, and South Korea.

A Changing World Foreign Direct Investment Picture

The source and destinations of FDI has also dramatically changed over recent years, with the US and industrialized countries becoming less important (although still dominant) as developing countries are becoming increasingly considered as an attractive and stable location for investment.

The U.S firms accounted for 66.3% of the worldwide FDI flow in 1960s. British firms were second, accounting for 10.5 % while Japanese firms were a distant third, with only 2%. However, with the barriers to the free flow of goods and capital fell, and as other countries increased their shares of world output, non U.S firms increasingly began to invest across national borders.

The share of FDI accounted by U.S firms declined substantially form around 44 percent in 1980 to 25 percent in 1994. Meanwhile the share accounted by Japanese, France, other developed nations and the world's developing nations reflects a small but growing trend in FDI.

Another trend shows an increasing tendency for cross border investments to be directed at developing rather than rich industrialized nations. (the flow of Foreign direct investment refers to the amounts invested across national borders each year.)

Among the developing nations China has received the greatest volume of inward FDI in recent years. Other developing nations receiving a large amount o of FDI included Indonesia, Malaysia, the Philippines, and Thailand, ($14 billion dollars.).

The Changing Nature of the Multinational Enterprise

Definition: A multinational enterprise is any business that has productive activities in tow or more countries.

The major trends in MNCs are the rise of non-US MNCs particularly Japanese Multinationals. The second is the growth mini multinationals.

A number of large multinationals are now non-U.S. based, and many are recognizable brand names in the worldwide (e.g. Sony, Philips, Toshiba, Honda, and BMW). The new large multinationals are not only are originating in other developed countries, but there are an increasing number of multinationals based in developing countries. The country focus on Korea's new multinationals clearly illustrates the growth of developing country multinationals.

An increasing number of small firms are becoming global leaders in their field, giving rise to the mini-multinationals. Although most international trade and investment are still conducted by large firms, many medium sized and small businesses are increasingly involved in international trade and investment.

E.g.: G.W Barth, manufacturer of cocoa beans roasting machinery based in Germany, employing just 65 people has captured 70 percent of the global market for cocoa bean roasting machines.

The Changing World Order

Between 1989 and 1991 a series of remarkable democratic revolutions swept the communist world. In country after country throughout Eastern Europe and eventually in the Soviet Union communist governments collapsed. The Soviet Union is now history, which is replaced by 15 independent republics. Czechoslovakia has divided itself into two states, while Yugoslavia has dissolved into a bloody civil war among its successor states.

For about half a century, these countries were closed for western international business. The fall of communism and the development of free markets in Eastern Europe and the former Soviet Union create profound opportunities, challenges, and potential threats for firms.

The economic development of China presents huge opportunities and risks, in spite of its continued Communist control. China seems to be moving progressively toward greater free market reforms. The southern China province called "Guangong" now has become the fastest growing economy in the world. Between 1983 and 1995, FDI in China increased from leas than $2 Billion dollars to over $38 Billion dollars. For North American firms, the growth and market reforms in Mexico and Latin America also present tremendous new opportunities both as markets and sources of materials and production.

The path to full economic liberalization and open markets is not without obstruction. Economic crises in Latin America, South East Asia, and Russia all caused difficulties in 1997 and 1998. In response, much trade was reduced, and some countries imposed new controls. Malaysia, for example, suspended foreigners from trading in its equity and currency markets to "prevent destabilizing influences." While firms must be prepared to take advantage of an ever more integrated global economy, they must also prepare for political and economic disruptions that may throw their plans into confusion.

The Globalization Debate: Prosperity or Impoverishment?

Is the shift toward a more integrated and interdependent global economy a good thing?

There are three major criticism against globalizations. These are:

- Reduced jobs and incomes

- It encourages poor labor practices and environmental policies
- National sovereignty of the countries are getting limited.

While many economists, politicians and business leaders seem to think so, globalization is not without its critics. Globalization stimulates economic growth, raises the incomes of consumers, and helps to create jobs in all countries that choose to participate in the global economy. Some of this growth, however, creates "sweatshop" jobs, increases pollution, and draws people from the countryside into ever more crowded cities and slums.

Globalization; Jobs and Incomes

One major criticism against globalization is that compared to creating jobs it actually destroys manufacturing jobs in the wealthy advanced countries like US. These critics argue that, falling trade barriers allow the firms to move their manufacturing activities to countries where wage rates are much lower.

In developed countries, labor leaders lament the loss of good paying jobs to low wage countries. When the NAFTA agreement was signed, some politicians warned of a hearing a "giant sucking sound" as jobs left USA for Mexico. Even if the jobs are not lost, it creates downward pressure on wages in industries where overseas production is a viable option. The availability of jobs for unskilled workers is clearly threatened when those jobs can be more efficiently performed elsewhere. One solution to this problem is to increase the education and training of workers in developed countries to maintain employment, and simply let the unskilled jobs go to locations where unskilled workers will accept lower wages.

Bartlett and Steele, two journalists form Philadelphia Inquirer News paper, cite the case of Harwood industries, a US clothing manufacturer that closed US operations, where it paid workers $9 per hour, and shifted manufacturing to Honduras, where workers receive 48 cents per hour. They argue because of free trade, the wage rates of poorer Americans have fallen significantly over the years.

Supporters of globalization reply that these critics miss the essential point about free trade- the benefits outweigh the costs. They argue that free trade results in countries specializing in the production of those goods and services that hey can produce more efficiently from other countries. Even though there is dislocation of jobs but the whole economy is better off as a result.

According to this view, it makes little sense for the US to produce textiles at home when they can produce textiles at la lower cost in Honduras or China. Importing textiles from China leads to lowering costs for cloths in US, which results in US consumers spend less on textiles and more on other items.

At the same time, the increased income generated in China, from textile exports increases income levels in that country, which helps the Chinese to purchase more products produced in US like, Boeing Jets, Intel Computers, Microsoft Software and Motorola cellular phones.

Therefore, supporter of global trade, argue that free trade benefits all countries.

LABOR POLICES AND GLOBALIZATION

One of the criticisms against globalization is that free trade encourages developed nations to move manufacturing facilities offshore to less developed countries that lack adequate regulations to protect labor and the environment. They feel that free trade can lead to an increase in pollution and exploitation of labor of less developed nations.

Lower labor costs are only one of the reasons why a firm may seek to expand in developing countries. These countries may also have lower standards on environmental controls and workplace safety. Nevertheless, since investment typically leads to higher living standards, there is often pressure to increase safety regulations to international levels. No country wants to be known for its poor record on health and human safety. Thus, supporters of globalization argue that foreign investment often helps a country to raise its standards.

There is also political and economic pressure on firms not to exploit labor or the environment in overseas operations. Western firms have been the subjects of consumer boycotts when it has been revealed that they, or their independent suppliers, operate at standards below that in developed countries.

National Sovereignty and Globalization

With the development of the WTO (World Trade Organization) and other multilateral organizations such as the EU (European Union) and NAFTA (North American Free trade Agreement), countries and localities necessarily give up some authority over their actions. If the USA wanted to "protect its domestic lumber industry" by preventing imports of lumber from Canada, the dispute would likely be settled by an international arbitration panel set up by the NAFTA agreement or the WTO. Because of its trade agreements, the USA would likely be forced to open its markets to importation of lower cost, higher quality Canadian lumber. While this would clearly be good for consumers, the domestic lumber industry would protest. While clearly some sovereignty (independence) has been surrendered, it has been done to protect the best interests of consumers. If a nation wanted to retreat into a more protectionist position, it could clearly choose to withdraw from its international agreements.

"Under the new system, many decisions, which affect billions of people, are no longer made by local or national Government, but instead, if challenged by any WTO member nation, would be deferred to a group of unelected bureaucrats sitting behind closed doors in Geneva, (HQs of WTO)... at risk is the very basis of democracy and accountable decision making." — *Ralph Nader, US environmentalist and consumer rights advocate.*

Managing in the Global Marketplace

Definition: An International business is any firm that engages in international trade or investment.

A firm does not have to be a MNC investing directly in operations in other countries to engage in International Business. All a firm has to do is to start exporting products or importing products from other countries. As the world shift toward a truly integrated global economy, more firms, both the large and small, are becoming intentional businesses.

As their organizations increasingly engage in cross-border trade and investment, it means managers need to recognize that the task of managing an international business differs from that of managing a purely domestic business in many ways. Countries differ in their cultures, political systems, economic systems, legal systems, and levels of economic development.

These differences require that business people vary their practices country by country, recognizing what changes are required to operate effectively. It is necessary to strike a balance between adaptation and maintaining global consistency, however. Coca-Cola would not be as successful, nor would Coke be Coke, if it tasted like ginseng in one country, lemon in another, and rhubarb in a third. Clearly, some adaptations need to be made to correspond with local regulations and distribution systems, but some things need also remain consistent in order to benefit from economies of scale in advertising and production.

As a result of making local adaptations, the complexity of international business is clearly greater than that of a purely domestic firm. Firms need to decide which countries to enter, what mode of entry to use, and which countries to avoid. Rules and regulations also differ, as do currencies and languages.

Managing an international business is different from managing a purely domestic business for at least four reasons:

(a) countries differ,

(b) the range of problems and manager faces is greater and more complex,

(c) an international business must find ways to work within the limits imposed by governmental intervention and the global trading system, and

(d) international transactions require converting funds and being susceptible to exchange rate changes.

Additional notes from Module 1

The Globalization Process

Definition: The globalization process is the structural and managerial changes and challenges experienced by a firm as it moves from domestic to global in operations.

This process happens in three phases.

Domestic operations.

International trade phase.

Multinational phase.

Take an example of Trident Corporation, a U.S based company, which transforms itself from being domestic to global company. The first phase is called domestic phase.

Phase One: Domestic Operations

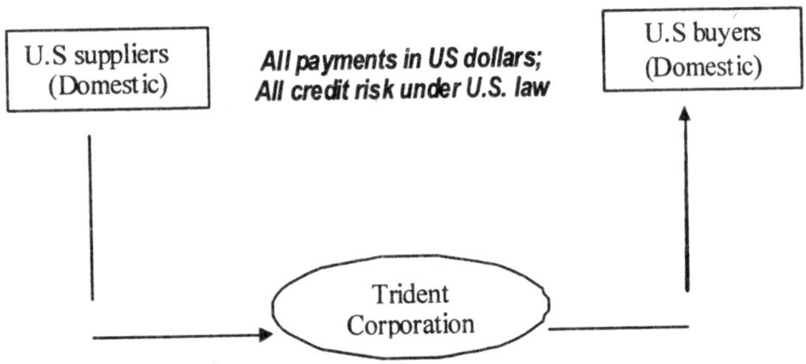

Trident may not be global or international itself, yet its competitors, suppliers and buyers may be working across borders. This is often a key driver to push a firm like Trident into first phase of globalization – international trade – The second half of this phase is the international trade phase

Phase 2: International trade phase

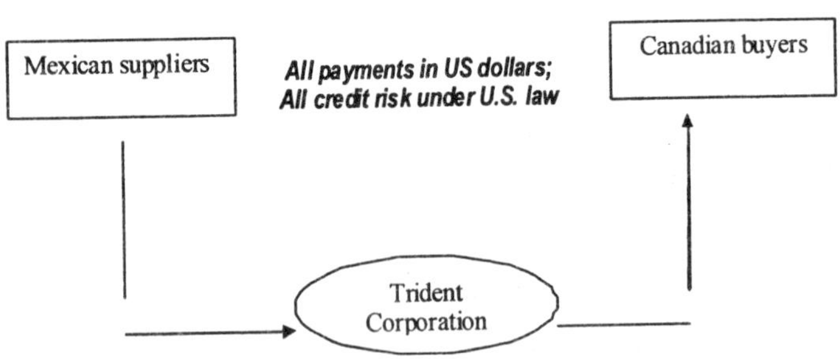

Trident responds to globalization factors by importing inputs from Mexican suppliers and making exports sales to Canadian buyers. This stage is called the *international trade phase.*

- Exporting and importing products increases the demands and requirements of a domestic business.
- The first is direct *foreign exchange risks* borne by Trident.
- Trident may have to quote prices and receive payments in foreign currencies.
- Trident will now experience significant risks from the daily volatility in exchange rates.
- Trident also faces risks associated with credit quality and evaluation of international counterparts.

- This *credit risk management* task is much more difficult in international business as buyers and suppliers are new and subject to differing business practices and legal systems.

Phase 3: Multinational Phase

If Trident is successful in international trade then the time will come for the next step in the globalization process, which is the move from the international trade phase to the multinational phase.

- Trident will eventually need to establish foreign sales and services affiliates
- This step is followed by the establishment of manufacturing operations or licensing agreements abroad
- Trident's continued globalization will require it to identify the sources of it competitive advantages
- This variety of strategic alternatives available to Trident is called the *foreign direct investment sequence.*
- These alternatives include the creation of foreign sales offices, licensing agreements, manufacturing, etc.

Once Trident owns assets and enterprises in foreign countries it has entered the *multinational phase* of globalization.

Globalization –Sequence:

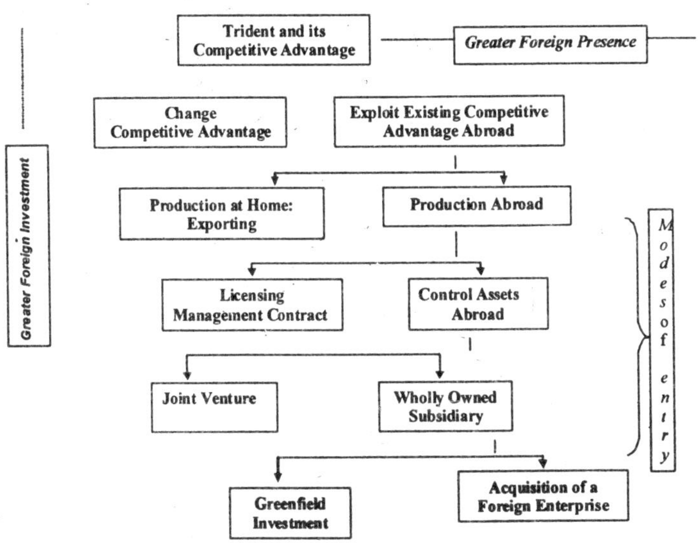

Green field investment: A long-term physical investment in productive capability in that country. (referred as new projects)

Acquisition: Identification, valuation, tender, and post-acquisition, management of an existing, going-concern.

Joint venture: Combining investment, capital and managerial know-how to reach specific opportunities

Ways to enter the new market: modes of globalization

- Simple export of the product
- Develop a joint venture to sell through an existing company in similar business
- Sell license to foreign company and collect royalties, or franchising, turnkey projects etc.
- Contract a foreign company to do the business for a % of the sales
- Overseas office and subsidiary company set up.

2

The International Business Environment

Contents: the influence of country's differences in political systems, economic systems, legal systems and cultural attitudes on international business and ethical issues in IBM.

- Understand how the political systems of countries differ.
- Understand how the economic systems of countries differ.
- Understand how the legal systems of countries differ.
- Understand how political, economic, and legal systems collectively influence a country's ability to achieve meaningful economic progress.
- Be familiar with the changes that are currently reshaping the political, economic and legal systems of countries.
- Ethical issues while doing international business.

INTRODUCTION

The issues that face international businesses are entirely different from those that face domestic firms. Whether the subject is political differences, cultural differences, trade and tariff issues or even corporate makeup, the major issues of international business are issues that simply do not occur in domestic businesses. One cannot expect to understand international business by learning the tenants of domestic business and then superimposing them on an international scene. Differences between countries are profound, and they have a powerful affect on how managers and firms work and act internationally. This chapter looks at the political, economic, and legal infrastructures of different countries.

The political economy of India shows the difficulty nations may experience .when they attempt to move from a largely state-driven economy to one of privatization. Even when change appears to be merited, the results of a particular change can be mixed and inconclusive. Changing political views on the ownership of business enterprises can have dramatic effects on economic efficiency and foreign investment.

POLITICAL SYSTEMS

Definition: Political system refers to the system pf Government in a nation. The economic and legal systems of the country are often shaped by its political system.

There are two separate polarities to consider when discussing political systems: collectivism vs. individualism and democracy vs. totalitarianism.

Political systems are assessed according two the two related dimensions. The first is the degree to which they emphasize collectivism as opposed to individualism. The second dimension is the degree to which they are democratic or totalitarian.

These two dimensions are interrelated, systems that emphasize collectivism tend to be totalitarian while, systems, that pace a high value on individualism tend to be democratic. However, there might be exceptions also.

Democracy and totalitarianism are at different ends of a political dimension. The democratic vs. totalitarian dimension is not independent of the collectivism vs. individualism dimension. Democracy and individualism go hand in hand, as do the communist version of collectivism and totalitarianism. However, gray areas also exist; it is possible to have a democratic state where collective values predominate, and it is possible to have a totalitarian state that is hostile to collectivism and in which some degree of individualism — particularly in the economic sphere — is encouraged.

COLLECTIVISM VS. INDIVIDUALISM

Collectivism

Definition: political system that stresses the primacy of collective goals over individual goals.

Here the needs of a society as a whole are generally viewed as being more important than individual freedoms. In this condition, an individual's right to do something may be restricted because it runs against, the good of society" or "the common good".

This concept originates from the Greek Philosopher Plato (427-347-BC), who in his book" the Republic" argued that individual rights should be sacrificed fro the good of the majority and that property should be owned in common.

The system, which advocates Collectivism, is called socialism and these activists are called socialists.

Socialism

Socialism roots from the intellectual lessons from Karl Marx (1818-1883). Marx's basic argument is that in a capitalist society where individual freedom is not restricted, the few benefit at the expense of many. Marx advocated state ownership of the basic means of production, distribution and exchange (business). His point is that if the state owned the means of production, the states could ensure that the workers were fully compensated for their labor. Thus, the idea is to manage state owned enterprise to benefit the society as whole, rather than individual capitalists.

The general premise of collectivism is that the state must manage enterprises if they are to benefit society. Democratic Socialism sees itself as part of the historical trend toward democracy and universal enfranchisement that has taken place worldwide since the 1700s. In fact, it sees socialism as the ultimate democracy — putting faith in the common person's ability not only to vote on Election Day, but also to govern his and her workplace and community.

In the early 20th century, socialist ideology split into two broad camps.. On the one hand, there were the communists, who believed that socialism could be achieved only through violent revolution and totalitarian dictatorship.

On the other hand, there were social democrats who committed themselves, to achieve socialism by democratic means, and who disagreed on violent revolution and dictatorship.

The communist version of socialism reached at the peak in the late 1970's, when the majority of the world's population lived in communist states. The countries under communist rule included:

- The former Soviet Union
- Its eastern European client nations (Poland, Czechoslovakia, Hungary)
- China
- The Southeast Asian nations of Cambodia, Laos and Vietnam
- Various African nations (Angola, Mozambique)
- Latin American nations(Cuba and Nicaragua).

By mid 1990's, however communism collapsed worldwide. The Soviet Union had collapsed and had been replaced by a collection of 15 republics. Communism was swept out of Eastern Europe by large bloodless revolutions of 1989. China remains the only major country in the world today under communist rule. However, China has recently moved significantly away from strict adherence to communist ideology and gives substantial limits to individual political freedom.

Social Democratic nations include Sweden, Germany, France, and Norway, although Social Democratic parties have not always held power in these nations.

Social democracy had its great influence in a number of democratic western nations, including, Australia, Britain, France, Germany. Norway, Spain and Sweden, where social democratic parties have from time to time held political power. Other countries where social democracy has had an important influence include India and Brazil.

Many social democratic governments have nationalized private companies in certain industries, transforming them into state owned enterprises to be run for "public good rather than private profit." In Britain for example, by 1970's state owned companies had a monopoly in industries like telecommunications, electricity, gas coal, railway and shipbuilding and have substantial shares in oil, airline, auto and steel industries.

The State owned firms promoting the public interest have had a poor record of accomplishment. The reasons are often obvious: state owned firms are often protected from competition and are poorly motivated to achieve any financial self-sufficiency. Often their major purpose is to carry on their existence, rather than bringing anything positive to the country they are supposed to serve. Thus, both former communist and Western European countries have privatized enterprises that were previously state owned. In a number of Western democracies, many social democratic parties were voted out of office in late 1970's and early 1980's. in Britain, this was replaced by, conservative party of Margaret Thatcher, sold the state's interests in telecommunications, electricity, gas, shipbuilding, oil, airlines, autos, and steel to private investors. Selling sate owned enterprises to private investors is known as privatization.

Many individuals are shocked to believe that a country could hope to control the ideology of its people by building a wall around a city (Berlin). In this day of rapid, instantaneous exchange of electronic information, the concept of a government trying to create physical barriers to control the flow of information is often difficult to grasp.

Individualism

This is the opposite of collectivism. Individualism refers to a philosophy that an individual should have the freedom in his or her economic and political pursuits.

In contrast to collectivism, individualism stresses that the interests of the individual should take precedence over the interests of the state. While advocated by Aristotle, individualism, in modern days was encouraged by David Hume, Adam Smith (Book- Wealth of Nations), John Stuart Mill, and most recently, Frederich Von Hayek and Milton Friedman (Nobel Prize winning economists).

Individualism focuses on (1) guaranteeing individual freedom and self-expression, and (2) letting people pursue their own economic self-interest in order to achieve the best overall good for society. The US Declaration of Independence and the Bill of Rights embody the spirit of individualism, but more familiar today are forces like MTV, which encourage people the world over to vote for their favorite video — even in countries where voting in elections is impossible and the concept of voting is not understood.

Collectivism advocates the primacy of the collective group over the individual; individualism asserts the opposite. This ideological difference shapes much of recent history and especially the Cold War. a war between collectivism championed by the now defunct Soviet Union and individualism, championed by U.S. In practical terms, individualism translates into an advocacy for democratic political systems and free market economies. Soviet Union, Eastern Europe etc have moved toward a greater individualism. Now as guiding political philosophy there is no doubt that individualism is currently rising over collectivism. This represents good news for international business since this creates a more favorable environment fro business and free trade.

An interesting deviation is environmentalism — in the context of collectivism vs. individualism. While one might expect that countries with a collectivist approach would have much higher environmental standards "for the common good" than individualist countries where "anyone can do what they want on their own land," the record is less clear.

While the Social Democratic countries of Norway and Sweden have some of the best overall environmental records, the pollution problems in many of the former communist states are unbearable. The USA has an environmental record that seems to lag behind many other social democratic countries in Western Europe. In fact, as we will see in later discussions on GATT and NAFTA, different countries' environmental standards are becoming an increasingly important issue in international trade negotiations.

DEMOCRACY VS. TOTALITARIANISM

Democracy

Definition: Democracy refers to apolitical system in which the government is by the people, exercised either directly or through elected representatives.

Democracy in its pure state, with each individual voting on every issue, has generally been replaced by representative democracy, where elected representatives vote on behalf of constituents. Yet, in Switzerland, many issues are decided by referendum, and in many US states, referendums decided directly by voters on Election Day are becoming increasingly common.

Democracy, in its pure from was originally practiced by several states in ancient Greece. In complex danced societies with millions of people, this is impractical. Most of the modern democratic states practice which is commonly known as 'representative democracy" in this system, the citizens periodically elect individuals to represent them these elected representatives then form a government, whose function is to make decisions on behalf of the electorate. A representative democracy rests on the assumptions that if elected represntives fail to perform this job adequately; they can and will be voted down at the next election. Democratic system guarantees constitutionally, a number safeguards to its citizens. These are:

An individual's right to freedom of expression, opinion, and organization, a free media, regular elections in which call eligible citizens are allowed to vote, universal adult suffrage, limited terms for elected representatives, a fair court system that is independent for the political system, a nonpolitical state bureaucracy, a non political police force and armed forces an relatively free access to state information etc. are some of these rights.

Totalitarianism

Definition: Totalitarianism is a form of Government in which one person or political party exercises absolute control over all spheres of human life, and opposing political parties are prohibited.

Under totalitarianism, a single political party, individual, or group of individuals monopolize the political power and do not permit opposition. There are four major forms of totalitarianism: communist, theocratic, tribal, right wing (often military).

Communist Totalitarianism

This is a form of totalitarianism that advocates achieving socialism through totalitarian dictatorship. Communism is in decline worldwide. The major exceptions to this trend are China, Vietnam, North Korea and Cuba. However, even these states show a decline in the communist party's monopoly.

Theocratic Totalitarianism

This is a form of totalitarianism in which political power is monopolized by a party, group or individual that governs according to religious principles. The most common theocratic totalitarianism is that based on Islam. It prevails in Iran, Saudi Arabia etc. in these states not only is freedom of political expression is restricted, but also is the freedom of religious expression, while the laws of the state are based on Islamic principles.

Tribal Totalitarianism

This is a form of totalitarianism found mainly in Africa, in which a political party that represents the interests of a particular tribe monopolizes the power. This is found in African countries like Zimbabwe, Tanzania, Uganda and Kenya. Such one party states are found throughout Africa where a political party that represents the interests of particular tribe(not necessarily, majority tribe) monopolizes the power.

Right Wing Totalitarianism

This is a form of totalitarianism in which individual economic freedom is allowed but individual political freedom is restricted in the belief that could leads to communism.

Many right wing dictatorships are backed by military and in some cases the government is made up of military officers. Many of the military dictatorship were common in Latin America. They were also found in south Korea, Taiwan, Singapore, Indonesia, Pakistan and the Philippines.

There has been a general trend away from communist and right wing totalitarianism and towards democracy in the 1980s and 1990s. Issues relating to theocratic and tribal totalitarianism are presently at the root of some unrest in Asia and Africa.

Economic System

A good way to understand countries' relative political and economic freedom is to draw a diagram with political freedom on one dimension and economic freedom on the other.. Then identify the relative position different countries on the dimensions of economic and political freedom.

The political environment of a country matters because:

(1) when economic freedoms are restricted so may be the ability of an international business to operate in the most efficient manner, and

(2) when political freedoms are restricted there are both ethical and legal risks concerns that have to be considered.

Economic Systems

There are four broad types of economic systems: market, command, mixed, and state-directed.

In reality almost all are mixed to some extent, for even the most market oriented systems have some governmental controls on business and even the most command based systems either explicitly allow some free markets to exist or have black markets for some goods and services. Yet, all countries can be considered to be at some point on a continuum between pure market and pure command.

Market Economy

In a pure market economy, the goods and services that a country produces, as well as the quantity in which they are produced, is not planned by anyone. Rather price and quantity are determined by supply and demand.

For a market economy to work, there must be no restrictions on either supply or demand — no monopolistic sellers or buyers. The recent legal battle with the federal government and Microsoft is an example of an attempt by government to remove from Microsoft what it perceived to be business restrictions that resulted in monopolistic operations.

Command Economy

In a pure command economy, the government plans what goods and services a country produces, the quantity in which they are produced, and the price at which they are sold. Resources are allocated "for the good of society." The government owns most, if not all, businesses, including even small businesses like the bread bakery and the local farm.

Command economies are found in communist countries where collectivist goals are given priority over individual goals. France and India have both experimented with extensive government planning and state ownership, although in both countries government planning has recently fallen into disfavor. In this system, state owned enterprises show little interest to control costs and be efficient. There is a general lack of dynamism and innovation in command economies are visible, since there is no incentives for individuals to look for better ways of serving customers.

Mixed Economy

A mixed economy includes some elements of each. In Canada, for example, while most business is privately owned and operated under market principles, health care, electrical power, and liquor distribution are run by state owned enterprises in most provinces.

In a state-directed economy, the government plays a significant role in directing the investment activities of private enterprises through "industrial policy." Both Japan and South Korea are often cited as examples of state-directed economies. In both situations, the government has played a significant role in directing investment. This direction has helped in the creation of some leading international firms. For a state-directed economy to work well, state bureaucrats must make better decisions than capital markets on the allocation of resources. While state bureaucrats may be able to take a longer-term perspective than capital markets, they may also prove to be intransigent and resistant to making necessary changes. The difficulties many South East Asian countries faced in 1997-98 highlight some of the limitations of a state-directed economy. Resisting whims of the market has both its good and bad points.

LEGAL SYSTEMS

The legal systems of a country refers to the rules, or laws that regulate behavior, along with the processes by which the laws of a country are enforced and through which redress for grievances is obtained.

The legal environment of a country is of immense importance to international business. A country's laws regulate business practice, define the manner in which business transactions are to be executed, and set down the rights and obligations of those involved in business transactions. Differences in the structure of law can have an important impact upon the attractiveness of a country as an investment site and/or market.

Legal systems and property rights: there are three aspects of legal systems that affect international business, i.e., laws of property rights, intellectual property rights, product safety and product liability laws and contract laws.

Property Rights

Property rights is the bundle of legal rights addressing the use to which a resource is put and the use made of any income that may be derived from that service.

Control over property rights are very important for the functioning of business. Property rights can be violated by either private action (theft, piracy, blackmail, Mafia) or public action (governmental bribery and corruption, nationalization). Lack of confidence in a country's fair treatment of property rights significantly increases the costs and risks of doing business.

The Country Focus on Corruption in Nigeria shows how a country that has huge natural resources can still remain poor when its political leaders conspire to damage its economic activity for their personal gain. High levels of corruption can naturally lead to a significant reduction in economic activity.

Intellectual Property Rights

Property such as computer software, screenplays, musical scores, or chemical formulas for new drugs that is the product of intellectual activity. (Patents, copyrights, and trademarks) are important for businesses if they are to capitalize on what they have developed.

Patents

Documents giving the inventor of a new product or processes exclusive rights to the manufacture, use, or sale of that invention.

Copyrights: are the excusive legal rights of authors, composers, playwrights, artists and publishers to publish and dispose their works as they see it.

Trademarks

Trademarks are designs and names, often officially registers, by which merchants or manufacturers designate and differentiate their products.

Firms like Microsoft, Levis, Coca-Cola, or McDonald's would have little reason to invest overseas if other firms in other countries were able to use the same name and copy their products without permission. For example, consider innovation in the pharmaceuticals firms an incentive to undertake the expensive, difficult and time consuming basic research required to generate new drugs(on average it costs $100 million in research and development and takes 12 years to get a new drug to the market.). Without the guarantee provided by patents, it is unlikely that companies would commit themselves to such research.

Paris convention for the protection of Industrial property: is an international agreement signed by 96 countries to protect intellectual property rights.

Estimates suggest that the Asian violations of intellectual property rights cost U.S computer software companies $ 6 billion annually and U.S pharmaceuticals companies at least $ 500 million annually. Because of all these violations, international laws are currently being strengthened. The world trade agreement which was signed in 1994 by 117 countries for the first time extends its scope of the General Agreement On Tariffs And Trade (GATT) to cover intellectual property. These regulations enforce WTO members to grant and enforce patents lasting at least 20 years and copyrights lasting 50 years.

Product Safety and Product Liability

Product safety laws set certain safety standards to which a product must adhere. Product liability involves holding a firm and its officers responsible when a product causes injury, death or damage. Product liability can be much greater if the product does not confirm to required safety standards. There are both civil and criminal liability laws. Civil laws calls for m0nuy and payment damages. Criminal laws result in fines or imprisonment.

Different countries have different product safety and liability laws. In some cases, US businesses must customize products to adhere to local standards if they are to do business in a country, whether these standards are higher or just different. The most strict liability laws are found in US and other western nations. Liability laws are typically least expensive in less developed nations.

When product standards are lower in other countries, 'firms face an important ethical dilemma. Should they produce products only of the highest standards even if this puts them at a competitive disadvantage relative other producers and results in not maximizing value to shareholders? On the other hand, should they produce products that respond to local differences, even if that means that consumers may not be assured of the same levels of safety in different countries? One serious example involves the flame retardant nature of children's pajamas. In many countries, restrictions on the level of flame retardency are very low and even nonexistent, thus it is legal to manufacture that product without protective standards. Should international firms continue to manufacture to higher protection levels, with resulting increased costs that may put them at a competitive disadvantage?

Contract Laws

A contract is a document that specifies the conditions, under which an exchange is to occur, and details the rights and obligations of the parties to a contract. Contract law is the body of law that governs contract enforcement. The parties can resort to contract law in case of violations. There are two legal traditions that are found in world today. The common law system and the civil law system.

The common law system evolved in England over hundred s of years ago. It is now found in most of Britain's former colonies including US. Common law is based on tradition, precedent and custom.

Civil law system is based on very detailed set of laws that are organizes into codes. These codes define the laws that govern business transactions. This is used in ore than 80 countries, including Germany, France, Japan and Russia.

Differences in contract law force firms to use different approaches when negotiating contracts. In countries with common law traditions, contracts tend to be much more detail oriented and need to specify what will happen under a variety of contingencies. Common law tends to interpret legal statutes according to the past decisions and rulings of courts. The United States uses a common law system. Under civil law systems, contracts tend to be much shorter and less specific since many of the issues relating to contracts are covered in the civil code of the country. Under common law, ownership is established by use; under civil law, ownership is determined by registration. Therefore, another firm may register a product first and prevail in a bid for ownership, even though the competition had been using the product for a long time but had failed to register it.

The Determinants of Economic Development

The major measures of economic development of courtiers are GDP, PPP, and HDI.

Different countries have dramatically different levels of development. GDP is often regarded as a good measure of economic activity of a country. GDP measures the total value of the goods and services produced annually. GDP/capita is also a good yardstick of economic activity, as it measures average value of the goods and services produced by an individual. (Refer map showing GDP / per capita).

Countries such as Switzerland, United States, Sweden, and Japan are among the richest with highest GDP, while the largest countries like China, India are the poorest. Japan's GDP per head is $28,217, whereas China has only $379 and India $307. (1993). Sudan has the lowest with GDP per head as $55. The world's richest Switzerland has $36,231.

However, GDP/capita does not consider the differences in costs of living. The UN's PPP index — shows the differences in the standards of living of people in different countries. PPP index shows GDP per head for the cost of living. The index is set equal to 100 for the country in which PPP is the highest, which happens to be US. (Refer the graph showing PPP index of selected countries.) This graph shows that an average Indian citizen can afford to consume only 5 percent of the goods and services consumed by the average US citizen.

A problem with both GDP/capita and PPP is that they are static in nature. From an international business perspective, it is good to look at the rate of growth in the economy as well as the status of its people. Map 2.3 shows that some of the fastest growing countries economically are those have been slower to develop.

A broader approach to assessing the overall quality of life in different countries is the Human Development Index developed by UN. This is based on life expectancy, literacy rates, and whether (based on PPP indices) incomes are sufficient to meet the basic needs of individuals. The map shows the Human Development Index. Notice that some of the worse off countries are heavily populated and have rapidly expanding populations. The human development index is scaled from 0 to 100. Countries scoring less than 50 are classified as having low human development; scoring 50 to 80 are classified as having medium human development while those countries that score above 80 are classified as having high human development. One of the reasons of low human development index is heavy and expanding population.

What is the relationship between political economy and economic progress? This is a difficult issue. One thing that is generally accepted is that innovation is the engine of long-run economic growth. Innovation is the process through which people create new products, new processes, mew organizations, new management practices and new strategies. Another thing is that a free market economy is better at stimulating innovation than a command economy that does not have the same types of incentives for individual initiative.

Innovation also depends on a strong protection of property rights, as innovators and entrepreneurs need some level of assurance that they will be able to reap the benefits of their initiative.

While it is possible to have innovation and economic growth in a totalitarian state, many believe that economic growth and a free market system will eventually lead a country to becoming more democratic.

Geography can also affect economic development. A landlocked country with an inhospitable climate, poor soil, few natural resources, and terrible diseases is unlikely to develop economically as fast as country with the opposite characteristics on each of these attributes.

While it can be hard to do much about unfavorable geography, education is something that governments can affect. Numerous studies suggest that countries that invest more in the education of their young people develop faster economically. Examples include Japan, South Korea, and many Asian countries.

STATES IN TRANSITION

Since the late 1980s, there have been two major changes in the political economy of many of the world's nations. First, a wave of democratic revolutions swept the world, and many of the previous totalitarian regimes collapsed. Secondly, there has been a move away from centrally planned and mixed economies towards free markets.

Eastern Europe and Soviet Union

Following the Second World War, Soviet backed Communist Governments took power in eight Eastern European sates: Poland, Czechoslovakia, Hungary, Bulgaria, Albania, Romania, Yugoslavia and East Germany. This set the scene for 40 years of ideological conflict between the Communist bloc, dominated by the Soviet Union and the democratic west.

The conflict started melting in 1985 when Mikhail Gorbachev became General Secretary of the Soviet Communist party and began his program of Glasnost and Perestroika. During 1989, communist governments fell globally. The biggest change occurred in 1991 in the Soviet Union. By 1991, the USSR had already moved significantly down the road toward political freedom, but not economic freedom. On January 1, 1992, the Union of Soviet Socialist Republics passed into history, to be replaced by 15 independent republics, 11 of which elected to remain associated as a commonwealth of independent states.

The post communist history has not been easy. The move toward greater political and economic freedom has often been accompanied by economic and political chaos. These countries stated dismantling decades of price controls, allowed private ownerships of businesses and permitted much greater competition and privatization of its sate owned enterprises.

But, most of these enterprises were inefficient and the private investors were not interested. The new democratic governments continued supporting these loss making enterprises to save from massive unemployment's. the resulted subsidies resulted in budget deficits that was balanced by "printing money". Along with lack of price controls, this led to inflation. In 1993, the inflation rate was 21 percent in Hungary, 38 percent in Poland, 841 percent in Russia and 10,000 percent in Ukraine. GDP also fell. However, there is improvement in economic conditions in Poland, Czech etc.

The revolutions in the USSR and Eastern Europe have (in general) moved these countries towards democracy (away from totalitarianism), towards individualism (away from collectivism), and towards mixed economies (away from command). The transitions have been difficult, however, and economic progress has not been easy. Recent elections have brought "reformed" communists back into power in some countries, and the economic problems facing the people are significant.

There are three main reasons for the spread of democracy. First, many totalitarian regimes failed to deliver economic progress to the vast bulk of their populations. Secondly, improved information technology limited the ability of the government to control citizens' access to information. Thirdly, increases in wealth and the standard of living have encouraged citizens to push for democratic reforms.

While there are general movements towards democracy and open economies, this does not mean that there is necessarily going to be a homogenization of civilization. At the same time, we see a further definition and development of both Islamic and Chinese civilizations.

Western Europe

In Western Europe, there has been a general trend towards privatization of state owned companies and deregulation of industry. In many western European countries, basic industries such as telecommunications, energy production, airlines and railroads were often state owned, while many other sectors were protected with heavy sate regulations.

Starting with Margaret Thatcher's conservative government in Britain during the early 1980's Britain has moved to privatization of these state owned enterprises. Sate owned industries have been privatized(sold to private investors) and restrictive regulations were lifted.

Asia

During the 1980's and early 1990's a shift toward greater political democracy occurred in the Philippines, Thailand, Taiwan and South Korea. In Vietnam, the ruling communist party removed many price controls and began to shift toward a market economy. In North Korea, also situation is changing to better relations with South Korea, which was their archrival. In India, in 1991, under the Government of P.V. Narasimha Rao, began a reform program aiming to free market economy.

In China too, the communist government started the shift from a pure command economy to a mixed economy. Private ownership was allowed. The most important of them was the creation of a number of special economic zones in which free markets were allowed to operate without any restrictions, private ownership was allowed and foreign companies were permitted to invest. China's economy as a whole has been growing at over 10 percent per year during 1990's. Japan's growth after Second World War also is phenomenal.

Latin America

During the 1980s, most Latin American countries changed from being run by dictatorship to democratically elected governments. While most countries previously had erected high barriers to imports and investment (to keep multinationals from "dominating" their economies), they now mostly are encouraging investment, lowering barriers, and privatizing state owned enterprises. The tide began to turn in the 1970's in Chile, under the military dictatorship, shifted sharply in the direction of a free market economy. The largest shift occurred in Mexico, then run by the civilian government of President Salinas, moved toward free market economy. Under him, Mexico, privatized many state owned enterprises, cancelled many of the laws that limited FDI, cut import tariffs to world levels, and in 1994, brought Mexico in to North American Free Trade Agreement (NAFTA) with the US and Canada. Two Latin American giants, Argentina and Brazil also followed Mexico to join NAFTA.

Africa

Africa is also moving toward more democratic modes of government and free market economies. Most African countries gained their independence from colonial powers particularly Britain, France and Portugal in the 1950's and 1960's.most of them became one party sates ruled by authoritarian leaders.

Today both socialism and totalitarianism are slowly ret4eraing form Africa. During 1994, South Africa, Malawi, and Mozambique all held their first democratic elections and 1996 in Sierra Leone and Uganda.

But according to the world bank's report, even of the African countries now achieve a 3 percent annual growth in GDP, it will take 40 years before many return to the level of economic growth they were at the early 1970's!!

Another report shows that foreign investors who are attracted to Africa because of cheap labor are deterred by the problem s of doing business in countries where the rules of law is so weak that even simple contracts can be difficult to enforce and they have to bribe poorly paid bureaucrats who can otherwise make business impossible.

The great hope for Africa is that the continent's potential economic powers, which include Nigeria, Kenya, and South Africa which might pull the rest of Africa along with them.

IMPLICATIONS FOR BUSINESS

These transitions are creating huge opportunities for international business, as well as creating huge risks. It is not clear what direction future changes will take, and if these will be entirely favorable for business. The shift toward a market-based economic system typically involves at least three distinct activities: deregulation, privatization, and legal enforcement of property rights. Deregulation involves removing restrictions on the free operation of markets. Privatization transfers the ownership of state property into the hands of private investors. In order to attract investment and protect the interests of the private enterprise encouraged by the first two activities, changes typically need to be made to legal systems to protect the property rights of investors and entrepreneurs.

Attractiveness of a Country

The political, economic, and legal environment of a country clearly influences the attractiveness of a country. A country's attractiveness can be best evaluated by looking at the benefits, costs, and risks of doing business in that country.

The long run monetary benefits of doing business in a country are a function of the size of the market, the present wealth (purchasing power) of consumers, and the likely future wealth of consumers. By identifying and investing early in a potential future economic star, firms may be able to gain first mover advantages (advantages that belong to an early entrants into the business market) and establish loyalty and experience in a country. Two factors that are reasonably good predictors of a country's future economic prospects are its economic system and property rights regime.

Cost of doing business: A number of political, economic, and legal factors determine the costs of doing business in a country. Political costs can involve the cost of paying bribes or lobbying for favorable or fair treatment. Economic costs relate primarily to the sophistication of the economic system, including the infrastructure and supporting businesses. Regarding legal costs, it can be more costly to do business in countries with dramatically different product, workplace, and pollution standards, or where there is poor legal protection for property rights.

Risks of doing business: Political risk is the likelihood that political forces will cause drastic changes in a country's business environment that adversely affects the profits or other goals of the business. Economic risk is the likelihood the economic mismanagement will likewise affect a business. Legal risk is the likelihood that a trading partner may opportunistically break a contract or expropriate intellectual property rights.

As a general point, it should be noted that the costs and risks associated with doing business in a foreign country are typically lower in economically advanced and politically stable democratic nations, whereas the risks are greater in less developed and politically unstable nations. The assessment is complicated, however, by the fact that the potential long-run benefits bear little relationship to a nation's current stage of economic development or political stability. Rather, they are dependent upon likely future economic growth rates. In turn, among other things, economic growth appears to be a function of a free market system and a country's capacity for growth (which may be greater in less developed nations). This leads one to the conclusion that, other things being equal, the benefit, cost, and risk tradeoff is likely to be most favorable in the case of politically stable developing nations that have free market systems. It is likely to be least favorable in the case of politically unstable developing nations that operate with a mixed or command economy.

Ethical Issues

Country differences give rise to some interesting ethical issues. Some of them are discussed below.

One major ethical dilemma facing firms from the Western democracies us whether they should do business in totalitarian countries that violates the human rights of their citizens (e.g.: China)

One ethical concern regards whether firms should invest in countries where the government represses its citizens in political and/or economic freedom. While some argue that investing in these countries is implicitly supporting the repression, others argue that the best way to encourage change is from within, and that increasing economic development of the country will lead to greater political and economic freedoms.

A second ethical concern regards whether an international firm should adopt consistent and high levels of product safety, worker safety, and environmental protection worldwide, or whether they should focus only on meeting local regulations. If they adopt high standards, and subsequently lose business to other competitors with lower standards, was this an ethically correct position for it to take in light its requirements to act in the best interest of shareholders and provide advancement opportunities for its personnel? If the question is taken to extremes, is it ethical for a company to make a decision that might ultimately put it out of business and put its employees out of work?

Another ethical concern regards whether firms should pay bribes to governmental officials or business partners in exchange for business access. Should paying bribes be completely avoided, or are bribes just another cost of doing business that "grease the wheels" and lead to benefits for both the firm and consumers.

If bribes are an integral part of business transactions in a country, is a firm being culturally insensitive and elitist if it finds bribes repulsive and refuses to pay them? One answer is that bribes are illegal, according to the regulations of the US government. Again, these considerations are not faced by executives in domestic firms as they only occur in international business.

Take for example the challenges involved in Microsoft's entry into China. Although the use of pirated software was out of control in China, the company found little solace in the courts when its tried to stop that piracy, despite prolonged, expensive attempts. One of the obvious problems is that the price of most of Microsoft's products far exceeds the financial ability of Chinese.

By steadfastly adhering to its principles of intellectual ownership, Microsoft gave birth to a competitor—the Linux operating system that appeared to be a good, cheap alternative to the Chinese.

Arguments for and against bribery

For	against
• Necessary to do business	• Wrong
• Common practice	• Illegal
• Accepted practice	• Compromise personal beliefs
• Form of commission, tax, or compensation	• Promotes government corruption
	• Prohibits taking a stand for honesty
	• Benefits recipient only
	• Creates dependence on corruption
	• Deceives stockholders

Four Actions for Improving International Business Ethics

- Create global codes of conduct
    - o Global codes and standards set by corporations
    - o Global Codes and standards set by international organizations
- Integrate ethics into a global strategy
- Suspend activities in host country
- Create ethical impact statements

Global Codes and Standards Developed by International Organizations

- Caux Principles
- Global Reporting Initiative
- Global Sullivan Principles
- OECD Guidelines for Multinational Enterprises
- Principles for Global Corporate Responsibility: Benchmarks
- UN Global Compact

Fundamental International Rights

1. The right to physical movement
2. The right to ownership of property
3. The right to freedom from torture
4. The right to a fair trial
5. The right to nondiscriminatory treatment
6. The right to physical security
7. The right to freedom of speech and association
8. The right to minimal education
9. The right to political participation
10. The right to subsistence.

Seven Moral Guidelines for MNCs

- Inflict no intentional or direct harm
- Produce more good than bad for the host country
- Contribute to host country's development
- Respect the human rights of their employees

- Pay their fair share of taxes
- Respect local cultural beliefs that do not violate moral norms
- Cooperate with the government to develop and enforce background institutions.

NATIONAL DIFFERENCES OF INDIA

India before the Reforms

After independence, India adopted a democratic system of Government. Our economic system is a mixed economy with a heavy dose of state owned enterprises, centralized planning and subsidies.

This system constrained the growth of private sector, which could expand only with the Government permission (License Raj). This resulted in long delays due to bureaucratic hurdles or red tapism.

In 1956, Industrial revolution reserved much of the heavy industries like auto, chemicals steel, mining etc. to state owned enterprises. Production quotas and high tariffs on imports also stunned the growth of a healthy private sector, and labor laws added to this.

Access to foreign exchange was limited. FDI was severely restricted. Land use was strictly controlled. In addition, the government managed prices as opposed to letting them set by market forces.

India: the Reform

By the early 1990's it was realized that this system was not capable of delivering the kind of economic progress that was anticipated due to poverty, illiteracy, health care problems etc. persisted. In 1991, an ambitious economic reforms program was initiated. Much of the industrial licensing was dismantled, several sectors are opened to private sector, and disinvestments of state owned companies were started. FDI in several sectors were allowed. 100 %foreign ownership allowed in some of the sectors. 51 %in some others.

Raw materials and many industrial goods were freely imported. In addition, the tariff on imports was reduced from 400% to 65%. The income and corporate tax rates reduced.

The responses to these reforms were impressive. Growth rate increased to 61 %in 199's. Exports and corporate profits gone up. FDI increased top 3.5$ billions inn 1997 from a meager 150Million$ in 1991.

However by the late 1990's economic reforms were stalled. Growth rate stagnated. High deficit at 9.6%of GDP, subsidies high at 15% of GDP. Infrastructure development were sluggish and poor. Privatization slowed down due to political opposition and trade unions.

Between 1991 and 1997, the government sold equity stakes in about 40 companies to private sector but, still, there are 240 state owned companies in 1999. Attempts to further reduce import tariffs were stalled by political opposition fearing that a flood of inexpensive Chinese products would enter if the barriers came down.

This is supported by labor laws and small sector problems. Due to these, the FDI decreased from its peak of 3.5 $ billion in 1997 to 2$ billion by 2000. (China FDI is 40$billion every year)

3

Differences in Culture

INTRODUCTION

International business is different from domestic business because countries are different. This is due to the differences in culture both across and within countries, which can affect the practice of international business.

Although many differences in culture are obvious, some are subtler. Many individuals are even often not aware of their own culture. The chapter describes some of the underlying characteristics of a country that help define the values and norms of a society. This affects not only how an individual from one country must adapt to work in another country, but also how organizations must recognize how cultural differences affect the way they work with other organizations. The rule of law, so common in countries of the West, does not work well in China, where personal relationships and connections are the key to getting things done. That concept is difficult for American businesspersons to understand because they have been trained to treat everyone as equal, and to seek the solace of the court system when problems arise.

Two themes run through the chapter:

(1) cross-cultural literacy is critical to success in a foreign country and

(2) the culture of a country can directly and indirectly affect the costs of doing business in country.

The opening case helps to highlight a number of cultural blunders that have affected the success of Euro Disney. It also implies that a company that has been so successful with similar enterprises elsewhere (Japan, for instance) as Disney had been, still needs to be sensitive to the cultures of the country in which it is doing business. Much of the reason for Disney's failure was its corporate ego that believed it could get things done by a "kick-down-the-door" mentality. Failure to recognize important cultural differences almost caused the demise of Euro Disney.

What is Culture?

Definition: Culture has been defined a number of different ways. Culture is a system of values and norms that are shared among a group of people and that when taken together constitute a design for living.

While culture is a characteristic of society as a whole, it shapes individual behavior by identifying appropriate and inappropriate forms of human interaction.

The fundamental building blocks of culture are values and norms.

Values are abstract ideas about what a society believes to be good, right, and desirable. As was discussed earlier, values affect political and economic systems as well as culture. Values include attitudes towards concepts like freedom, honesty, loyalty, justice, responsibility, and personal relations including marriage. Values from the bedrock of ac culture. People argue, flight, even die over values such as "Freedom."

Norms are social rules and guidelines that prescribe the appropriate behavior in particular situations. Norms shape the actions of people towards one another. Norms can be divided into folkways and mores.

Folkways are the routine conventions of everyday life, but generally have little moral significance. Examples would be dress, eating habits, and social graces. Foreigners may be easily excused for making a few *faux pas*. (blunder) Timeliness is a good example, when timeliness is critical (test days) as well as when one may be expected to be "fashionably late." Americans tend to arrive a few minutes early fro business appointments. When invited fro dinner at someone's home it is considers polite to arrive on time or just a few minutes late. Typically, "American" individuals will have different concepts about lateness. In Britain when someone says" come fro dinner at 7 pm" he or she means come for dinner at 7.30 at 8 pm. The concept of time as a commodity is peculiar to Western society. Time can be spent, saved, wasted. That is quite different from many other societies, especially some areas of Latin

America, where time is seen as an item to be enjoyed and savored. Mores are more serious standards of behavior, the breaking of which may be very inappropriate or even illegal. Examples would be theft, adultery, murder, or use of mind-altering substances (including alcohol, caffeine, and marijuana). Mores can vary greatly between countries: what in one country may be viewed, as an innocent flirt in another may constitute a serious affront to someone's dignity or even harassment. While it is acceptable, and even expected, to consume alcohol with business associates in Japan, where evening business contacts often border on drunkenness, such actions would be disallowed and is punishable by imprisonment in the United Arab Emirates.

Norms and values are an evolutionary product of a number of factors that are at work in a society, including political and economic philosophy, social structure, religion, language, and education. Culture affects both of these factors and is affected by them.

CULTURE WITHIN NATION-STATES

The nation-state is only a rough approximation of a culture. Within a nation-state, multiple cultures can easily exist (as we can only too painfully see in the former Yugoslavia), and cultures can also cut across national borders. That can often be easily illustrated by describing the differences that exist between people in a country. It is quite easy to get individuals in the Western US to agree that the people in New York are really different and generally rude, while people in the Eastern will comment on Californians or Southerners, etc. Likewise, individuals in Stockholm will have clear opinions about how different Swedes are from the far North or far South. In virtually any country or state people will easily be able to describe the differences between city-folks and country-folks, and some will "defend" their culture while making disparaging remarks about the other.

The determinant of culture: are political and economic philosophy, the social structure of a society, and the dominant religion, language and education.

Social Structure

The social structure of a country can be described along two major dimensions: individualism vs. group and degree of stratification into classes or castes.

Individuals and Group

A group is an association of two or more individuals who have a shred sense of identity and who interact with each other unstructured ways on the basis of common set of expectations about each other's behavior.

While groups are found in different societies, societies differ according to the degree to which the group is viewed as the primary means of social organization. In some of societies individual attributes and achievements are viewed as being more important than group memberships while in some the opposite is true.

Individual: A focus on the individual and individual achievement is common in many Western societies. Earlier we discussed the implications of this for political and economic systems. An emphasis on individual achievement has positive and negative implications. On the positive side, the dynamism of the US economy owes much to people like Sam Walton, Steve Jobs, and Bill Gates - people, who took chances, tried new things, succeeded, and encouraged others to do likewise. They have an admiration of "rugged individualism and entrepreneurship". On the other hand, individualism can lead to a lack of company loyalty and failure to gain company-specific knowledge, competition between individuals in a company rather than team building, and limitation of people's ability to develop a strong network of contacts within a firm.

While moving from company to company may be good for individual mangers it may not be good for companies. The lack of loyalty and commitment to an individual company and the tendency to move on when a better offer comes can result in mangers, who have good general skills but lack in depth knowledge. The emphasis on individualism may make it difficult to build within an organization to perform collective tasks. If individuals are always competing with each other on the basis of individual performance, it may prove difficult for them to cooperate in group.

The group: In sharp contrast to the Western emphasis on the individual, in many Asian societies the group is the primary unit of social organization. While in earlier times the group was usually the family or the village, today the group may be a work team or business organization. In a social setting, Asian employees may often say they work for Sony, while a Western employee may say he/she is an electrical engineer. In Asia, the worth of an individual is more linked to the success of the group rather than individual achievement. This emphasis on the group may discourage job switching between firms, encourage lifetime employment systems, and lead to cooperation in solving business problems.

Some argue that competitive advantage of Japanese enterprises in the global economy is based on their ability to achieve close cooperation between individuals within a company and between companies. (Suppliers). Lifetime employment is the norm is most Japanese companies, where managers and workers build up knowledge, experience and a network of interpersonal business contacts. All these things can help managers perform their jobs more effectively and achieve cooperation with others.

On the other hand, it tends to suppress individual creativity and initiative. US may continue to be more successful than Japan at pioneering radically new products and new ways of doing business.

Social Stratification

Social categories in a society defined in the basis of characteristics such as the family background, occupation and income.

All societies have some sort of stratification, where individuals in higher strata or castes are likely to have a better education, standard of living, and work opportunities. What matters is less what these strata are, but rather the mobility between strata and the significance of strata levels for business.

The term social mobility refers to the extent to which individuals varies significantly from society to society. A caste system is closed system of stratification in which social position is usually is not possible during an individual's lifetime. (i.e., social mobility is very limited.)

The mobility permitted by culture affects whether individuals can move up (or down) in strata, and can limit the types of jobs and education available. In the USA, individuals are very mobile ("anyone can become president"), in Britain, there is less mobility, and the caste system in India severely limits mobility. Despite the laws against it, the effects of the caste system in India still exist today, and are especially prevalent in the practice of people in non-urban areas. The significance of the social strata can have important implications for the management and organization of businesses. In cultures where there is a great deal of consciousness over the class of others, the way individuals from different classes work together (i.e. management and labor) may be very prescribed and strained in some cultures (i.e. Britain), or have almost no significance in others (i.e. Japan). The class of a person may be very important in some hiring and promotion decisions, particularly in sales organizations where the person will be dealing with customers that may also come from a particular class.

Religious and Ethical Systems

Religion can be defined *as a system of shared beliefs and rituals that are concerned with the realm of the sacred.*

Ethical systems refer to a set of moral principles, or values, that are used to guide and shape behavior. The ethical practices of individuals within a culture are often closely intertwined with their religion. While there are literally thousands of religions worldwide, four that have the largest following are discussed: Christianity, Islam, Hinduism, and Buddhism. Confucianism, while not a religion, influences behavior and shapes culture in many parts of Asia. Refer the Map to see dominant religions across the world.

Christianity is the largest religion and is common throughout Europe, the Americas, and other countries settled by Europeans. Within Christianity, there are three major branches: Protestant, Roman Catholic, and Eastern Orthodox. At the turn of the century Max Weber suggested that is was the "Protestant work ethic", that was the driving force of capitalism. This focus on hard work, wealth creation, and frugality encouraged capitalism while the Catholic promise of salvation in the next world did not foster the same kind of work ethic. The Protestant emphasis on individual religious freedom, in contrast to the hierarchical Catholic Church, was also consistent with the individualist economic and political philosophy discussed earlier.

Islam: with 750 million followers this is the second largest of the world's major religions. Islam dates back to AD 610 when Prophet Mohammed began spreading the word. Muslims constitute a majority of aver 35 countries and inhabit a nearly continuous stretch of land from the north west coast of Africa , through the middle east, to china and Malaysia and far east.

Islam extends this to more of an all-embracing way of life that governs one's being. It also prescribes many more "laws" on how people should act and live. These are laws that are entirely counter to the US "separation of church and state." In Islam, people do not own property, but only act as stewards for God and thus must take care of that with which they have been entrusted. They must use property in a righteous, socially beneficial, and prudent manner; not exploit others for their own benefit; and they have obligations to help the disadvantaged. Thus while Islam is supportive of business, the way business is practiced is strictly prescribed. For instance, no interest may be paid on business loans.

Hinduism: approximately 500 million followers, practiced primarily on the Indian sub-continent, over 4,000 years ago, making it the world's oldest major religion. Hinduism focuses on the importance of achieving spiritual growth and development, which may require material and physical self-denial. Since Hindus are valued by their spiritual rather than material achievements, there is not the same work ethic or focus on entrepreneurship found in some other religions. Likewise, promotion and adding new responsibilities may not be the goal of an employee, or may be infeasible due to the employee's caste.

Buddhism: Buddhists also stress spiritual growth and the afterlife, rather than achievement while in this world. Buddhism, practiced mainly in Southeast Asia, does not support the caste system, however, so individuals do have some mobility not found in Hinduism and can work with individuals from different classes. There are around 250 million Buddhists, most of who are found in Central and Southeast Asia, China, Korea and Japan.

Confucianism: practiced mainly in China, Korea, and Japan. This teaches the importance of attaining personal salvation through right action. Unlike religions, Confucianism is not concerned with the supernatural and has little to say about the concept of a supreme being or an afterlife. The needs for high moral and ethical conduct and loyalty to others are central in Confucianism. Three key teachings of Confucianism - loyalty, reciprocal obligations, and honesty - may all lead to a lowering of the cost of doing business in Confucian societies. The close ties between Japanese auto companies and their suppliers, called keiretsus, have been an important ingredient in the Japanese success in the auto industry. They have facilitated loyalty, reciprocal obligations, and honesty. In countries where these relationships are more adversarial and not bound by these same values, the costs of doing business are probably higher.

Language

The language of a society allows it to communicate but also directs the attention of people towards certain features of the world and human interactions. A good example is how the Inuit (Eskimos) have 24 words for snow, but no word for the overall concept. (Powder snow, falling snow, wet snow, drifting snow etc.) Language helps describe how different people see the world.

Since language shapes the way people perceive the world, it also helps define the culture. In countries with more than one language, one also finds often more than one culture. In Canada, there is English speaking culture and a French speaking culture. Tensions between the two run often high demanding independence from a Canada

"Dominated by English speakers."

While English is clearly the language of international business, knowing at least some of the local language can greatly help when working in another country. In some situations, knowing the local language can be critical for business success. Knowledge of the local language is often taken as an indication that the businessperson is willing to meet the local firm "on its own court."

Unspoken language can be just as important for communication. Using a few facial expressions and hand gestures to the class can illustrate the point. The fact that these can have different interpretations in different cultures, and that many of these actions may be automatic or reflexive, obviously complicates international communication. Not only may the person you are dealing with be unintentionally sending non-verbal signals that you do not understand or find misleading, you may be unconsciously sending your own signals. For example, consider different perceptions of "personal space" in communications. Have a conversation with an individual (about sports or the weather) standing "a long distance apart" and a similar conversation with someone else with your faces only a few inches apart. Most individuals find both of these extreme, although a few reserved Midwesterners will find the long distance quite acceptable. People from different countries will also comment on their perceptions, and how distance varies with familiarity with the person.

Education

Schools, as a part of the social structure of a society, and one that individuals are exposed to in their formative years, convey many cultural values and norms. Education plays an important role as determinant of national business competitive advantage. The availability of a pool of skilled and educated human resources seems to be major determinant for the economical success of a country.

The knowledge base, training, and educational opportunities available to a country's citizens can also give it a competitive advantage in the market and make it a more or less attractive place for expanding business. In nations that have a ready trained workforce for particular types of jobs, it is easier to start operations than in nations where an investor will also have to undertake time-consuming and costly training.

Michael Porter notes that Japan's excellent education system was an important factor explaining the country's post war economic success.

The general education level of a country is also a good index of the kind of products that might sell in a country and of the type of promotional material that should be used.

Although there is not a perfect correspondence between educational spending and literacy rates, a relation does exist, and spending on education does give an indication of a country's commitment to education.

CULTURE AND THE WORKPLACE

For an international business with operations in different countries, it is important to understand how a society's culture impacts on the values found in the workplace. The opening and closing cases both provide examples of culture affecting the workplace.

Hofstede's model

The most famous study of how culture relates to values in the workplace was undertaken by Geert Hofstede. As part of his job as a psychologist working for IBM, from 1967 to 1973, Hofstede collected data on employee attitudes and values for over 1, 00,000 individuals.

This data enabled him to compare dimensions of culture across 40 countries. Geert Hofstede made a study of IBM employees worldwide, and identified four dimensions that summarize different cultures: power distance, individualism vs. collectivism, uncertainty avoidance, and masculinity vs. femininity.

- Power distance dimension focused on how a society deals with the fact that the people are unequal in physical and intellectual capabilities. According got Hofstede, high power distance cultures were found in countries that let inequalities grow over time into inequalities of power and wealth. Low power distance cultures were found in societies that tried to play down such inequalities as much as possible.
- The individualism versus collectivism dimension focused on the relationship between individuals and his or her fellows. In individualistic societies, the ties between individuals were loose and individuals achievement and freedom were highly valued. In societies where collectivism was emphasized the ties between individuals were tight. In such societies people were born into collectivists, such as extended families and everyone was supposed to look after the interests of his or her near ones.
- Uncertainty avoidance dimension measured the extent to which different cultures socialized their members into accepting ambiguous situations and tolerating uncertainty. Members of high uncertainty avoidance cultures placed a premium on jib security, career patterns, and retirement benefits and so on. They also had a strong need for rules and regulations, the manager was expected to issue clearer instructions, and subordinates initiatives were highly controlled. Lower uncertainty avoidance cultures were characterized by greater readiness to take risks and less emotional resistance to change.
- Masculinity Vs femininity dimension looked at the relationship between the gender roles and work roles. In masculine cultures, sex roles were sharply differentiated and traditional masculine values such as achievement and the effective exercise of power, determined cultural ideals. In feminine cultures sex roles were less sharply distinguished and little differentiation was made between men and women in the same job.

Hofstede created an index score for each of four dimensions that range from 0 to 100 and scored high for high individualism, high power distance, high uncertainty avoidance and high masculinity. He averaged the score of all employees from a given country and plotted the result scores of each country on series of graphs.

	Power Distance	Uncertainty Avoidance	Indivi-dualism	Masculinity
Argentina	49	86	46	56
Brazil	69	76	38	49
France	68	86	71	43
India	77	40	48	56
Japan	54	92	46	95
Mexico	81	82		69
Netherlands	38	53	80	14
U.S.A.	40	46	91	62

Criticisms against the Study:

- First Hofstede assumes that there is a one to one correspondence between culture and the states of a country, many countries have more that one culture.
- Second, the research tem was composed of Europeans and Americans. The questions and answers may have been shaped by their own cultural biases.
- Third, his research worked only within a single industry, the computer industry, but also within a single company, IBM. It is possible that the values of IBM employees are different in important respects from the cultures of the countries they originally come from.
- Fourth, the study, which is conducted between 1960s and 1970, may not be reasonable today, and may be outdated.

While critics have concerns about Hofstede's methodology, and it is important not to take it all too seriously, the study does suggest what individuals should consider when doing business from individuals from another country.

CULTURAL CHANGE

Culture is not a constant, but does evolve over time. What was acceptable behavior in the US in the 1960s is now considered "insensitive" or even harassment. Language and sensuality that was not allowed on Indian TV in the 1960s is now commonplace. Changes are taking place all the time. As countries become economically stronger and increase in the globalization of products bought and sold, cultural change is particularly common.

IMPLICATIONS FOR BUSINESS

Countries are so different because of cultural changes. Two important implications of international business flow from these differences. The first is to appreciate not only that cultural differences exist, but also what such differences mean for the practice of international business. The second is due to the cultural differences, the cost of doing the business in a country, and national competitive advantage may vary.

Cross Cultural Literacy

Individuals and firms must develop cross-cultural literacy. International businesses that are ill informed about the practices of another culture are unlikely to succeed in that culture. One way to develop cross-cultural literacy is to regularly rotate and transfer people internationally.

One must also beware of ethnocentric behavior, or a belief in the superiority of one's own culture. Along with this superiority, they may develop contempt for all the other cultures. Some people have been unable to find some of the obvious weaknesses in our own culture and strengths of other cultures. Some people are unaware of the uniqueness of the culture. One good example on the uniqueness of American culture is the second free cup of coffee. It is so common in American restaurants, yet is unheard of in many European or Asian countries. People who have traveled internationally can often identify many other examples.

Culture and Competitive Advantage

Cultural values can influence the costs of doing business in different countries, and ultimately the competitive advantage of the country. The text suggests some positive and negative aspects of US and Japanese culture than may have contributed to the economic success of these countries. Understanding what countries may have a competitive advantage has implications both for looking for potential competitors in world markets and for deciding where to undertake international expansion.

1. Discuss the implications of international business arising out of cultural differences between countries? (June-July 2003-10 marks)
2. Discuss and evaluate Geert Hofstede's model of culture at work place? (June-July 2003- 7 marks)
3. What is social mobility and how does it affect international business? (3 marks)

Additional notes:

The debate of globalization VS anti-globalization

IMPACT ON		Globalists	Antiglobalists
	Consumers	Free trade promotes lower costs and quality products.	Benefits the wealth at the expense of the poor
	Employees	Faster economic growth promotes Higher wages, etc.	Places profits above people
	Environment	Creates resources needed to address the issue	Exploits and destroys ecosystems
	Developing Nations	Promotes national economic development, higher standard of living, etc.	World financial institutions conspire to keep poor nations in debt
	Human Rights	Creates cultures that support law and free expression	Corporations pursing profits ignore human rights violations

4

Regional Economic Integration

INTRODUCTION

Definition: Regional Economic Integration means agreements between groups of countries in a geographic region to reduce and ultimately remove tariff and non-tariff barriers tot eh free flow of goods, services and factors of production between each other.

GATT and WTO are the biggest association of more than 140 member countries, which strive to reduce the barriers. However, more than regional, WTO has a global perspective.

By entering into regional agreements, groups of countries aim to reduce trade barriers more rapidly than can be achieved under WTO. While there have been decreases in the global barriers to trade and investment, the greatest progress had been made on a regional basis.

There are many examples in the current popular push on the European Union (EU) and the effects the EU have on a particular business or industry that illustrates this point.

Perhaps the best example of the benefits of economic integration and political union is the USA. Before the current constitution was written, the thirteen colonies had erected significant barriers to trade between each other and had separate currencies. Seeing that this was not working well, and wanting a better system for their citizens, the founding fathers agreed to combine their separate states into a United States. Whether the EU, with its significant cultural and language differences in neighboring countries, can achieve similar benefits remains to be seen. Nevertheless, major gains have already been made. The notion of regional economic integration is becoming increasingly important as countries strive to work together better and become more productive. While integration takes place at a much broader level under the WTO, it is within local regions — with fewer countries — that have the ability to make much greater steps.

Integration creates both winners and losers, however. An important challenge facing many firms and governments is what should be done to minimize the costs of transition to freer markets regionally as well as internationally.

LEVELS OF ECONOMIC INTEGRATION

Free Trade Area: All barriers to trade among members are removed, but each member can determine its own trade policies with non-members. Theoretically free trade are

Customs Union: All barriers to trade among members are removed and a common external trade policy is adopted.

Common Market: All barriers to trade among members are removed, a common external trade policy is adopted, and factors of production allow mobility between countries.

Economic Union: All barriers to trade among members are removed, a common external trade policy is adopted, factors of production allow mobility between countries, a common currency is established, tax rates are harmonized, and a common monetary and fiscal policy is established.

Political Union: Separate nations are essentially combined to form a single nation. The establishment of the European Parliament suggests that Europe is moving towards political union. Giving up this last bit of sovereignty, however, is a big step psychologically and philosophically.

THE ARGUMENTS FOR REGIONAL INTEGRATION

The economic case for integration has been largely presented in the previous chapters. Free trade and movement of goods, services, capital, and factors of production allow for the most efficient use of resources. That is positive sum game, as all countries can benefit.

Regional economic integration is an attempt to go beyond the limitations of WTO. While it is hard for 100 countries to agree on something, (e.g. the United Nations) it is much more likely that only a few countries with close proximity and common interests will be able to agree to even fewer restrictions on the flows between their countries. The political case for integration has two main points:

(1) By linking countries together, making them more dependent on each other, and forming a structure where they regularly have to interact, the likelihood of violent conflict and war will decrease.

(2) By linking countries together, they have greater influence and are politically much stronger in dealing with other nations.

In the case of the EU, both a desire to decrease the likelihood of another world war and an interest in being strong enough to stand up to the US and USSR were factors in its creation.

There are two main impediments(obstacles) to integration:

(1) there are always painful adjustments, and groups that are likely to be directly hurt by integration will lobby hard to prevent losses,

(2) concerns about loss of sovereignty and control over domestic interests.

For example, Canada has always been concerned about being dominated by its southern neighbor, and Britain is very hesitant to give much control to European bureaucrats (it still has not adopted the euro)

The case on NAFTA and the US Textile Industry shows that although the effects of NAFTA have hurt employment in the US textile industry, the overall effect has actually been positive. The reason: clothing prices have fallen, exports have increased, and sales to apparel factories have surged. Those factors more than compensate for the loss of jobs.

THE ARGUMENTS AGAINST REGIONAL INTEGRATION

Many groups within a country do not accept the case for integration, especially those that are likely to be hurt or those that feel that sovereignty and individual discretion will be reduced. Thus, it is not surprising that most attempts to achieve integration have progressed slowly and with hesitation. Whether regional integration is in the economic interests of the participants depends upon the extent of trade creation as opposed to trade diversion.

Trade creation occurs when low cost producers within the free trade area replace high cost domestic producers.

Trade diversion occurs when higher cost suppliers within the free trade area replace lower cost external suppliers.

A regional free trade agreement will only make the world better off if the amount of trade it creates exceeds the amount it diverts.

REGIONAL ECONOMIC INTEGRATION IN EUROPE

Refer Map to identify the member countries of the EU. The EU is large economically and politically, and many of the independent countries that were under the influence of the former USSR have sought to join the EU.

- Hungary
- Ireland
- Italy
- Latvia
- Lithuania
- Estonia
- Finland
- France
- Germany
- Greece
- Austria
- Belgium
- Czech Republic
- Cyprus
- Denmark
- Slovakia
- Slovenia
- Spain
- Sweden
- United Kingdom
- Luxembourg
- Malta
- Netherlands
- Poland
- Portugal

MEMBER COUNTRIES OF EUROPEAN UNION

The forerunner of the EU was the European Coal and Steel Community, which had the goal of removing barriers to trade in coal, iron, steel, and scrap metal formed in 1951. The Treaty of Rome formed the EEC in 1957. While the original goal was for a common market, progress was generally very slow.

Over the years, the EU expanded in spurts, as well as moved towards ever-greater integration.

Many countries that are now members of the EU were initially members of EFTA who felt either that the EU were pushing for too much integration too fast, or were denied entry by other member states. Norway, while always a member of EFTA, has twice had its citizens vote down membership in the EU because they felt they would lose too much control to their much bigger neighbors to the south. Being a small country, they felt they would have little say in policies, and would be forced to adopt policies that were unfavorable to their prospering oil and fisheries industries. (And it is generally true that the EU would like to have the benefits from these industries spread around.) Nevertheless, since most of Norway's trade is with EU member countries, it has chosen to adopt many EU regulations — and is in fact in greater compliance with EU regulations than some of the EU member states.

The economic policies of the EU are formulated and implemented by a complex and still evolving political structure. The five main institutions are the European Council, the Council of Ministers, the European Commission, the European Parliament, and the Court of Justice.

The problems with lack of progress on the objectives of the EU resulted in a number of problems for firms and governments, and led to adoption of the Single European Act in 1987. The Single European Act called for the removal of border controls, mutual recognition of standards, open public procurement, a barrier free financial services industry, no currency exchange controls, free and open freight transport, and freer and more open competition.

The Management Focus on the EU and the media industry mergers shows the power that the EU has acquired in controlling and regulating mergers of international companies. Through the use of concessions, the EU has been able to dramatically change the shape of an entire industry.

The Treaty of Maastricht took the EU one step further, by specially spelling out the steps to economic union and partial political union. In addition to simply spelling out the steps needed, the Treaty also laid out the future outlines of a common foreign policy, economic policy, defense policy, citizenship, and currency, as well as strengthened the role of the European Parliament. The single currency will eliminate exchange costs and reduce risk, making EC firms more efficient.

The Euro was officially launched on January 1, 1999. It became into full use On January 1, 2002. Member states that have entered into monetary union have fixed exchange rates with the Euro, and hence with each other. The Euro reduces both exchange rate costs and risks, and has been used for many business transactions. The use of national currencies was discontinued in 2002 in favor of the euro, although many member banks will accept their national currency in exchange for the euro. Adoption of the Euro will help citizens more easily compare prices, should increase cross border competition, and lead to lower costs for consumers.

Britain, Denmark, and Sweden have chosen to opt out of joining EMU for now. One reason is a concern over losing control over monetary policy to the European Central Bank. Some believe that currency union should only take place after political union.

A number of countries have applied for membership in the EU, particularly from Eastern Europe. Given the profound differences in income, development, and systems, however, makes near term integration of these countries into the EU difficult.

Many firms and countries (including the EFTA countries) are concerned that the EU will result in a "fortress Europe," where insiders will be given preferential treatment over outsiders. That clearly already exists in agriculture, although whether it will be extended to other areas is a matter of debate.

REGIONAL ECONOMIC INTEGRATION IN THE AMERICAS

Refer map to see the primary areas of integration in the Americas.

These are:

- The North American Free Trade Agreement (NAFTA)
- The Andean Pact
- MERCOSUR
- Other Latin American trade pacts like Central American common market, CARICOM etc.
- The North American Free Trade Agreement (NAFTA)

In 1988, the USA and Canada agreed to form a free trade area, with the goal of gradually eliminating all barriers to the trade of goods and services between the countries. In 1991 the US, Canada, and Mexico signed an agreement aimed at forming a free trade area between all three countries known as NAFTA.

The agreement became law in January 1, 1994. it contains the flowing actions.

- Abolishes within 10 years tariffs on 99 percent goods traded between Mexico, Canada and United States.

- Removes barriers on cross border flow of services, e.g., allowing financial institutions unrestricted access to Mexican markets by 2000.
- Protects intellectual property rights.
- Removes restrictions on FDI between three member countries
- Allow each country to apply its own environmental standards, lowering of standards to lure investments is described as inappropriate and establish twocommissions with the power to impose fines to protect these standards.

In all three countries the political and economic consequences of the agreement are still being felt, and politicians in all countries are able to strike a cord with workers who perceive that they lost their jobs as a result of the agreement.

Arguments for NAFTA

Proponents of NAFTA argue that it will provide economic gains to all countries: Mexico will benefit from increased jobs as low cost production moves south, and will attain more rapid economic growth as a result. The US and Canada will benefit from the access to a large and increasingly prosperous market and from the lower prices for consumers from goods produced in Mexico. In addition, US and Canadian firms that have production sites in Mexico will be more competitive on world markets.

Arguments against NAFTA

Opponents of NAFTA argue that jobs will be lost and wage levels will decline in the US and Canada, Mexican workers will emigrate north, pollution will increase due to Mexico's more lax standards, and Mexico will lose its sovereignty.

Since NAFTA is an ongoing process, and the implications are still unclear, it likely will be another decade before the true costs and benefits are known. Nevertheless, recent articles in the popular press help illustrate many opportunities and some concerns.

The Andean Pact

The Andean Pact, originally formed in 1969, when Bolivia, Chile, Ecuador, Colombia and Peru signed the Cartagena agreement. The

Andean pact was largely based on EC model, and reformed and renegotiated several times, has made little progress due political and economic turmoil in most of the countries. The integration steps begun in 1969 included an internal tariff reduction program, a common tariff, a transportation policy, ac common industrial policy and special concessions for the smallest members Bolivia and Ecuador.

However, by the mid 1980's the Andean pact had collapsed. It has failed to achieve any of its stated objectives. In 1990, the heads of five current members of the Andean group-Bolivia, Ecuador, Peru, Colombia and Venezuela met in Galapagos Islands. The resulting Galapagos declaration effectively relaunched the Andean group.

The countries are making another strong attempt again, and their initial progress on removing trade barriers is promising. However, the tremendous differences between the countries will make agreement on many issues difficult.

MERCOSUR

MERCOSUR originated in 1988 as a free trade pact between Brazil and Argentina. In 1990, it was expanded to include Paraguay and Uruguay. MERCOSUR has been making progress on reducing trade barriers between member states. Today, most goods go tariff free within MERCOSUR, except sugar and cars. Trade among MERCOSUR's four core members grew from $4 billion in 1990 to $14.5 billion in 1995.

Given some high tariffs for goods from other countries, it would appear that in some industries MERCOSUR is trade diverting rather than trade creating, and local firms are investing in industries that are not competitive on a worldwide basis.

Other Latin Americans Trade Pacts

The countries of Central America are trying to revive their trade pact. In the early 1960's Costa Rica, El Salvador, Guatemala, Honduras and Nicaragua attempted to set up Central American common market. it collapsed in 1969 when the war broke out between Honduras and El Salvador. Now five countries are trying to revive their agreement.

A Customs Union was to have been created in 1991 between English speaking Caribbean countries under the name of Caribbean community. This is refereed to as CARICOM, was established in 1973.

Attempts at the creation of trade pacts between Central American and Caribbean countries have not been particularly successful thus far. There has been a goal to create a Free Trade Area of the Americas that would encompass most nations in North and South America. Thus far, there has been little progress.

REGIONAL ECONOMIC INTEGRATION ELSEWHERE

While there was clearly economic integration with COMECON, the "agreement" between the USSR and most of Eastern Europe, had little rational economic basis and has collapsed with the collapse of the central planning system.

Association of Southeast Asian Nations (ASEAN)

Formed in 1967, ASEAN currently include Brunei, Indonesia, Malaysia, Philippines, Singapore, Thailand and Vietnam. These countries are characterized by an abundance of natural resources, large international trade sectors most successful economic policies.

The basic objectives of ASEAN are to foster free trade between member countries and to achieve some cooperation in their industrial policies.

The ASEAN pact has had little impact on trade and integration, although most of the countries have grown very quickly.

Asia Pacific Economic Cooperation (APEC)

APEC is a broader Pacific organization that meets yearly and includes the US, Japan, China, and 15 other countries. These 18 countries account for half of the world's GDP, 46 percent of world trade and most of the growth in the world economy. The stated aim of APEC is to increase multilateral cooperation in view of the economic rise of the pacific nations and the growing interdependence within the region. Thus far, the goals of APEC and the photo opportunities for the leaders have been far loftier than the success.

IMPLICATIONS FOR BUSINESS

Economic integration creates a number of significant opportunities for business. Larger markets can now be served, additional countries open to trade, and greater economies of scale achieved.

The greatest implication for MNEs is that the free movement of goods across borders, the harmonization of product standards, and the simplification of tax regimes, makes it possible for them to realize potentially enormous cost economies by centralizing production in those locations where the mix of factor costs and skills is optimal. By specialization and shipping of goods between locations, a much more efficient web of operations can be created.

The lowering of barriers to trade and investment between countries will be followed by increased price competition, requiring firms to rationalize production and reduce costs if they are to remain competitive.

As other firms become more competitive in their home markets (now expanded), they may be able to enter additional markets and threaten local firms' positions.

Firms also must be concerned that they may be "locked out" of "fortress Europe" or "fortress North America," and thus may need to establish operations with a region if they are to remain an active player in the market.

5

Multinational Corporation—Organization, Design and Structures

THE STRATEGY OF INTERNATIONAL BUSINESS

Contents: how firms can increase their profitability by expanding their operations in foreign markets, different strategies that firms can pursue when competing internationally, and the pros and cross of these strategies. In addition, various factors affecting the firms' choice of strategy.

INTRODUCTION

When we think of international businesses, we often focus on the big MNEs (Multinational Enterprises). However, all of these were once small firms just beginning to expand internationally. Small firms undertake a great deal of international business.

The book to this point has looked primarily at the environment in which international business takes place, and suggested some implications for business. With this chapter, it moves into looking more specifically at firms, and the actions that they can take to both respond to and shape their environment.

STRATEGY AND THE FIRM

Firms are in the business of making profits by value creation — being able to sell what they make for more than it costs to make it. Thus, they create value by either lowering the costs of production or raising the value so that consumers will pay more. A firm can add more value to a product when it improves the product's quality, provides a service to the consumer or customize the product to consumer needs in such away that the consumers will pay more for it.

Firms can lower the costs of value creation when they find ways to perform value creation activities more efficiently. Thus, there are ttwo basic strategies for improving a firm's profitability- a differentiation strategy and a low cost strategy.

To extend this, it is useful to use the value creation approach, as shown in Figure.

Support activities

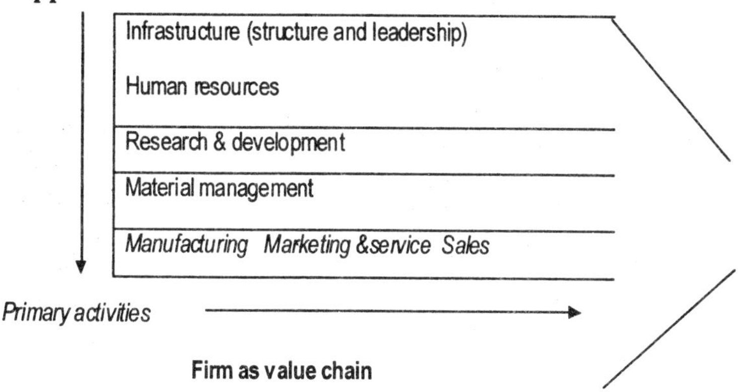

Firm as value chain

Firm is value chain composed of a series of distinct value creation activities, including production, marketing, materials management, R&D, human resources information systems and the firms;' infrastructure.

These value creation activities are classified into primary activities and support activities.

Primary activities: these have to do with creating the product, marketing and delivering the product to buyers and providing support and after sales service to the buyers of the product. Efficient production can reduce the costs of crating value (by realizing scale economies) and can add value by increasing product quality (by reducing the number of defective products)

Support activities: these provide the inputs that allow the primary activities of production and marketing to occur. The material management function controls the transmission of physical materials through the value chain from procurement through production into distribution. It also can monitor the quality of inputs into the production process. The R&D function develops new products and process technologies, which can reduce production costs and can result in the creation of more useful and more attractive products than can demand a premium price. An effective human resources function ensures that the firm has an optimal mix of people to perform the primary function efficiently. Information systems helps in getting the information it needs to maximize the efficiency of it value chain and to exploit information based competitive advantages. Firm's infrastructure with factors such as organizational structure, general management, planning, finance and legal environment also help the firm achieve more value in the primary activities.

The Role of Strategy

Strategy can be defined as the actions that managers take to attain the goals of the firm.

To be profitable in a competitive environment, affirm must pay continual attention to both reducing the costs of value creation and to differentiating its product offering in such a manner that consumers are willing to pay more for the product than it costs to produce it.

Strategy is about identifying how best a firm can go about creating value. It is often helpful for a firm to base each value creation activity at the location where factors are most conducive to the performance of that activity.

PROFITING FROM GLOBAL EXPANSION

Expanding globally allows firms both large and small to increase their profitability in a number of ways not available to purely domestic enterprises.

Firms that operate internationally have the ability to:

(1) earn a greater return from their distinctive skills or core competencies,

(2) realize location economies by dispersing individual value creation activities to those locations were they can be performed most efficiently, and

(3) realize greater experience curve economies, thereby lowering the costs of value creation.

For some companies international expansion represents a way of earning greater returns by transferring the skills and product offerings derived from their *core competencies* to markets where indigenous competitors lack those skills.

Definition: Core competence refers to skills within the firm that competitors cannot easily match or imitate.

These skills may exist in any of the value creation activities of the firm. Production, marketing, R&D, human resources, general management etc. E.g. Mc Donald's ahs a core competency in managing fast food operations, Toyota can produce high quality, well designed cats at a lower delivery costs than any other firm's in the world. For such firms' global expansions is a ay f further exploiting the value potential of their skills and the product offerings by applying those skills and the product s in larger market.

Location Economies

Due to national differences, it pays a firm to base each value creation activity it performs at that location where economic, political, and cultural conditions, including relative factor costs, are most conducive to the performance of that activity (transportation costs and trade barriers permitting). This strategy is referred as focusing upon the attainment of *location economies.* MNEs that take advantage of different locational economies around the world create a *global web* of activities. In the worldwide market, a local economy may have some specific locational advantages. For example, Silicon Valley may have a location specific advantage in a technological work force. Galveston, Texas has a port location that serves the U.S. southwest, (although it lost much of its shipping trade when the city of Houston deepened its shipping channel.)

Definition: locational economies are the economies that arise from performing a value creation activity in the optimal location for that activity, wherever in the world that might be.

E.g.: General Motors's Pontiac is marketed widely in United States, the car was designed in Germany, key components were manufactured in Japan, Taiwan, Singapore, the assembly operations was performed in South Korea, and the advertising strategy was formulated in Great Britain.

The management focus on McDonald's shows how a successful U.S. firm could export its core competency in managing fast-food operations into far reaching areas of the world.

Other implications: New Zealand may have a competitive advantage for automobile assembly operations but due to high transportation costs would make it an uneconomical location for them. U.S firms are now shifting their production form Asia to Mexico due to less transportation costs and trade barriers. Mexico has three distinct advantages over many Asian nations such as low labor costs; its proximity to large US market reduces its transportation costs; NAFTA has removed many trade barriers among Mexico, US and the Canada.

Experience Curve Economies

Definition: experience curve is the systematic reductions in the production costs that occur over life of a product.

A number of studies show that a product's production costs decline by some characteristics about each time accumulated output doubles. E.g. in aircraft industry, where each time accumulated output f airframes was doubled, unit costs typically declined to 80 percent of their previous level. That is the production costs of the fourth airframe would be 80 percent less of the production costs for the second airframe, the eighth airframe's production costs is 80 percent less of he fourth's, the sixteenth's airframe costs is 80 percent less of the eighth's and so on.

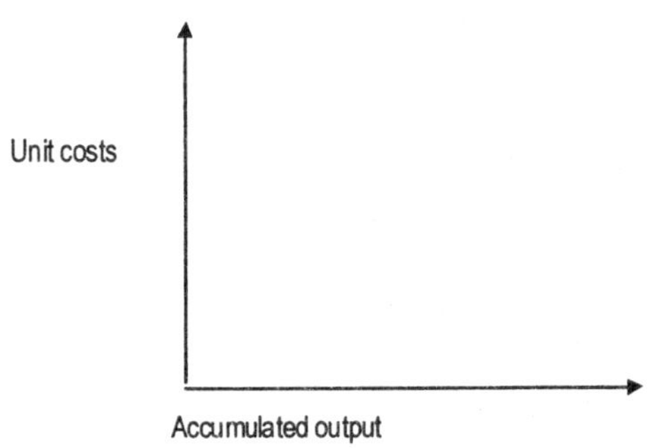

The Experience Curve

The Figure shows the experience curve that normally allows costs to be reduced with additional output.

This is due to two reasons: learning effects and economies of scale.

Learning effects: refers to the cost savings that come from learning by doing. Labor productivity increases as individuals learn the most efficient ways to perform particular tasks. Management also typically learns how to mange the new operation costs efficiently over time. But it has been suggested that learning effects are important only during the start up period of a new process and that they cease after two or three years. After that, any decline in the experience curve is due to economies of scale.

Economies of scale: refers to the reduction in unit cost achieved by producing a large volume of a product. This is mainly due to the ability to spreads fixed costs over large volume.

By building sales volume more rapidly, international expansion can assist a firm in the process of moving down the experience curve. By lowering the costs of value creation, *experience economies* can help a firm to build barriers to new competition.

PRESSURES FOR COST REDUCTIONS AND LOCAL RESPONSIVENESS

Firms that compete globally typically face two types of competitive pressures: pressures for cost reductions, and the pressures for local responsiveness in the industry in which it competes.

These competitive pressures place conflicting demands on firms.

Pressures for Cost Reductions

Responding to cost pressures requires that a firm try to lower the costs of value creation by mass-producing a standard product at the optimal locations worldwide. Pressures for cost reductions are greatest in industries producing commodity type products where price is the main competitive weapon. Pressures for cost reductions are also intense when major competitors are based in low cost locations, where there is persistent excess capacity, and where consumers are powerful and face low switching costs.

Pressures for Local Responsiveness

Pressures for local responsiveness arise from differences in consumer tastes and preferences, differences in national infrastructure and traditional practices, differences in distribution channels, and host government demands. Pressures for local responsiveness imply that it may not be possible for a firm to realize the full benefits from experience curve and location economies.

The management focus on tailoring cars to the USA market reflects how foreign automotive producers have had to change their product offerings to appeal to the American market. But, Theodore Levitt (Harvard Business school professor) has predicted emergence of enormous global markets for standardized consumer products. Levitt cites the worldwide acceptance of mc Donald's hamburgers, Coca-Cola, Levi's Strauss blue jeans and Sony televisions, which are sold as standardized products as evidence of increasing similarity of global marketplace.

STRATEGIC CHOICE

Firms use four basic strategies to enter and compete in the international environment: an international strategy, a multi domestic strategy, a global strategy, and a transnational strategy. Figure illustrates when each of these strategies is most appropriate.

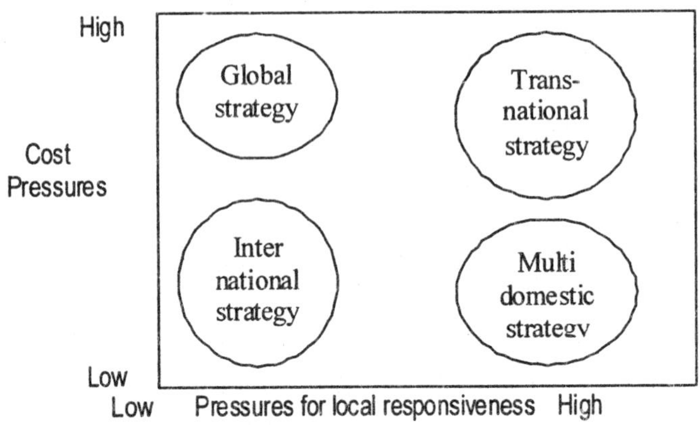

An International Strategy

Firms pursuing an international strategy transfer the skills and products derived from core competencies to foreign markets, while undertaking some limited local customization.

Most international firms have created value by transferring differentiated products developed at home to new market overseas. Accordingly, they tend to centralize product development functions at home (R&D). They also tend to establish manufacturing and marketing functions in each major country in which they do the business.

However, they may suffer from a lack of extensive local responsiveness and from an inability to exploit experience curve and location economies.

International firms include Toys R Us, McDonald's, IBM, Kellogg's and Procter &Gamble.

This strategy makes sense if the firm has valuable core competency that indigenous competitors in foreign markets lack and if the firm face relatively weak pressures for local responsiveness and cost reductions.

An international strategy makes sense if a firm has valuable core ·competency that indigenous competitors in foreign markets lack and if the firm faces relatively less pressures for local responsiveness and cost reductions. These firms tend to suffer from high operating costs due to duplications of manufacturing facilities. They may alos loose out to firms that place high emphasis on customizing the product offerings according to local needs.

Multidomestic Strategy

Firms pursuing a multidomestic strategy customize their product offering, marketing strategy, and business strategy to national conditions. They tend to transfer skills and products developed at home to foreign markets.

They have the tendency to establish a complete set of each major value creation activities including productions, marketing and R&D in each major national markets in which they do business. Most of the multidomestic firms have a high cost structure. However, they may suffer from an inability to transfer skills and products between countries, and from an inability to exploit experience curve and location economies.

This strategy makes sense when there are high pressures for local responsiveness and low pressures for cost reductions. The high cost is due to the duplications of production facilities.

Strategy	Advantages	Disadvantages
Global	Exploit experience curve effects Exploit location economies	Lack of local responsiveness
International	Transfer distinctive competencies to foreign markets	Lack of local responsiveness Inability to realize location economies Failure to exploit experience curve effects
Multidomestic	Customize product offerings and market accordance with local responsiveness.	Inability to realize location economies Failure to exploit experience curve effects Failure to transfer distinctive competencies to foreign markets
Transnational	Exploit experience curve effects Exploit location economies Customize product offerings and marketing in accordance with local responsiveness	Difficult to implement due to organizational problems.

Global Strategy

Firms pursuing a global strategy focus on reaping the cost reductions that come from experience curve and location economies. That is they are pursuing a low cost strategy. The production, marketing and R&D

activities of firms pursuing global strategy are concentrated in a few favoured locations. They tend not to customize their product offerings and market strategy to local conditions. However, they may suffer from a lack of local responsiveness. They tend to market a standardized product worldwide so that they can reap maximum benefits from economies of scales.

This strategy makes sense where there are strong pressures for cost reductions and where demands for local responsiveness are minimal. Intel, Texas Instruments, Motorola etc follow global strategy.

Transnational Strategy

In a transnational strategy, firms must exploit experience curve cost economies and location economies, transfer distinctive competencies within the firm, and pay attention to pressures for localization. To do this, there need to be flows of knowledge from the parent to subsidiaries, flows from foreign subsidiary to home country, and from foreign subsidiary to foreign subsidiary — a process called "global learning".

This strategy makes sense when a firm has high pressures for cost reductions and high pressures for local responsiveness. E.g.; Caterpillar, Unilever etc.

The approach of the transnational is not appropriate in all situations, nor is it without costs. Where demands for local responsiveness is low, a global strategy may still be the most appropriate. The coordination and management challenges of a transnational also create higher costs (and sometimes benefits) than with one of the more traditional strategies.

6

The Organization of International Business

INTRODUCTION

The theme of this chapter is that in order to succeed an international business must have the appropriate formal and informal organizational structure and control mechanisms.

Organizational architecture: this term refers to the totality of firm's organization including the formal organization structure, control systems and incentives, organizational culture, process and people.

What is appropriate depends upon the strategy of the firm, which as we saw in the last chapter is inter-related with the demands of the industry environment.

The organization structure means three things: the formal division of the organization into sub units such as product divisions, national operations and functions. (Organizational charts), the location of decision making responsibilities within that structure (e.g., centralized or decentralized etc) and the establishment of integrating mechanisms to coordinate the activities of sub units including cross functional terms or regional committees.

Control systems: are the metrics used to measure the performance of sub units and make judgments about how will the mangers are running the sub units. Unilever measured the performance of its subsidiary companies according to profitability. Profitability was the control systems.

Incentives: are the devices used to reward the appropriate managerial behavior. Incentives are very ties to performance metrics. E.g. a bonus for exceeding performance targets.

Process: are the manners in which the decisions are made and work is performed within an organization. Examples are the processes for formulating strategy, for deciding how to allocate the resources within the firm, or for evaluating the performance of managers and giving feedback.

Origination culture: Are the norms and value systems that are shared among the employees of an organization. Just are societies having distinct patterns of culture and sub couture. The organizational culture can have a profound impact on how a firm performs.

Structure

People: means nor just the employees of the organization but also the strategy used to recruit, compensate and retain those individuals and the types of people that they are in terms of their skills values and orientation.

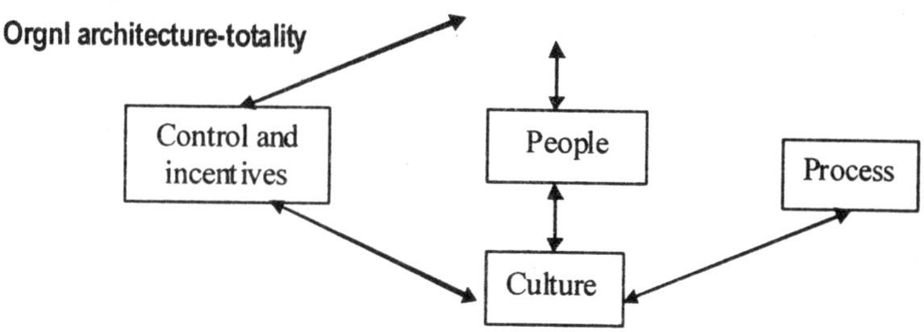

Just as there were trade-offs between different strategies, there are trade-offs between different organizational choices — advantages and disadvantages to different approaches.

Structure

Vertical differentiation is principally about the centralization and decentralization of decision making responsibilities. It is concerned with identifying where in a hierarchy decision making power should be concentrated.

There are four main arguments for centralization:

(1) Facilitating coordination,

(2) Ensuring consistency between decisions and organizational objectives,

(3) Providing top managers the means to push through major changes, and

(4) Avoiding duplication of activities.

There are five main arguments for decentralization:

(1) Overburdened and hence poor decision-making at the top of the organization,

(2) Increased motivation at lower levels,

(3) Greater flexibility,

(4) Better decisions on the spot by the people directly involved, and

(5) Increased accountability and control.

The choice between centralization and decentralization is not an absolute one. Frequently it makes sense to centralize some decisions and decentralize others depending upon the type of decision and the strategy of the firm.

For firms pursuing a global strategy, there is clearly more of a need for centralized decision making than for firms pursuing a multidomestic strategy. For transnational, it is less clear, as some decisions should perhaps be centralized while others are decentralized.

HORIZONTAL DIFFERENTIATION

Horizontal differentiation is concerned with how the firm decides to divide into sub-units. The decision is typically made upon the basis of functions, business areas, or geographical areas.

In many firms, just one of these is predominant, while in others there are difficult trade-offs to be made. The management focus on Dow Chemicals helps illustrate how different demands can pull a firm in different directions.

Most firms start out with no formal structure. After growth, a functional orientation usually develops as shown in Figure. These functions reflect the firm's value creation captivities. These functions are controlled and coordinated by the management. The decision-making is centralized.

Functional organization

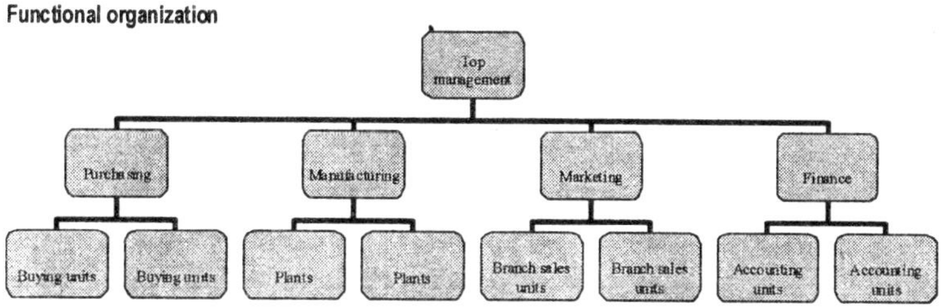

Product Organization

As firms diversify into multiple product lines, a product division structure that allows autonomy responsibility in the operating units is usually chosen as shown in Figure. Then each division is responsible for a distinct product line.

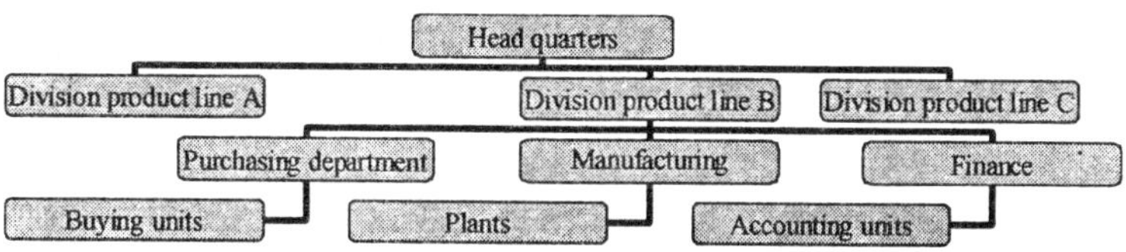

International Division (functional)

Historically, when many firms began to expand abroad they typically grouped their international activities into an international division. This tended to be the case whether the firm was organized on a functional basis or based on product divisions. No matter whether the domestic structure of the firm was based primarily upon functions or upon product divisions, the international division tends to be organized on geographical lines. This is illustrated in Figure for a firm whose domestic organization is based on product divisions.

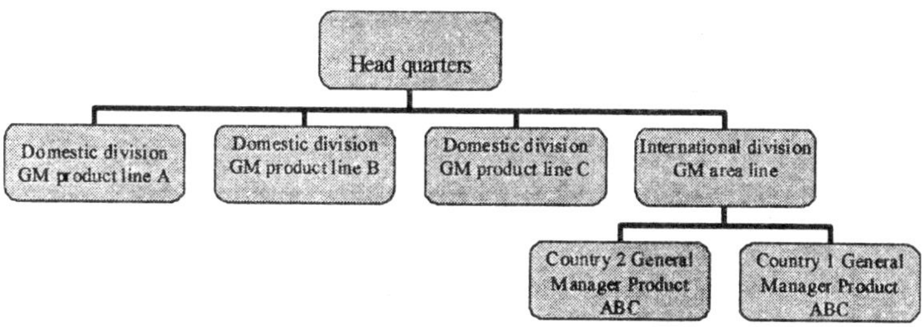

International Division (product)

This structure rarely lasts due to the inherent potential for conflict and coordination problems between domestic and foreign operations. Firms then switch to one of two structures — a worldwide area structure (undiversified firms) and a worldwide product division structure (diversified firms).

WORLDWIDE AREA STRUCTURE

A worldwide area structure tends to be favored by firms that have a low degree of diversification and domestic structure based on functions as illustrated in Figure. Each area tends to have a self contained largely autonomous entity with tits own set of value creation activities. Operations authority and strategic decisions relating to each of these activities are typically decentralized to each area. This structure facilitates local responsiveness and is consistent with a multidomestic strategy.

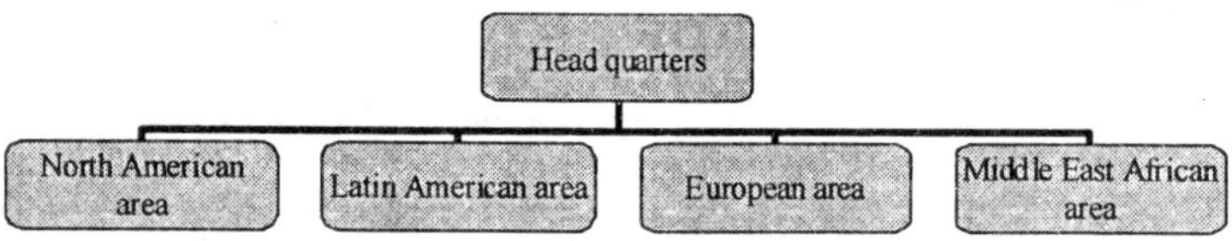

WORLDWIDE AREA STRUCTURE

Worldwide Product Division Structure

A worldwide product division structure tends to be adopted by firms that are reasonably diversified and accordingly, originally had a domestic structure that was based on product divisions as illustrated in Figure. The great strength of such a structure is that it provides an organizational context within which it is easier to pursue the rationalization of value creation activities necessary to realize location and experience curve economies. Thus, it is consistent with a global strategy.

The Global Matrix Structure

Since neither of these structures achieves a balance between the need to be both locally responsive and to achieve location and experience curve economies, many multinationals adopt matrix type structures. However, global matrix structures have typically failed to work well, primarily due to bureaucratic problems.

The Global Matrix Structure contains simultaneous, intersecting differentiation bases, with employees reporting to a functional and a product manager simultaneously

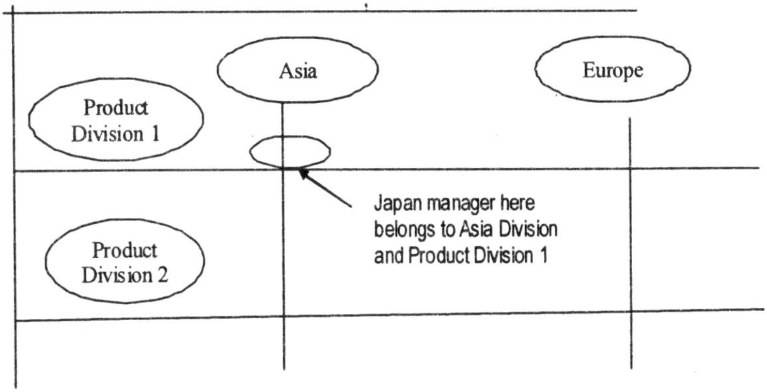

GLOBAL MATRIX STRUCTURE

Transnational firms attempt to overcome the problems inherent in the matrix structure by being more flexible and working to create networks of individuals and a shared culture.

The Mixed Structure is most common in the Multinational Enterprises. It uses localization in product development, marketing, sales, and service. At the same time functions that benefit from scale advantages, like purchasing, are centralized

Subsidiary Roles and Imperatives

Corporations commonly have *subsidiaries* that operate in host environments. They play a key part in balancing integration and local responsiveness through playing an autonomous role, a receptive role, or an active role.

The Autonomous Role has a subsidiary performing most activities of the value chain independently of HQ, selling output in a local market or in markets the autonomous subsidiary can arrange. This role is commonly used with Multi-Domestic Strategy.

The Receptive Role has subsidiary functions that are integrated with HQ for other units. An example is where the subsidiary imports or exports components to other subsidiaries for redistribution or final assembly. Commonly used with Global Strategy. The Active Role has many activities performed locally, but coordinated with subsidiaries. Commonly used with Transnational Strategy, with mandate from HQ, and flexibility for adaptation.

Integrating Mechanisms

Both formal and informal mechanisms can be used to help achieve coordination.

The need for coordination (and hence integrating mechanisms) varies systematically with the strategy of the firm. It is lowest in multidomestic firms, higher in international firms, higher still in global firms, and highest of all in transnational firms.

Integration is inhibited by a number of impediments to coordination, particularly different sub-unit orientations. To the extent that different sub-units have different objectives and ways of operating, integration becomes more difficult.

Integration can be achieved through formal integrating mechanisms. Formal integrating mechanisms vary in complexity from direct contact and simple liaison roles, through teams, to a matrix structure. However, formal integrating mechanisms can become bureaucratic.

To overcome the bureaucracy associated with formal integrating mechanisms, firms often use informal mechanisms. These include management networks and organization culture.

For a network to function effectively it must embrace as many managers within the organization as possible. Information systems and management development policies (including job rotation and management education programs) can be used to establish firm wide networks.

For a network to function properly, managers in different sub-units must be committed to the same goals. One way of achieving this is to foster the development of a common organization culture. Leadership by example, management development programs, and human relations policies are all-important considerations in building a common culture.

Taken together, managerial networks and a common culture can serve as valuable coordination mechanisms in international firms that can help overcome the deficiencies of formal mechanisms.

Control Systems

One of the major tasks of a firm's headquarters is to control the various sub-units of the firm to ensure consistency with strategic goals. The headquarters can achieve this through its use of control systems. There are four main types of controls — personal controls, bureaucratic controls, output controls, and cultural controls. In most firms, all four are used, but the relative emphasis tends to vary with the strategy of the firm.

Personal control involves control by personal contact with subordinates. This type of control system tends to be most widely used within small firms where it finds expression in the direct supervision of the actions of subordinates, but is also applicable in large international firms.

Bureaucratic control involves control through the establishment of a system of rules and procedures that are used to direct the actions of sub-units. With regard to headquarters control of sub-units within multinational firms, the most important form of bureaucratic controls are sub-unit budgets and capital spending rules.

Output controls involve setting goals for sub-units to achieve, expressing those goals in terms of relatively objective criteria such as profitability, productivity, growth, market share, or quality, and then judging the performance of sub-unit management by their ability to achieve these goals.

Cultural controls exist when employees buy into the norms and value systems of the firm. When this occurs, employees tend to control their own behavior, which reduces the need for direct management supervision. Cultural controls require substantial investments of time and money by the firm in building organization wide norms and value systems.

The key to understanding the relationship between international strategy and control systems is the concept of performance ambiguity. Performance ambiguity arises when the causes of poor performance by a sub-unit are ambiguous — when there is a high degree of interdependence between sub-units within the organization.

The degree of interdependence, and hence performance ambiguity and the costs of control, is a function of the international strategy of the firm. It is lowest in multidomestic firms, higher in international firms, higher still in global firms, and highest of all in transnational.

The costs of control can be defined as the amount of time that top management has to devote to monitoring and evaluating the performance of sub-units. This will be greater the greater the amount of performance ambiguity.

SYNTHESIS: STRATEGY AND STRUCTURE

The implications of the four main strategies on organizational structure and control systems are identified.

To underline the scheme is the notion that a *fit* between strategy and structure is necessary if the firm is going to achieve high performance. For a firm to succeed two conditions must be fulfilled. First, the strategy of the firm must be consistent with the environment in which the firm operates. Second, the organizational structure and control systems of the firm must be consistent with its strategy.

- What is a strategic alliance in International business?
- What are the factors to be considered in designing an organization structure of a MNC?
- What is global management?
- Discuss the different strategic choices available to compete in the international business.

MARKET ENTRY STRATEGIES AND STRATEGIC ALLIANCES

Which Foreign Markets to Enter?

The choice between foreign markets must be made on an assessment of their long-term profit potential. This is a function of a large number of factors, many of which we have already discussed earlier like political, economic, legal and cultural differences. The attractiveness of a country as potential market for an international business depends on balancing the benefits, costs and risks associated with doing business in that country.

The most attractive foreign markets tend to be found in politically stable developed and developing nations that have free market systems and where there is not a dramatic upsurge in either inflation rates or private sector debt.

Other markets that do not fit this description may be attractive for other reasons. The size of the Chinese market certainly makes it attractive to firms with a long-term perspective.

Timing of Entry

Once attractive markets have been identified, it is important to consider the timing of entry.

There are several advantages associated with entering a national market early, before other international businesses have established themselves. These advantages are called "first mover advantages." These advantages must be balanced against the pioneering costs that early entrants often have to bear including the greater risk of business failure.

There can also be disadvantages associated with entering a foreign market before other international business known as "first mover disadvantages". These disadvantages may give rise to "pioneering costs", or costs that an early entrant has to bear that a later entrant can avoid.

Scale of Entry

Large-scale entry into a national market constitutes a major strategic commitment (a decision that has a long-term impact and is difficult to reverse). That is likely to change the nature of competition in that market and limit the entrant's future strategic flexibility. A firm needs to think through the implications of such a commitment before embarking on a large-scale entry.

INTRODUCTION AND BASIC ENTRY DECISIONS

When a firm that wishes to enter a foreign market, it has several options, including exporting, licensing or franchising to host country firms, setting up a joint venture with a host country firm, or setting up a wholly owned subsidiary in the host country to serve that market. Each of these options has its advantages and each has its disadvantages.

The magnitude of the advantages and disadvantages associated with each entry mode are determined by a number of different factors, including transport costs and trade barriers, political and economic risks, and firm strategy. The optimal choice of entry mode varies from situation to situation depending upon these various factors. Thus, while it may make sense for some firms to serve a given market by exporting, other firms might serve the same market by setting up a wholly owned subsidiary in that market, or by utilizing some other entry mode.

We can define strategic alliances as cooperative agreements between actual or potential competitors. The term "strategic alliances" is often used rather loosely to embrace a wide range of arrangements between firms, including cross-share holding deals, licensing arrangements, formal joint ventures, and informal cooperative deals.

Strategic alliances have both advantages and disadvantages, and require significant effort if they are to work successfully.

Entry Modes

(The management focuses on the Fuji-Xerox merger show how two foreign competitors could successfully merge and deliver product development and marketing inroads that neither alone would have been able to achieve. (Read case study in Charles Hill)

The various modes of entry are:

- Exporting
- Turnkey projects
- Licensing
- Franchising
- Joint ventures
- Wholly owned subsidiaries
- Exporting.

Many manufacturers begin their global expansion as exporters and later switch to another mode for serving a foreign market. Manufacturing in existing locations and transporting into new markets is called exporting.

Advantages

- Avoid costs of investing in new location.
- Realize experience curve and location economies. By manufacturing the product in a centralized location and exporting it to other national markets, the firm may be able to realize substantial sale economies from its global sales volume.

Disadvantages

- new locations may have lower manufacturing costs

- High transport costs can make exporting uneconomical, particularly for bulk products.
- Tariff and non-tariff barriers by the host country government can make it risky and costly.
- Agents in the foreign country may not act in exporter's best interest.

Turnkey Projects

A project in which contractor handles every detail of the project for a foreign client, including the training of operating personnel, and then hands over the foreign clients the "key" to a plant that is ready for operation. (Setting up a new plant ready for operation). Turnkey projects are most common in the chemical, pharmaceutical, petroleum refining and metal refining industries, all of which use complex, expensive production technologies.

Advantages

- This is the best way of earning greater economic returns from that asset. Obtain returns from know-how about a complex process.
- Government restrictions may limit other options therefore; this strategy is best in case where FDI is limited by government. (Middle East countries and petroleum refining.)
- Lower risk if unstable economic/political situation in country

Disadvantages

- The firm that enters into the turnkey deal will have no long-term interest in the foreign country. Less potential to profit from success of plant.
- Creating a competitor by transferring the technical know-how to a foreign firm.
- Give away technological know-how to potential competitor

Licensing

Licensing agreement is an arrangement whereby a licensor grants the rights to intangible property to the licensee for specified time in exchange for royalties. Foreign licensee buys rights to manufacture a firm's product. Intangible property includes patents, inventions, formulations, processes, designs, copyrights and trademarks. Originally, Fuji-Xerox joint venture started as licensing agreement with Xerox. Licensed its xerographic know-how to Fuji-Xerox. In return, Fuji-Xerox paid Xerox a royalty fee equal to 5 percent of the net sales revenue that Fuji-Xerox earned from the sales of photocopiers based on Xerox's patented know-how.

Advantages

- The firm does not have to bear the costs and risks of investment, it is an attractive option for firms lacking capital to develop operations overseas.
- Avoid political/economic problems or restrictions in a country. This is used when a firm wishes to participate in a foreign market but is prohibited from doing so by barriers to investment.

Disadvantages

- Licensing does not give a firm tight control over manufacturing, marketing and strategy that is required for realizing experience curve and location economies. Loss of control over operations (marketing, manufacturing, strategy)
- Unable to realize experience curve and locational economies
- Limited in coordinating international strategy against competitors
- Loss of technological know-how

Cross licensing can minimize some of the disadvantages of direct licensing if there is a potential for two-way licensing; it creates interdependencies between the parties.

Meaning: Cross licensing, is an arrangement whereby a company grants the rights to intangible property to another firm for a special time in exchange for royalties and a license from the foreign partners for some of its technological know-how.

Franchising

Franchising is similar to licensing. This tends to involve a longer-term commitments than licensing. Selling limited rights to use of a brand name and service know-how.

Meaning: franchising is a specialized form of licensing in which the franchiser not only sells intangible property to the franchisee (normally trademark) but also insists that the franchisee agree to abide strict rules as to how to do the business. The franchiser will assist the franchisee to run the business on an ongoing basis. The franchiser in turn receives a royalty payment, which amounts to some percentage of the franchise's revenues.

Advantages

- Franchisor do not bear the costs and risks of investment
- Avoid political/economic problems and restrictions in a country
- Quicker international expansion possible

Disadvantages

- Limited in coordinating international strategy against competitors
- Loss of control over quality and service

Joint Ventures

A joint venture is an establishment of a firm that is jointly owned by tow or more otherwise independent firms. Work with a local partner and share in the costs/profits of an operation. The most typical joint venture is a 50/50 venture, in which there are tow parties, each of which holds a 50 percent ownership stake and contributes a team of managers to share operating control, however, there are joint ventures in which tone from has a majority share and thus tighter control.

Advantages

- Benefit from local firm's knowledge about the host country's competitive conditions, culture, language, political systems and business systems.
- shared costs/risks of development
- political constraints on other options

Disadvantages

- Loss of control over technology to its partner.
- JVs do not give the firm the tight control over subsidiaries that it might need to relisse experience curve or location economies. Limited ability to realize experience curve and location economies

- limited ability to coordinate international strategy against competitors
- conflicts between partners over goals and objectives of the JV.

Wholly Owned Subsidiaries

In wholly owned subsidiary, the firm owns 100 percent of the stock. Establishing a wholly owned subsidiary in a foreign market can be done in two ways. The firm can either set up a new operation in that country or it can acquire an established firm and use that firm to promote its products in the country's market.

Advantages

- Control over technological know-how ensured, especially when a firm' competitive advantage is based on technological competence. Many high tech firms prefer this entry mode for overseas expansion.(firms in semiconductor, electronics and pharmaceuticals).
- control over ability to coordinate international strategy
- ability to realize location and experience economies
- ability to coordinate with other subsidiaries

Disadvantages

- Most costly method of serving a foreign market.
- The firm entering through this mode must bear the full costs and risks of setting up overseas operations.

Selecting an Entry Modes

A brief summary of the advantages and disadvantages of each of the modes is shown. The optimal choice of entry mode for firms pursuing a multinational strategy depends to some degree on the nature of their core competency.

If a firm's competitive advantage (its core competence) is based upon control over proprietary technological know-how, licensing and joint venture arrangements should be avoided if possible in order to minimize the risk of losing control over that technology, unless the arrangement can be structured in a way where these risks can be reduced significantly.

Mode of Entry	Advantages	Disadvantages
Exporting	Economies of scale Lower foreign expenses	No low cost sales High transportation costs Potential tariffs
Turnkey Project	Access to closed markets	Competition from local client Loss of competitive advantage
Licensing	Quick expansion Lower expenses and risks Lower political risk	Loss of competitive advantage Limited ability to use profits in one country to increase competition in another country
Franchising	Quick expansion Lower development costs and risks Lower political risk	Loss of competitive advantage Potential quality control problems Limited ability to use profits in one country to increase competition in another country
Joint Venture	Knowledge of local markets Lower development costs and risk Access to closed markets	Potential for conflict of interest Loss of competitive advantage
Wholly Owned Subsidiary	Maximum control over proprietary knowledge / technology Greater strategic flexibility Efficiencies of global production system	Large capital outlay Lack of local knowledge Increased risk
Strategic Alliance	Access to closed markets Pooled resources increase partner's capabilities Complementary skills & assets	Loss of competitive advantage Potential overestimation of partner's capabilities

When a firm perceives its technological advantage as being only transitory, or the firm may be able to establish its technology as the dominant design in the industry, then licensing may be appropriate even if it does involve the loss of know-how. By licensing its technology to competitors, a firm may also deter them from developing their own, possibly superior, technology. The competitive advantage of many service firms is based upon management know-how. For such firms, the risk of loosing control over their management skills to franchisees or joint venture partners is not that great, and the benefits from getting greater use of their brand names can be significant.

The greater the pressures for cost reductions, the more likely it is that a firm will want to pursue some combination of exporting and wholly owned subsidiaries. This will allow it to achieve location and scale economies as well as retain some degree of control over its worldwide product manufacturing and distribution.

Strategic Alliances

The Term Strategic Alliances refers to Cooperative Agreements between Potential or Actual Competitors

The advantages of alliances are that they facilitate entry into foreign markets, enable partners to share the fixed costs and risks associated with new products and processes, facilitate the transfer of complementary skills between companies, and help firms to establish technical standards.

The disadvantage of a strategic alliance is that the firm risks giving away technological know-how and market access to its alliance partner, while getting very little in return.

Making Alliances Work

When considering the selection of a partner, a firm must be certain that the partner is one that can help the firm achieve its goals, share the firm's vision for the purpose of the alliances, and not act opportunistically to exploit the alliance for purely its own ends. Partner selection can be critical to success, and requires a significant investment in researching the skills and traits of potential partners.

A firm should structure the alliance to avoid unintended transfers of know-how. This can be done by walling-off (wall-off) sensitive technologies, by writing contractual safeguards into alliance agreements, by agreeing in advance to engage in reciprocal swaps of technological know-how, and by seeking credible commitments from alliance partners.

Two of the keys to making alliances work seem to be (1) building trust and informal communications networks between partners, and (2) taking proactive steps to learn from alliance partners. Overall, strategic alliances tend to have quite high failure rates. Many times this failure is a result of unrealistic expectations and conflicts between the partners. It should be noted, however, that just because an alliance is terminated it may not have necessarily failed — some perfectly acceptable alliances can serve mutual interests for short periods of time where both parties benefit, and then end when the benefits no longer exceed the costs. You can draw analogies between alliances and the dating practices of people to help illustrate the benefits, costs, risks, as well as the long vs. short-term nature of the "alliances"!

EXPORTING, IMPORTING, AND COUNTERTRADE

The previous chapter presented exporting as just one of a range of strategic options for profiting from international markets. This chapter looks more at how to export.

Exporting is not just an activity of large multinationals to obtain scale and location economies, but is also an activity for small firms. Almost all large multinationals today started their expansion overseas via exporting.

Exporting can be a very challenging activity for many firms — unfortunately, it usually takes more effort than just placing goods in a box and slapping on foreign shipping label as we will see, although sometimes, it is almost that easy.

The Promise and Pitfalls of Exporting

The potential benefits from exporting can be great. Regardless of the country in which a firm has its base. The rest of the world is a much larger market than the domestic market. While larger firms may be proactive in seeking out new export opportunities, many smaller firms are reactive and only pursue international opportunities when the customer calls or knocks on the door.

Many new exporters have run into significant problems when first trying to do business abroad, souring them on following up on subsequent opportunities.

Common pitfalls include poor market analysis, poor understanding of competitive conditions, lack of customization for local markets, poor distribution arrangements, bad promotional campaigns, as well as a general underestimation of the differences and expertise required for foreign market penetration.

If basic business issues were not enough, the tremendous paperwork and formalities that must be dealt with can be overwhelming to small firms.

Improving Export Performance

National differences in the governmental and business infrastructure available for supporting exporting vary considerably. German and Japanese firms have relatively easy access to information and assistance. While US firms are not left totally to their own devices, the amount of direct and indirect assistance to them is much less developed.

One of the biggest impediments to exporting is ignorance of foreign market opportunities.

The best way of overcoming ignorance is to collect more information. In the USA, there are a number of institutions, most importantly the US Department of Commerce, which can assist firms in the information gathering and matchmaking process.

Business and trade associations can also provide valuable assistance to firms.

One way for first-time exporters to identify opportunities and help avoid pitfalls is to hire an Export Management Company. A good EMC will have a network of contacts in potential markets, will have multilingual employees, will have knowledge of different business mores, and will be fully conversant with the ins and outs of the exporting process and with local business regulations.

One drawback of relying on EMCs is that the company fails to develop its own exporting capabilities.

The probability of exporting successfully can be improved by utilizing an EMC or export consultants, focusing on only one or a few markets at first and get them working effectively, starting out on a small scale, having realistic expectations about the time and commitment required, developing good relations with local distributors, and hiring local personnel. The example of 3M helps illustrate one firm's approach.

Export and Import Financing: Procedure

Firms engaged in international trade face a problem — they have to trust someone who may be very difficult to track down if they default on an obligation.

Due to the lack of trust, each party to an international transaction has a different set of preferences regarding the configuration of the transaction.

Firms can solve the problems arising from a lack of trust between exporters and importers by using a third party who is trusted by both-normally a reputable bank.

A bank issues a letter of credit, abbreviated as L/C at the request of an importer. It states that the bank promises to pay a beneficiary, normally the exporter, upon presentation of documents specified in the letter of credit.

A draft (bill of exchange) is the instrument normally used in international commerce to effect payment. It is an order written by an exporter instructing an importer, or an importer's agent, to pay a specified amount of money at a specified time. Drafts fall into two categories — sight drafts and time drafts. Time drafts are negotiable instruments.

The bill of lading is issued to the exporter by the common carrier transporting the merchandise. It serves three purposes; it is a receipt, a contract, and a document of title.

The entire 14-step process for conducting an export transaction is summarized. Take for example an Indian importer and US exporter.

- Step1: The Indian importer places an order with the US exporter and asks the American if he would be willing to ship under a letter of credit.
- Step 2: the US exporter agrees to ship under a letter of credit and specifies relevant information such as price and delivery terms.
- Step 3: the Indian importer applies to (e.g.) State bank of India for a letter of credit to be issued in favor of the US exporter fro the merchandise the importer wishes to buy.
- Step 4: the state bank of India issues a letter of credit in the Indian importer's favor and sends it to the US exporter's bank, the bank of New York.
- Step 5: the bank of New York advices the US exporter of the opening of a letter of credit in his favour.

- Step 6: the US exporter ships the goods to the Indian importer on a common carrier. An official of the carrier gives the exporter a bill of lading.
- Step 7: the US exporter presents a 90 day-time draft (bill of exchange) drawn on the State Bank of India, in accordance with its letter of credit and the bill of lading to the bank of New York. The US exporter endorses the bill of lading so title of goods is transferred to the Bank of New York.
- Step 8: the bank of New York sends the draft and the bill of lading to the State Bank of India. The State Bank of India accepts the draft, taking possession of the documents and promising to pay the now accepted draft in 90 days.
- Step 9: State Bank of India returns the accepted draft to the bank of New York.
- Step 10: the bank of New York tells the US exporter that it has received the accepted bank draft, which is payable in 90 days.
- Step 11: the exporter sells the draft to the bank of New York at a discount from its face value and receives the discounted cash value of the daft in return.
- Step 12: State Bank of India notifies the Indian importer of the arrival of the documents. He agrees to pay the State Bank of India in 90 days. State Bank of India releases the documents so the importer can take possessions of the shipment.
- Step 13: in 90 days, the State Bank of India receives the importer's payment, so it has funds to pay the maturing draft.
- Step 14: in 90 days the holder of the matured acceptance ie, bank of New York presents it to the State Bank of India fro payment. The State Bank of India pays.

Export Assistance

Exporters in the India can draw upon two types of government-backed assistance to help finance their exports; the Export-Import bank and Export Credit Guarantee Corporation (ECGC)

The Export-Import Bank (EXIM BANK) is a public sector financial institution established in January 1, 1982. it was established by an act of parliament fro the purpose of financing, facilitating, and promoting foreign trade in India.

Export Credit Guarantee Corporation (ECGC): this institution covers the exporter against various risks. It also provides guarantees to the financing banks to enable them to provide adequate finances to exporters.

Counter trade

Counter trade is a term that covers a whole range of barter like agreements. It is primarily used when the firm is exporting to countries whose currency is not freely convertible, and who may lack the foreign exchange reserves required to purchase the imports. By some estimates, counter trade accounted for 20% of world trade by volume in 1998There are five distinct types of countertrade — barter, counter purchase, offset, switch trading, and buy back.

7

The Global Trading System

INTRODUCTION

While earlier Chapter discussed the economic/trade theories of international trade and outlined the case free trade, it was mostly silent on the political aspects of trade policy. This chapter focuses on the political systems and tools of trade policy.

The major objective of this chapter is to describe how political realities have shaped, and continue to shape, the international trading system.

While in theory, many countries adhere to the free trade ideal outlined in Chapter 4, in practice most have been reluctant to engage in unrestricted free trade.

Free trade environment in which a government does not attempt to restrict what its citizens can buy from another country or that they can sell to another country. However, in reality this does not happen due to political interferences known as trade policies formed by government.

For example, the USA continues to restrict trade in textiles, sugar, and other basic products in response to domestic political pressures, in addition to technological and militarily sensitive products.

INSTRUMENTS OF TRADE POLICY

- Tariffs and
- Non-tariff barriers:
    - o Subsidies
    - o Import quotas

  - o Voluntary export restraints (VER)
  - o Antidumping policies and,
  - o Administrative policies.

- Tariffs are one of the oldest and easiest to recognize and regulate, and simplest forms of trade policy.

Definition: a tariff is a tax levied on imports. Tariffs fall into tow categories. Specific tariffs and ad- valorem tariffs.

Specific tariffs specify an amount that will be levied on each unit of imported good. ($10/ton of tea or $5 on a barrel of oil.) Ad valorem tariffs are based on a percentage of the value of the imported good (5% of the import value). Anyone who pays property taxes has seen the tern ad valorem (an amount based on the value of the property). Tariffs raise the cost of foreign goods relative to domestic goods, making the consumer pay more.

Tariffs benefit the government due to the revenue raised, benefit domestic producers since they can charge higher prices, and hurt domestic consumers. Tariffs are unambiguously pro-producer and anti-consumer. They reduce the overall efficiency of the world economy — a protective tariff encourages domestic firms to produce products at home that in theory could be produced more efficiently abroad.

- A subsidy: definition: is a government payment to a domestic producer. Subsidies take many forms including cash grants, low interest rate loans, tax breaks, and government equity participation in domestic firms. Subsidies help domestic producers in two ways:
  - (1) subsidies help domestic producers compete against low cost foreign imports, and
  - (2) subsidies help domestic producers gain export markets.

Subsidies clearly benefit domestic producers, and damage foreign producers. Domestic consumers, however, must pay for subsidies, usually through taxes. When subsidies are in the form of price supports (i.e. often in agriculture), domestic consumers may also pay directly.

Subsidies generally help support inefficient industries and keep productive assets employed in industries that do not make most effective use of these assets. According to official figures, the government subsidies to industry in most industrialized countries amount to between 2 percent and 3.5 percent to the value of industrialized output.

- An import quota: Definition: is a direct restriction on the quantity of some good that can be imported into a country. Usually, governments regulate import quotas by issuing import licenses for the import of some specific quantity of goods to a group of individuals or firms.
- A voluntary export restraint (VER) may have the same effect as a quota.

Definition: VER is the quota on trade imposed by the exporting country, typically at the request of the importing country.

In a VER, another country or countries agree not to export more than a certain quantity to another country or countries. VERs is usually only enacted when it is feared that a more restrictive tariff or quota will be levied unless exports are "voluntarily" reduced. In other words, the threat of retaliation encourages compliance.

Import quotas and VERs benefit domestic producers and harm domestic consumers. They can also even help foreign producers, as foreign producers can raise the price they charge for the limited supply they can sell, and take the difference as additional profit.

- Local content requirements specify that firms must produce some portion of a good domestically. The purpose of a local content requirement is usually to aid the formation of domestic industries, to keep manufacturers from switching to foreign suppliers, or to keep foreign firms from setting up "screwdriver plants." where imported manufactured components undergo simple assembly in order to avoid some other trade restriction on the importation of the fully assembled product. Domestic suppliers benefit, and domestic consumers must bear the costs. Local content regulation may mean the formation of strange bedfellows in certain markets. For example, the market for automobiles in Argentina is too small to support local production by all the competing firms. Therefore, the firms agreed to let one of them build engines in Argentina for all the vehicles assembled there.
- Antidumping polices: Dumping occurs when a country sells goods in another country below cost or below fair market value.

> Dumping is a way firms can unload excess production into foreign markets. When plants must operate at a certain level regardless of domestic demand, the producer may find it appropriate to export some portion of the factory's output abroad. At times dumping may also be done for predatory reasons, hoping to drive other producers out of the market, and subsidizing foreign sales with higher domestic prices.

Antidumping policies are assigned to punish foreign firms that engage in dumping. These are designed to prevent dumping from occurring, or by instituting import taxes in order to bring prices of "dumped" goods back up to fair levels. The ultimate objective is to protect domestic producers from unfair foreign competitors.

Administrative policies: these are bureaucratic rules that are designed to make it difficult for imports to enter a country. A wide range of administrative barriers can be enacted. Some say the Japanese are the masters of this trade barrier. In recent years Japan's formal tariff and non tariff barriers have been he lowest in the world. However, critics charge that their informal administrative barriers to importsmore than compensate fro this. Taking so much time to inspect goods that they spoil or setting down specific regulations on "product standards" that are very expensive to meet.

THE ARGUMENTS FOR GOVERNMENT INTERVENTION

"Protecting Jobs and Industries."

The most common political reason for trade restrictions is "protecting jobs and industries." Usually this results from political pressures by unions or industries that are "threatened" by more efficient foreign producers, and have more political clout than the consumers that will eventually pay the costs.

"Vital for National Security"

Keeping industries "vital for national security" viable is an oft used argument for trade restrictions. While this may be reasonable for industries like steel, aerospace, and electronics; in the USA the shoe industry has regularly lobbied that soldiers need boots. Thus, the USA needs to have a viable shoe industry in order to be able to provide shoes during a time of war.

"Retaliation"

Government intervention in trade can be used as part of a "get tough" policy to open foreign markets. By taking, or threatening to take, specific actions, other countries may remove trade barriers. However, when threatened governments do not back down, tensions can escalate and new trade barriers may be enacted.

"Protecting Consumer"

Consumer protection can also be an argument for restricting imports. The opening case suggests that the EU's concern over bananas was, in part, due to an interest in protecting consumers. Since different countries do have different health and safety standards, what may be acceptable in one country, may be unacceptable in others.

"Protecting Human Rights"

Concern over human rights in other countries plays an important role in foreign policy. Governments sometimes use trade policy to improve the human rights policies of trading partners. Governments also use trade policies to put pressure on governments to make other changes. In recent years, the USA has had trade restrictions against Libya, Iran, Iraq, North Korea, Cuba, and other countries whose governments were pursuing policies that were not viewed favorably by the US government. Unless a large number of countries choose to take such action, however, it is unlikely to prove successful.

"Infant Industry"

The "infant industry" argument suggests that an industry should be protected until it can develop and be viable and competitive internationally. Unless an industry is allowed to develop and achieve minimal economies of scale, foreign competitors may undercut prices and prevent a domestic industry from developing. The infant industry argument has been accepted as a justification for temporary trade restrictions under the WTO.

A problem with the infant industry argument is determining when an industry "grows up." Some industries that are just plain inefficient and uncompetitive have argued they are still infants after 50 years. The other problem is that given the existence of global capital markets, if the country has the potential to develop a viable competitive position, its firms should be capable of raising the necessary funds without additional support from the government.

Strategic trade policy suggests that in cases where there may be important first mover advantages, governments can help firms from their countries attain these advantages.

Strategic trade policy also suggests that governments can help firms overcome barriers to entry into industries where foreign firms have an initial advantage.

THE REVISED CASE FOR FREE TRADE

While strategic trade policy identifies conditions where restrictions on trade may provide economic benefits, there are two problems that may make restrictions inappropriate: retaliation and politics.

Intervening to aid domestic firms will only be successful if other countries do not take similar actions that offset the effects.

While it could be very difficult to identify situations where strategic intervention in trade is economically appropriate, various interest groups will be certain to lobby that particular firms should be aided. Given the ease with which special interest groups seem to be able to capture the attention of the government, it is more likely that consumers will be harmed more needlessly than producers will. It is unreasonable to expect the government to be completely fair and objective in "targeting" industries, when different industries, lobbies, and politicians all have there own objectives for "getting their paws in the honey pot" of governmental funds.

THE DEVELOPMENT OF THE WORLD TRADING SYSTEM

Up until the Great Depression of the 1930s, most countries had some degree of protectionism. Great Britain, as a major trading nation, was one of the strongest supporters of free trade.

Although the world was already in a depression, in 1930 the USA enacted the Smoot-Hawley tariff, which created significant import tariffs on foreign goods. As other nations took similar steps and the depression deepened, world trade fell further.

After WWII, the US and other nations realized the value of freer trade, and established the General Agreement on Tariffs and Trade

(GATT). [Referred to sometimes as the General Agreement to Talk and Talk.]

The approach of GATT was to gradually eliminate barriers to trade. Over 100 countries became members of GATT, and worked together to further liberalize trade. Figure 5.1 shows the different rounds of GATT negotiations and the resulting reductions in tariffs.

During the 1980s and early 1990s, the world trading system as "managed" by GATT underwent strains. First, Japan's economic strength and huge trade surplus stressed what had been more equal trading patterns, and Japan's perceived protectionist (neo-mercantilist) policies created intense political pressures in other countries. Second, the persistent trade deficits by the US, the world's largest economy, caused significant economic problems for some industries and political problems for the government. Thirdly, many countries found that although limited by GATT from utilizing tariffs, there were many other more subtle forms of intervention that had the same effects and did not technically violate GATT (e.g. VERs).

Against the background of rising protectionist pressures, in 1986 GATT members embarked on their eighth round of negotiations to reduce tariffs (called the Uruguay Round). This was the most ambitious round to date, as the goal was to expand beyond the regulation of manufactured goods and address trade issues related to intellectual property, agriculture, services, and enforcement mechanism. Table 5.1 illustrates the main features of the agreement that was finally reached in 1993.

The agreement, however, left several important matters unaddressed: financial services, broadcast entertainment, environmental matters, worker's rights, and foreign direct investment. Those items were left to further negotiations under the auspices of the World Trade Organization.

When the WTO was established, its creators hoped the WTO's enforcement mechanisms would make it a more effective policeman of the global trade rules than the GATT had been. The WTO has handed down a number of rulings that have led to changes in governmental policies that restricted trade; in other cases, governments had made changes in advance of WTO rulings.

Under the WTO, 68 countries that account for more than 90% of world telecommunications revenues pledged to open their markets to foreign competition and to abide by common rules for fair competition in telecommunications. The WTO has also made headway in liberalizing trade in financial services, although the current agreement still includes a number of exceptions.

Substantial work still remains to be done on the international trade front. Environmental policies are one area of concern, as are regulations regarding foreign direct investment.

IMPLICATIONS FOR BUSINESS

Clearly, trade barriers negatively impact the ability of firms to locate activities in the economically optimal location or source materials from the best producers. Trade barriers can change the underlying costs and benefits of different locations, and force firms to undertake operations in specific locations rather than import or export.

Even if specific quotas, tariffs, local content, etc. regulations do not specifically require that certain actions be taken, a firm may choose to locate facilities or buy from certain suppliers in order to reduce the threat of mandatory and more punitive governmental intervention.

Certain trade barriers may even make some operations no longer viable, and force a firm to give up particular markets or production sites.

In general, international firms have an incentive to lobby for free trade, and keep protectionist pressures from causing them to have to change strategies. While there may be short-term benefits to having governmental protection in some situations, in the long-run, these can back fire and other governments can retaliate.

8

International Trade Theory

INTRODUCTION AND OVERVIEW OF TRADE THEORY

This chapter reviews a number of different theories of international trade to show why it is beneficial for a country to engage in trade and what patterns of international trade might be expected. Take Iceland for example: "What would life be like on Iceland if it did not trade?" Clearly there would be few if any autos or electronic products, and the diet would consist mainly of fish - very inexpensive fish. While it would clearly be technically possible for Iceland to make greenhouses, use heat from its abundant geothermal resources, and supply artificial light to produce all sorts of tropical fruits, these would be very expensive fruit. Thus, it makes sense for Iceland to trade some its abundant fish for other goods produced at lower costs in the rest of the world.

While it is easy to see why it makes sense to trade for goods that a country cannot easily produce, it is sometimes harder to understand why a country should not make goods that it can easily produce. There is little reason why the USA should not be able to produce all the sneakers and jeans demanded by its citizens. All of the raw materials required for these goods are available in the USA, as is labor. Nevertheless, the USA imports most of the sneakers and jeans consumed. This is because production is fairly labor intensive, and American labor is much more costly than labor in other parts of the world. American consumers would have to pay a great deal more for these goods if they were made only domestically. Thus, it is beneficial for consumers to purchase goods from their least expensive source, and better that labor produce goods that take advantage of the educational level of most American workers.

Having completely free trade is certain to hurt some domestic industries that are not competitive on a worldwide basis. Workers in the textile industry do not like losing their jobs to workers in other countries who are willing to work for lower wages. Yet, consumers want to purchase goods with the best price/quality tradeoff.

Some patterns of trade are easy to explain - it is obvious why Saudi Arabia exports oil, the US exports agricultural products, and Mexico exports labor-intensive goods. Yet, others are not so obvious or easily explained. The US ships Jeep Cherokees to Scandinavia, while Sweden ships Volvo (Ford) station wagons to the US. Clearly, it would be technically possible for Ford's Swedish subsidiary to produce durable four-wheel-drive SUVs and for American firms to produce "status" station wagons.

There are many examples regarding trade issues in the news. Recently, the USA and the EU were involved in trade disputes over bananas and beef. The banana dispute revolved around the EU providing preferential treatment to former colonies. There always seem to be election campaigns with rhetoric on "protecting jobs" or industries, and the steel unions are considering public demonstrations against steel dumping in the USA. As a candidate, George W. Bush promised job protection to coal and steel workers in West Virginia that undoubtedly helped him in putting the state on his side in the Electoral voting system.

Nevertheless, a president cannot change global economic reality. Bethlehem Steel is in bankruptcy protection, citing "unfair" foreign imports as a major reason that it has not been able to be internationally competitive. There is usually some dispute between the US and Japan, or some posturing going on in the EU regarding its Eastern neighbors or former colonies over trade. Last year, for the first time in world history, a foreign entity — the EU — prohibited two American companies (General Electric and Honeywell) from merging even after that merger had been approved by all the governmental agencies in the USA. Clearly, the sovereignty of American businesses has become globalized.

The trade theories:

- Mercantilism
- Absolute advantage
- Comparative advantage

- Heckscher-Ohlin theory
- Leontief paradox
- The product life cycle theory
- The new trade theory
- Porter's Diamonds: national competitive advantage
- Mercantilism and Early Classical Thought (c. 1500 - c. 1790).

Since gold and silver were viewed as valuable and a sign of wealth, mercantilism suggested that countries should design policies that led to an increase in their holdings of gold and silver.

Mercantilism believed that it was the country's best interests to maintain a trade surplus, to export more than it imported. By doing so, a country would accumulate gold and silver and consequently increase its national wealth and prestige.

Countries should run a balance of trade surplus, and have exports of greater value than imports. Thus, tariffs and quotas limited imports, while exports were subsidized.

David Hume pointed out how a persistent trade surplus would begin to affect money supply and in the long-run close the trade surplus.

The key problem with the mercantilist view is that it views trade as a zero sum game, where if one country benefits, the other must lose.

As an economic philosophy, mercantilism is flawed and invalid. Yet, many political views today have the goal of boosting exports while limiting imports by seeking only selective liberalization of trade.

Absolute Advantage

Adam Smith (Wealth of Nations (1776), argued that countries differed in their ability to produce goods efficiently, and they should specialize in the production of the goods they can produce the most efficiently.

If Britain were to specialize in textile production and France in wine production, Smith argued that both Britain and France could consume more textiles and wine than if each only produced for their own consumption. Thus, trade is a positive sum game.

These gains from trade can be showed graphically by looking again at Ghana and South Korea.

When each country has an absolute advantage in one of the products, it is clear that trade is beneficial. However, what if one country has an absolute advantage in both products? Then we should consider the country's comparative advantage.

Comparative Advantage

Ricardo showed how it makes sense for a country to specialize in the production of goods in which it simply has a comparative advantage, even if it can produce both more efficiently than the other country.

The case shows the production possibilities frontiers for Ghana and South Korea when Ghana has an absolute advantage in both cocoa and rice.

Ghana has a comparative advantage in the production of cocoa since it can produce 4 times as much cocoa as South Korea, but only 1.5 times as much rice. Ghana is comparatively more efficient at producing cocoa than rice.

This simple example makes a number of assumptions: only two countries and two goods; zero transportation costs; similar prices and values; resources are mobile between goods within countries, but not across countries; constant returns to scale; fixed stocks of resources; and no effects on income distribution within countries. While these are all unrealistic, the general proposition that countries will produce and export those goods that they are the most efficient at producing remains quite valid.

Diminishing returns to specialization simply suggest that after some point, the more of a good that a country produces, the greater will be the units of resources required to produce each additional item. If crops are grown on increasingly less fertile land, mining is done on less productive ore regions, or less skilled personnel need to be hired to perform high skilled jobs, production per unit of input will decrease. Diminishing returns implies a PPF that is convex. In reality, countries do not specialize entirely, but produce a range of goods. It is worthwhile to specialize up until that point where the resulting gains from trade are offset by diminishing returns.

Opening an economy to trade is likely to generate dynamic gains of two types. First, trade might increase a country's stock of resources as increased supplies become available from abroad. Secondly, free trade might increase the efficiency of resource utilization, and free up resources for other uses. Figure 4.4 shows how dynamic gains can shift a country's PPF outwards.

Heckscher-Ohlin Theory

The Heckscher-Ohlin theory predicts that countries will export those goods that make intensive use of factors of production that are locally abundant, while importing goods that make intensive use of factors that are locally scarce. Thus, it focuses on differences in relative factor endowments rather than differences in relative productivity.

When we look at US agricultural exports (abundant fertile land), Icelandic and Norwegian fish exports (coastal waters climates conducive to good fish), Canadian lumber exports (plentiful forests with few people), Saudi oil exports, and South African gold exports, the Heckscher-Ohlin theory seems to make sense.

Leontief paradox:

Using the Heckscher-Ohlin theory, Wassily Leontief in 1953, postulated that the US should be an exporter of capital-intensive goods and an importer of labor intensive goods. To his surprise, however, he found that US imports were less capital intensive than US exports. Since this result was at variance with the predictions of the theory, it has become known as the Leontief paradox. Hence, while we can see some support for Heckscher-Ohlin, other evidence contradicts it.

The Product Life Cycle Theory

Vernon suggested that as products mature, both the location of sales and the optimal production location would change, affecting the direction and flow of imports and exports.

While the product life cycle theory accurately explains what has happened for products like photocopiers and a number of other high technology products developed in the US in the 1960s and 1970s, the increasing globalization and integration of the world economy has made this theory less valid in today's world.

The New Trade Theory

New trade theory suggests that because of economies of scale and increasing returns to specialization, in some industries there are likely to be only a few profitable firms. Thus, firms with first mover advantages will develop economies of scale and create barriers to entry for other firms. The commercial aircraft industry is an excellent example. Boeing, established in the early 1910s, has long had a superior advantage over other aircraft manufacturers that have not had the advantage of governmental subsidies (like Airbus).

Productive efficiency may not be the result of factor endowments or specific national characteristics, but instead be a result a firm's first mover advantages. New trade theory does not contradict the theory of comparative advantage, but instead identifies a source of comparative advantage.

An obvious and controversial extension of new trade theory is the implication that governments should consider strategic trade policies. Strategic trade policies would suggest that governments should nurture and protect firms and industries where first mover advantages and economies of scale are likely to be important, as doing so can make it more likely that a firm will build economies of scale and eventually end up a winner in the global competitive race.

National Competitive Advantage: Porter's Diamond

Porter's study tried to explain why a nation achieves international success in a particular industry. This study found four broad attributes that promote or impede the creation of competitive advantage.

Factor Endowments: A nation's position in factors of production such as skilled labor or infrastructure necessary to compete in a given industry can be critical. These factors can be either basic (natural resources, climate, location) or advanced (skilled labor, infrastructure, technological know-how). While either can be important, advanced factors are more likely to lead to competitive advantage

Demand Conditions: The nature of home demand for the industries product or service influences the development of capabilities. Sophisticated and demanding customers pressure firms to be competitive.

Relating and Supporting Industries: The presence in a nation of supplier industries and related industries that are internationally competitive can spill over and contribute to other industries. Successful industries tend to be grouped in clusters in countries - having world class manufacturers of semi-conductor processing equipment can lead to (and be a result of having) a competitive semi-conductor industry.

Firm Strategy, Structure, and Rivalry: The conditions in the nation governing how companies are created, organized, and managed, and the nature of domestic rivalry impacts firms' competitiveness. Firms that face strong domestic competition will be better able to face competitors from other international firms.

In addition to these four main attributes, government policies and chance can influence any of the four. Government policy can affect demand through product standards, influence rivalry through regulation and antitrust laws, and affect the availability of highly educated workers and advanced transportation infrastructure.

The four attributes of the diamond, government policy, and chance work as a reinforcing system, complementing each other and in combination creating the conditions appropriate for competitive advantage. The Management Focus on Nokia provides a good example of how this Finnish firm built its competitive advantage because of factors in Porter's diamond.

Like the other theories we have studied in this chapter, the diamond makes sense in some situations. There is also anecdotal evidence of its applicability in certain situations. Yet, some forms of trade are much more simply explained by simple absolute advantage (Saudi Arabia's oil exports). Moreover, this, or any theory, does not easily explain other trade patterns.

IMPLICATIONS FOR BUSINESS

Most of the theories discussed have implications for the location of production activities. Firms will attempt to locate different activities in the location that is optimal for the production of that good, component, or service.

Being a first mover can have important competitive implications, especially if there are economies of scale and the global industry will only support a few competitors. Firms need to be prepared to undertake huge investments and suffer losses for several years in order to reap the eventual rewards.

Governmental policies with respect to free trade or protecting domestic industries can significantly impact global competitiveness. The opening case showed how Ghana's policies negatively influenced the global success of its cocoa business. While new trade theory may suggest that governments subsidize specific industries, Porter's theory focuses how policies can influence the attributes of the diamond.

One of the most important implications for business is that they should work to encourage governmental policies that support free trade. If a business is able to get its goods from the best sources worldwide, and compete in the sale of products into the most competitive markets, it has a good chance to survive and prosper. If such openness is restricted, a business's long-term survival will be in greater question.

9

Global Manufacturing and Materials Management

INTRODUCTION

The company's decisions regarding global manufacturing and outsourcing and globally dispersed supply chain management are important in controlling their activities to deliver its products to customers who are dispersed all over the world.

Definition: the activities involved in the procurement of inputs into production process, the creation of product and its delivery to customers are called operations. Managers in an international business have to make a number of critical decisions in the operational arena. They have to decide where in the world to locate productive activities, how much production to outsource to foreign suppliers, and how bet to coordinate globally dispersed supply and distribution.

Production: definition: are the activities involved in creating a product.

Materials management: definition: is the activity that controls the transmission of physical materials through the value chain, from procurement through production and into distribution.

STRATEGY, MANUFACTURING, AND MATERIALS MANAGEMENT

The objectives of manufacturing and materials management are to lower the costs of value creation and add value by better serving customer needs. This can be done by lowering costs and increasing product quality. These two aspects are related.

There are three ways in which improved quality control reduces costs.

- First, productivity increases because time is not wasted manufacturing poor quality products that cannot be sold. This saving leads to a direct reduction in unit costs.
- Second, increased product quality means lower re-work and scrap costs.
- Third, greater product quality means lower warranty and re-work costs. The net effect is to lower the costs of value creation by reducing both manufacturing and service costs.

Added to the objectives of lowering costs and improving quality are two further objectives of manufacturing and materials management that take on particular importance for international businesses.

- First, manufacturing and materials management must be able to accommodate demands for local responsiveness.
- Second, manufacturing and materials management must be able to respond quickly to shifts in customer demand.

The main management technique that companies are utilizing to boost their product quality is Total Quality Management. TQM was developed by a number of American consultants such as Edward Deming, Joseph Juran etc. TQM focuses on the need to improve the quality of a company's products and services.

Where to Manufacture

For the firm that considers international production to a feasible option, three broadly defined factors need to be considered when making a location decision - country factors, technological factors, and product factors etc.

- Country factors: As discussed earlier in the book, country factors suggest that a firm should locate it various manufacturing activities in those locations where economic, political, and cultural conditions, including relative factor costs, are most conducive to the performance of that activity. However, regulations affecting FDI and trade can significantly affect the appropriateness of specific countries as can expectations about future exchange rate changes.

- Technological factors include the fixed costs of setting up manufacturing facilities, the minimum efficient scale of production, and the flexible manufacturing etc. in some countries setting up of a manufacturing plant are so high that a firm must serve the world market from a single location or from a very few locations. Minimum efficient scale is another technological factor, which tells us that as plant output expands, unit costs decrease. The reasons for this relationship include the greater utilization of capital equipment and the productivity gains that come from with greater specialization f employees within the plant. Manufacturing technologies designed to reduce setup times, increase use of individuals machines through between scheduling, and improve quality control at all stages of manufacturing.
- Product factors: the first is the product's value to weight ratio because it influence on transportation costs. Many electronic components have high value to weight ratios, they are expensive and they do not weigh much. Thus even if they are shipped halfway around the world, their transportation costs account for a very small percentage of total costs. The other product feature that can influence location decisions is whether the product serves that can influence location decisions all over the world. (e.g. Many industrial products)

Locating Manufacturing Facilities

There are two basic strategies for locating manufacturing facilitates, concentrating them in optimal location and serving the world market from there, and decentralizing them in various regional or national locations that are close to major markets. The appropriate strategic choice Is determined by the various country, technological and product factors.

Concentration (centralization) of manufacturing make most sense when;

- Differences in factor costs, political economy and culture have substantial impact on the costs of manufacturing in various countries.
- Trade barriers are low.

- Important exchange rates are expected to remain relatively high.
- The production technology has high fixed costs or a high minimum efficient scale or a flexible manufacturing technology exists.
- The product's value to weight ratio is high.
- The product serves universal needs.

Alternatively, decentralization of manufacturing is appropriate when;

- Differences in factor costs, political economy etc do not have substantial impact on the costs of manufacturing in various countries.
- Trade barriers are high.
- Important exchange rates are expected to remain relatively low.
- The production technology has low fixed costs or a low minimum efficient scale or a rigid manufacturing technology exists.
- The product's value to weight ratio is low.
- The product does not serve universal needs.

In practice location decisions are seldom clear.

Make or Buy Decisions

Sourcing decisions: The key issue in many international businesses is identifying which component parts should be manufactured in-house, and which should be out-sourced to independent suppliers.

The advantages of making components in-house are: making components in house is also called vertical integration.

Lower costs: if the firm is more efficient at that production activity than any other company is, then it must make the product or component in house.

- Investments in specialized assets: if the company's core competency lies in developing a high performance, high quality component, then it must decide to make it in house. When substantial investments in specialized assets are required to manufacture a component part, the firm will prefer to make that component internally rather than contract out to an independent supplier.
- Helps the firm protect its proprietary technology: if it enables the firm to produce a product containing superior features,

proprietary technology can give the firm a competitive advantage. Obviously the firm runs the risk of loosing this technology if it outsource this technology. In order to maintain control over its technology, a firm might prefer to make component parts that contain proprietary technology in-house, rather than have them made by independent suppliers.

- Improves scheduling between adjacent stages in the value chain: the product cost savings resulting from vertical integration is because it makes the panning, coordination and scheduling of adjacent processes easier. This important in firms with just in time inventory systems. When a firm needs to tightly control scheduling, planning, and coordination of adjacent production processes, vertical integration can be preferable to being dependent on independent suppliers.

The Advantages of Buy

The advantages of buying components from independent suppliers are that it helps preserve strategic flexibility, and it helps the firm to avoid many of the organizational problems associated with extensive vertical integration.

- *Strategic flexibility*: The great advantage of buying component parts from independent suppliers is that the firm can maintain its flexibility, switching orders between suppliers as circumstances dictate. This is particularly important in the international context where changes in exchange rates and trade barriers might alter the attractiveness of various supply sources over time.
- *Lower costs*: outsourcing may be associated with the lowering the firm's cost structure.

Vertical integration into the manufacture of component parts involves an increase in the scope of the organization. Although there may be advantages in costs and in maintaining control of delivery of component parts, the resulting increase in organizational complexity can be costly. There are three reasons for this.

(1) The greater the numbers of sub-units within an organization, the greater are the problems of coordinating and controlling those units.

(2) The firm that vertically integrates into component part manufacture may find that because its internal suppliers have

a captive customer in the firm, internal suppliers lack an incentive to reduce costs.

(3) Leading directly on from the previous point, vertically integrated firms have to determine the appropriate price for goods transferred between sub-units within the firm. Setting appropriate transfer prices is a problem in any firm. The firm that buys its components from independent suppliers can avoid all of these problems.

Several firms have tried to capture some of the benefits of vertical integration, without encountering the associated organizational problems, by entering into long-term strategic alliances with key suppliers. Although alliances with suppliers can help the firm to capture the benefits associated with vertical integration without dispensing entirely with the benefits of a market relationship, alliances do have their drawbacks. The firm that enters into a strategic alliance may find its strategic flexibility limited by commitments to alliance partners.

COORDINATING A GLOBAL MANUFACTURING SYSTEM

Materials management encompasses the activities necessary to get materials to a manufacturing facility, through the manufacturing process, and out through a distribution system to the end user. The materials management function is complicated in an international business by distance, time, exchange rates, customs barriers, and the like. Efficient materials management can have a major impact upon a firm's bottom line.

Just-in-time: systems generate major cost savings from reduced warehousing and inventory holding costs. In addition, JIT systems help the firm to spot defective parts and take them out of the manufacturing process - thereby boosting product quality.

For a firm to establish a good materials management function it needs to legitimize materials management within the organization. It can do this by putting materials management on an equal footing with other functions in the firm.

The role of information technology: Information technology and particularly electronic data interchange play a major role in materials management. EDI (electronic data interchange) facilitates the tracking of inputs, allows the firm to optimize its production schedule, allows the firm and its suppliers to communicate in real time, and eliminates the flow of paperwork between a firm and its suppliers.

GLOBAL MARKETING AND R&D

The focus of this chapter is on how marketing and R&D can be performed in order to:

(1) lower the costs of value creation, and

(2) add value by better serving customer needs.

The tension that exists in most international businesses between, on the one hand, the need to reduce costs, and on the other hand, the need to be responsive to local conditions is particularly predominant in this chapter as we look at the development and marketing of products.

The Globalization of Markets?

This topic is not new — it was discussed several times in earlier chapters. The general view is usually that while Theodore Levitt overstates the case, he does identify a clear trend. "a powerful force drives the world toward a converging commonality and that force is technology... the result is a new commercial reality- the emergence of global markets for standardized consumer products on a previously unimagined scale of magnitude."

Market Segmentation

Market segmentation refers to identifying distinct groups of consumers whose purchasing behavior differs from others in important ways. Firms must adjust their marketing mix from segment to segment. In international business, segmentation needs to consider the existence of segments that transcend national borders and understand differences across countries in the structure of segments.

For a segment to transcend national borders, consumers in that segment must have some compelling similarities that lead to similarities in purchasing behavior. Where such similarities do not exist, there must be some customization if the firm is to maximize performance in the market. This customization may be in the product, the packaging, or simply the way in which the product is marketed. Global market segments are much likely to exist in industrial products (e.g., memory chips, chemical products, corporate bonds) than in consumer products.

PRODUCT ATTRIBUTES

A product can be viewed as a bundle of attributes. Different customers value different attributes, as well as value the same attributes differently. A soccer mom in the USA may value her automobile for its ease of use, but her Latin American counterpart may value its durability.

Product attributes have to be varied from country to country to account for differences in consumer tastes and preferences. Differences in consumer tastes and preferences between countries are a function of differences in culture and economic development.

Differences in product and technical standards may require the firm to customize product attributes from country to country. Within the EU, the need to meet differing technical standards is being reduced - but some of these previous technical standards have shaped consumer preferences as well. Even in advanced products like cellular phones, the new "global" GSM standard for digital communication (which allows customers to travel in many countries and still receive calls) has not been approved in North America.

Distribution Strategy

Distribution strategy is about choosing the best channel to deliver a product to the consumer. Figure 17.1 illustrates a typical distribution system.

Significant country differences with regard to distribution systems exist. In some countries, the retail system is very concentrated, whereas in others it is very fragmented. In some countries channel length is short, whereas in others it is long. While in some countries access to distribution channels may be difficult.

In countries with concentrated retail systems, a few retailers supply most of the market. In Germany, for example, four retail chains control 65% of the food market. In nearby Italy, no chain controls more than 2% of the market. Such differences clearly affect how a firm gets its products to consumers.

The longer the channel, the greater the aggregate mark-up and the higher the price that consumers are charged for the final product. Despite this, the benefits of using a longer channel may outweigh the drawbacks, particularly if the retail market is very fragmented. The benefits of using a longer channel are that longer channels may economize on selling costs and assist the firm to gain market access.

When there are exclusive distribution channels, it can be difficult for outsiders to obtain access to markets. Exclusive channels are often based on long established and successful relationships.

Occasionally in order to gain market access a firm may have to devise an entirely new distribution strategy. While costly, that may be the only way to obtain access, and it may even give the firm a competitive advantage.

COMMUNICATION STRATEGY

A critical element in the marketing mix is communication strategy. This is the process of communicating the attributes of a product to prospective customers.

A number of different communications channels are available to a firm. These include direct selling, sales promotion, direct marketing, and advertising via many different media. A firm's communications strategy is partly defined by its choice of channel.

The effectiveness of international communication can be hindered by three potentially critical variables - cultural barriers, source effects, and noise levels. Cultural barriers arise from the difficulty of communicating messages across cultures. The best way for a firm to overcome cultural barriers is for it to develop cross-cultural literacy, although that is often difficult to achieve.

Source effects occur when the receiver of the message (the potential consumer) evaluates the message based upon the status or image of the sender. Source effects can be either positive or negative. For example, think of some positive and negative source effects — such as German autos vs. French wine or Italian cuisine vs. British cuisine.

Noise tends to reduce the chance of effective communication. In this context, noise refers to the amount of other messages that are competing for a potential consumer's attention.

Push Strategy and a Pull Strategy

The main choice with regard to communication strategy is between a push strategy and a pull strategy. A push strategy emphasizes personnel selling which requires a competent sales force and is costly. Whereas a pull strategy emphasizes mass media advertising to communicate the marketing message to potential customers. The choice between push and pull strategies depends upon product type and consumer sophistication, channel length, and media availability.

Push strategies tend to be emphasized more in the following circumstances:

(1) for industrial products and/or complex new products,

(2) when distribution channels are short, and

(3) when few print or electronic media are available.

Pull strategies tend to be emphasized more in the following circumstances:

(1) for consumer goods products,

(2) when distribution channels are long, and when

(3) sufficient print and electronic media are available to carry the marketing message.

A globally standardized advertising campaign is one in which the same marketing message is used the world over. The major benefits of standard advertising are lower costs of ad creation, better utilization of creative talent, and the avoidance of confusion created by differences in message. While a standardized campaign has economic advantages, it usually fails to account for differences in culture and advertising regulations between countries.

Pricing Strategy: the concept of strategic pricing has tow aspects, which are refereed as predatory pricing and experience curve pricing.

Price discrimination exists whenever consumers in different countries are charged different prices for the same product. Price discrimination can assist a firm in the process of maximizing its profits.

For price discrimination to work, the firm must be able to keep national markets separate and different price elasticities of demand must exist in different countries. The elasticity of demand is determined by a number of factors, of which income level and competitive conditions are probably the most important. In general, price elasticities tend to be greater in countries with lower income levels and greater numbers of competitors. The concept of strategic pricing has two aspects, which are refereed as predatory pricing and experience curve pricing.

Predatory pricing involves using the profit gained in one market to support aggressive pricing in another market, the objective being to drive competitors out of the market. Here the price is used as competitive weapon to drive weaker competitors out of a national market by pricing very low. Once the competitors have left the market, the firm can raise prices and enjoy high profits. Many Japanese firms have been accused of pursuing this strategy.

Experience curve pricing involves aggressive pricing to build up accumulated global volume as rapidly as possible, thereby moving the firm down the experience curve as rapidly as possible. A firm builds its accumulated production volume over time, unit costs fall due to "experience effects" due to learning curves and economies of scale.

The ability of a firm to engage in price discrimination or strategic pricing is limited by antidumping regulations and nation competition policy. Antidumping regulations limit firms' ability to price below cost or below the price in its domestic market. Competition regulations can limit firm's ability to charge monopoly prices.

CONFIGURING THE MARKETING MIX

Standardization versus customization is not an all or nothing concept. In reality, most firms standardize some things and customize others. When looking at the overall marketing mix and message, one often finds some aspects of standardization and some aspects of customization in all products depending on local requirements and overall cost structures.

NEW PRODUCT DEVELOPMENT

New product development is a high risk but high return activity. In order to build up a competency in new product development, the international business must do two things:

(1) disperse R&D activities to those countries where new products are being pioneered and

(2) integrate R&D with marketing.

Innovations can make established products obsolete overnight. At the same time, innovations can create a host of new product possibilities.

To stay abreast of competitors' innovations, as well as develop their own, firms should have R&D activities in locations that are on the cutting edge of technology.

The need to adequately commercialize new technologies poses special problems in international businesses, since commercialization may require different versions of the product is produced for different countries.

A firm's new product development efforts need to be closely coordinated with the marketing, production, and materials management functions. This integration is critical to making certain that customer needs are met and that the company performs all its value creation activities efficiently.

One way to achieve cross-functional integration is to have cross-functional product development teams. Effective cross-functional teams should be led by a heavyweight project manager with status in the organization, have members from all the critical functional areas, have members located together, have clear goals, and have an effective conflict resolution process.

This all becomes more difficult when developing products for multiple worldwide markets. Many large firms have research centers in limited locations, with product development activities more dispersed.

10

The International Monetary System

INTRODUCTION

This chapter discusses how the international monetary system works and to point out its implications for international business. To understand this we must study the international monetary system's evolution. It all started with the gold standards and its break up in 1930's. Then in 1944, Bretton Woods conference, which established the basic framework fir the post world war II, international monetary system. This system called for fixed exchange rates against the US dollar.

Under this fixed exchange rate, system the value of the most currencies in terms of the US dollar was fixed for long periods and allowed to change only under specific terms.

The Bretton Woods conference also created two major international institutions, The International Monetary Fund IMF and the World Bank.

The Bretton woods system of fixed exchange rates collapsed in 1973. Since then the world has operated with a managed float system ,under the managed float system some currencies are allowed to float freely, but the majority are either managed in some way by the government intervention or pegged into other currency.

Over the past 100 years, the world has gone through eras with a gold standard, fixed exchange rates, and the current managed float system, with periods of high instability at several times.

Since WWII, the IMF and the World Bank have played an important role in the world economy. Their role going forward is currently under debate.

Exchange rates are not free to move in the way we assumed. This chapter focuses on the institutional context within which exchange rates are free to move and do so.

THE GOLD STANDARD

The gold standard has its origin in the use of gold coins as medium of exchange, unit of account and store of value-a practice that stretches back to ancient times. In the days when international trade was limited in volume. Payments of goods purchased from another country was typically made in gold and silver. However as the volume of international trade expanded after the industrial revolution, a more convenient means of financing international trade was needed. Shipping large quantities of gold and silver around the world was impractical.

The solution was to arrange fro pare currency and for governments to agree to convert the paper currency into gold on demand at a fixed rate.

Under the gold standard, countries pegged their currency to gold by agreeing to exchange a particular quantity of money for an ounce or grain of gold. At one time, for example, the US government would agree to exchange one dollar for 23.22 grains of gold. British Pound was defined as containing 113 grains of fine gold.

480 grains of gold = 1 ounce of gold

i.e., 1 ounce of gold = $20.67 (480/23.22) or,

1 ounce of gold = 4.25 pounds (480/113)

Therefore, the exchange rate for converting pounds into dollars = 1 pound = $4.87 ($20.67/4.25 pounds)

The exchange rate between currencies was determined based on how much gold a unit of each currency would buy.

The gold standard provides a powerful mechanism to pull trade imbalances between countries back into equilibrium - in fact; this is one of the key reasons why some advocate returning to the gold standard. A country is said to be in balance of trade equilibrium when the income its resident earn from exports is equal to the money its residents pay to people in other countries for imports.

The gold standard worked fairly well until the inter-war years and the great depression. Trying to spur exports and domestic employment, a number of countries started regularly devaluing their currencies, with the end result that people lost confidence in the system and started to demand gold for their currency. That put pressure on countries' gold reserves and forced them to suspend gold convertibility.

THE BRETTON WOODS SYSTEM

A key problem with the gold standard was that there was no multinational institution that could stop countries from engaging in competitive devaluations.

During The World War I, in 1914, gold standard was abandoned. During the war several governments financed their massive military expenditures by printing money. This resulted in inflation and by the end of world war, 198, the price levels were higher everywhere. Later the great Britain and United States returned to gold standard by pegging their currencies at a prewar gold parity level of £ 4.25 per ounce, despite substantial inflation, which priced British goods out of foreign goods out of foreign markets which pushed the country into deep depression. The US also did the same. The result was shattering of confidence in the gold standard system.

In 1944, at the height of World War II, representatives of 44 countries met at Bretton Woods, New Hampshire, to design a new multinational monetary system. With the collapse of gold standards and the great depression these members wanted to build economic order that facilitate growth.

The agreement reached at Bretton Woods's system established two multinational institutions - the IMF and the World Bank. The task of IMF was to maintain an order in the international monetary system and that of the World Bank was to promote general economic development. The Bretton woods agreement called for as system of fixed exchange rate that would be policed by IMF.

Fixed Exchange Rate

The US dollar was to be pegged and convertible to gold, and other currencies would set their exchange rates relative to the dollar. Devaluations were not to be used for competitive purposes, and a country could not devalue the currency by more than 10% without IMF approval.

The Role of IMF

The main aim of IMF was do act as a custodian was to try and avoid a repetition of the chaos due to financial collapse, competitive devaluations, trade wars, high unemployment and hyperinflation etc.

The fixed exchange rates were supposed to force countries to have greater monetary discipline through a need to maintain a fixed exchange rate, which puts a brake on the competitive devaluations and brings stability to the world trade environment.

The system also provided some flexibility, and countries could use short-term funds from the IMF to help support currencies during temporary pressures for revaluation.

IMF Tried Stabilize the Monetary System through and Discipline Flexibility

Discipline: the fixed exchange rate regime impose discipline in tow ways; first the need to maintain a fixed exchange rate puts a brake on competitive devaluations and brings stability to the world. Second the fixed exchange rate system imposes monetary discipline on countries thereby reducing price inflation. (Suppose if India rapidly increased its money supply by printing rupees.

This will lead to more supply of money which would leads to increased price. Or price inflation. In turn fixed exchange rate, would make Indian goods uncompetitive in world makers, while the prices of imports would become more attractive in India.

The result would be a widening trade deficit in India, with the country importing more than it exports. To correct his trade imbalance, under a fixed exchange rate regime, India would be required to restrict the rate of growth n its money supply to bring price inflation back under control.

Flexibility: two major features of IMF Articles of Agreement fostered flexibility: IMF lending facilities and adjustable parities. The IMF was ready to lend foreign currencies to members to tide them over during short periods of balance of payments deficit. When rapid tightening or monetary policy would hurt domestic employment. A pool of gold and currencies contributed by IMF members provided the resources for these lending operations. By providing funds would buy countries time which bring down their inflation rates and reduce balance of payments deficit.

The system of adjustable parities allows the devaluation of country's currency by more than 10 percent, if the OMF agrees that the country's balance of payments is in "fundamental disequilibrium." "Fundamental disequilibrium" means such countries, which had suffered permanent adverse effect in the demand for their products. Without devaluation, such a country would experience high unemployment and a persistent trade deficit until the domestic price level fallen far enough to restore a balance of payment equilibrium. Refer solved answers notes for information.

The Role of World Bank

The official name of the World Bank is the International Bank for Reconstruction and Development (IBRD). The World Bank's (IBRD) major purpose was to provide funds to help in the reconstruction of Europe and the development of third world economies.

The IBRD lends money at generous interest rates, primarily for improvements in a country's infrastructure (roads, bridges, etc). During the 1960s, the IBRD also lent money to support farming, education, population control, and urban development.

The World Bank lends money under two schemes. Under the IBRD scheme, money is raised through bonds sales in the international capital market. Borrowers pay what the bank calls a market of interest-the bank's cost of funds plus a margin for expenses. In fact, this market rate is lower than commercial banks interest rates. Under the scheme IBRD offers low interest loans to customers whose credit rating is often poor.

A second scheme is through resources raised through subscriptions from wealthy members such as US, Japan, Germany. (Refer solved answers notes for information.)

THE COLLAPSE OF THE FIXED EXCHANGE RATE SYSTEM

The fixed exchange rate system established in Bretton Woods collapsed mainly due to the economic management of the USA. To understand why the system failed one must understand the special role of the US dollar in the system.

As the only currency that would be converted into gold, and as the currency that served as the reference pint for all others, the dollar occupied a central place in the system. Any pressure on the dollar to devalue would play havoc with the system and that is what it happened. Under Lyndon Johnson, the US financed huge increases in poverty reduction programs, as well as the Vietnam War by increasing its money supply.

Speculation that the dollar would have to be devalued relative to most other currencies, as well as underlying economics and some forceful threats by the US forced other countries to increase the value of their currency relative to the dollar. The key problem with the Bretton Woods system was that it relied on an economically well managed US, since the dollar was the base currency. When the US began to print excess amounts of money, run high trade deficits, and experience high inflation, the system was strained to the breaking point.

THE FLOATING EXCHANGE RATE REGIME

The Jamaica agreement called for floating exchange rates (although countries could intervene to smooth out speculative spurts), the end of gold as a reserve asset, and more funds in the IMF to help countries overcome short-term problems.

Since 1973, exchange rates have been relatively volatile. Figure 10.1 shows movements in exchange rates over the past three decades.

The rise of the $ from 1980-5 is interesting, as this is a time where the underlying fundamentals discussed in Chapter 9 would have predicted that the $ should fall, not rise. The subsequent fall was both a result of governmental intervention and underlying market forces.

The regularity of governmental intervention in the foreign exchange markets explains why the current system is sometimes referred to as a "managed" or "dirty" floating system.

FIXED VERSUS FLOATING EXCHANGE RATES

The case for a floating exchange rates regime claims that such a system gives countries autonomy regarding their monetary policy and that floating exchange rates facilitate smooth adjustment of trade imbalances.

The case for a fixed exchange rate regime claims that:

(1) the need to maintain a fixed exchange rate imposes monetary discipline on a country,

(2) floating exchange rate regimes are vulnerable to speculative pressures,

(3) the uncertainty that accompanies floating exchange rates hinders the growth of international trade and investment, and

(4) far from correcting trade imbalances, depreciating a currency on the foreign exchange market tends to cause inflation.

While we know that the past attempts at fixed exchange rates have not held up, perhaps there is another new approach. The floating system clearly works, but it causes great volatility.

EXCHANGE RATE REGIMES IN PRACTICE

Under a pegged exchange rate regime, a country will peg the value of its currency to that of another major currency. Pegged exchange rates are popular among the world's smaller nations, as they peg their exchange rate to that of other, larger currencies that are presumed to be more stable.

There is some evidence that adopting a pegged exchange rate regime does moderate inflationary pressures in a country.

A country that introduces a currency board commits itself to converting its domestic currency on demand into another currency at a fixed exchange rate. To make this commitment credible, the currency board holds reserves of a foreign currency equal at the fixed exchange rate to at least 100% of the domestic currency issued.

European Monetary Union

Chapter on regional economic integration provided some information on the Euro and European Monetary union. Some background on how the current European system developed may provide background relevant to understanding this particular form of exchange rate stabilization.

The objectives of the European Monetary System (EMS) were to:

(1) create a zone of monetary stability in Europe,

(2) control inflation, and

(3) to coordinate exchange rate policies with third currencies.

The ECU was created as a basket of currencies that served as the unit of account for the EMS. Each national currency in the EMS was given a central rate vis-à-vis the ecu. From this central rate flow a series of bilateral rates.

Currencies were not allowed to depart by more than 2.25% from their bilateral rate with another EMS currency. Countries could borrow from each other to defend their currency against speculative pressure.

The EMS was fairly successful in stabilizing exchange and interest rates between countries, although a clear crisis occurred in 1992 that showed the difficulty in maintaining the bands when pressured by the currency markets.

RECENT ACTIVITIES AND THE FUTURE OF THE IMF

With the introduction of the floating rate system and the emergence of global capital markets, much of the original reason for the IMF's existence has disappeared. Financial difficulties have not disappeared, however, and the IMF has found away to grow and redefine its mission.

The IMF has gotten involved in helping third world countries out of their debt crises. Relatedly, the IBRD has found that economic mismanagement by various nations can make good projects turn out to be inappropriate. Moreover, the line between the role of the IBRD and the IMF has become increasingly blurred.

The Third World debt crisis had its roots in the OPEC oil price hikes of 1973 and 1979, when banks recycled money from OPEC countries into debt by developing countries. When these countries took on too much debt and were unable to even make interest payments, the IMF stepped in to help reschedule debt.

The Mexican currency crisis of 1995 was a result of high Mexican debts, and a pegged exchange rate that did not allow for a natural adjustment of prices. In order to keep Mexico from defaulting on its debt, a $50 billion aid package was put together. The effect of the

Mexican currency crisis on the US automobile industry, described in the Management Focus box, was to allow the peso to float freely, to cause the prices of imported autos to rise, and for the entire auto industry to plummet.

Russian ruble crisis: Between 1992 and 1995, the value of the Russian ruble relative to the dollar fell from 125 to 5130. That fall occurred while Russia was implementing an economic reform program designed to transform the country's crumbling centrally planned economy into a dynamic market economy. The fall was directly related to the hyperinflation in Russia, in line with what would be expected by purchasing power parity. The financial crisis that erupted across Southeast Asia during the fall of 1997 were sown in the previous decade when these countries were experiencing unprecedented growth. Huge increases in exports, and hence the incoming funds, helped fuel a boom in commercial and residential property, industrial assets, and infrastructure. As the volume of investments grew, the quality of these investments declined, leading to significant excess capacity. These investments were often supported by dollar-based debts. When inflation and increasing imports put pressure on the currencies, the resulting devaluations led to default on dollar denominated debts.

In helping bail out countries under financial crisis, the IMF's policies have come under criticism. One criticism is that the IMF has a "one size fits all" policy that does not adequately deal with the differences across countries. Another is that the IMF creates a moral hazard - since people and governments believe that the IMF will bail them out, they undertake overly risky investments. While it may be that the IMF has become too big and does not have enough accountability for its actions, it has also been extremely helpful to many countries.

IMPLICATIONS FOR BUSINESS

The present floating rate system makes it important that firms carefully manage their foreign exchange transactions and exposure to changes.

Given that currencies can change, and that the relative appropriateness of different locations for production and sales can change with changing exchange rates, it is important that MNEs have strategic flexibility to transfer production to locations where the exchange rates are the most favorable. Using contract manufacturing from different countries can also provide flexibility in low value added manufacturing.

Firms have an incentive to both encourage governments to undertake policies that provide favorable exchange rates, as well as encourage that a system of more stable exchange rates be established. The relative stability of exchange rates in Europe has clearly helped European firms in managing their cross-border activities.

11

The Global Capital Market

INTRODUCTION

There has been a dramatic growth in the international capital market over the past 15 years.

Companies are increasingly turning to the global capital market for funds, as the opening China Mobile case illustrates. By using international capital markets, firms can lower the costs and increase their access to funds.

Investors are also diversifying their portfolios and reducing their systematic risk by investing internationally, although new risks are created in the process.

BENEFITS OF THE GLOBAL CAPITAL MARKET

In the case of international capital markets, there are simply more of players and a greater diversity in the players and the possible combinations.

Firms can obtain funds via both debt and equity. To raise funds via debt, a firm owes investor money (They borrow). To raise funds via equity, a firm sells partial ownership (stock) to an investor.

There are two main reasons why an international capital market offers an improvement over a purely domestic capital market:

(1) from a borrower's perspective, it increases the supply of funds available for borrowing and lowers the cost of capital; and

(2) from an investor's perspective, it provides a wider range of investment opportunities, thereby allowing investors to build a portfolio of international investments that diversifies risk.

If there is limited liquidity in a purely domestic capital market, the cost of capital is higher relative to what would be found in an international market.

With an increase in the choices available to an investor, the investor is able to diversify holdings internationally, thereby reducing systematic risk below what could be achieved in a purely domestic market.

While the systematic risks are reduced with international portfolio investments, exchange rate risks now come into play.

GROWTH OF THE GLOBAL CAPITAL MARKET

De-regulation and improvements in technology have facilitated the growth of the international capital market.

Due to advances in communications and data processing capabilities, the international capital markets are always active around the globe. International trading is an information intensive activity that would not have been possible only a few decades ago when computing and telecommunication capabilities were much less developed.

The deregulation of capital flows, a removal of limitations on the types services that can be provided by foreign financial services firms, and a reduction in the restrictions imposed on domestic financial services firms have all contributed to the growth of the international capital market.

While capital is generally free to move internationally, evidence to date suggests that most investors choose to make long term investments in their home country and only make short term opportunistic investments elsewhere.

A lack of information about the fundamental quality of foreign investments may encourage speculative flows in the global capital market.

The Country Focus on Mexico and the global capital markets shows that a country cannot count on capital inflows to finance its deficits, especially when the money that is being invested is not there for the long term..

THE EUROCURRENCY MARKET

A Eurocurrency is any currency that is banked outside of its country of origin. Eurodollars, which account for about two-thirds of all Eurocurrencies, are dollars banked outside of the United States. The Eurocurrency got its origin as holders of dollars outside the USA, initially communist countries but later also middle eastern countries, wanted to deposit their dollars but were afraid that they may be confiscated if deposited in the USA.

The lack of government regulation makes the Eurocurrency market attractive to both depositors and borrowers. Due to the lack of regulation, the spread between the Eurocurrency deposit rate and the Eurocurrency lending rate is less than the spread between the domestic deposit rate and the domestic lending rate. This gives Eurobanks a competitive advantage. The lack of regulation is also a drawback of Eurocurrency deposits, as the risk of forfeiture is greater than for domestic deposits. However, this is not a major problem. There is also a risk of currency fluctuations that would not arise if funds were held domestically in the domestic currency.

THE GLOBAL BOND MARKET

The international bond market falls into two general classifications; the foreign bond market and the Eurobond market. Eurobonds account for the lion's share of international bond issues.

Foreign bonds are sold outside of the borrower's country and are denominated in the currency of the country in which they are issued.

A Eurobond issue is normally underwritten by an international syndicate of banks and placed in countries other than the one in whose currency the bond is denominated.

The Eurobond market is an attractive way for companies to raise funds due to the absence of regulatory interference, less stringent disclosure requirements than in most domestic bond markets, and the favorable tax status of Eurobonds.

ECU and Euro denominated bonds became increasingly common in the 1990s. One advantage of these bonds is that the risks associated with exchange rates are lower, since the ECU and Euro are actually a basket of currencies.

THE GLOBAL EQUITY MARKET

There is no international equity market in the same sense that there are international currency and bond markets. Instead there are a number of separate equity markets that are linked via specific equities and overall market fundamentals.

Foreign investors are increasingly investing in different national equity markets, primarily as a way of diversifying risk by diversifying their portfolio of stock holdings across nations.

As firms are listed on multiple national exchanges and have their shares owned by an even greater number of shareholders from different nationalities, it is becoming increasingly meaningless to refer to firms as "American" or "Dutch." For example, the "nationality" of DaimlerChrysler does not matter.

Companies are beginning to list their stock in the equity markets of other nations, primarily as a prelude to issuing stock in the market to raise additional capital. Other reasons for foreign listings include facilitating future stock swaps, using the company's stock and stock options to compensate local management and employees, satisfying local ownership desires, providing access to funding for future acquisitions in a country, and increasing the company's visibility to local employees, customers, suppliers, and bankers

Foreign Exchange Risk and the Cost of Capital

When borrowing funds from the international capital market, companies must weigh the benefits of a lower interest rate against the risks of an increase in the real cost of capital due to adverse exchange rate movements.

Using forward rates cannot typically remove the risk altogether, particularly in the case of long-term investments.

Implications for Business

By utilizing international capital markets, firms can often borrow funds at a lower cost than they could domestically — regardless of whether the funds are in the form of cash loans, equity, or bonds.

The minimal regulation in international capital markets helps lower the cost of capital, but also increases risk in both currencies and security.

For investors, the international capital market provides opportunities for portfolio diversification and the lowering of systematic risk. At the same time, it creates new currency risks.

FOREIGN DIRECT INVESTMENT

With FDI, a firm has a significant ownership in a foreign operation and the potential to affect managerial decisions of the operation.

The goal of our coverage of FDI is to understand the pattern of FDI that occurs between countries, and why firms undertake FDI and become multinational in their operations.

This chapter will describe some of the basic theories of FDI, and why firms undertake FDI rather than simply exporting products or licensing their know-how.

Foreign Direct Investment in the World Economy

When discussing foreign direct investment, it is important to distinguish between the flow of FDI and the stock of FDI. The flow of FDI refers to the amount of FDI undertaken over a given time period (normally one year). The stock of FDI refers to the total accumulated value of foreign owned assets at a given point in time.

The significant growth in FDI during 1999-2001 has both to do with the political economy of trade as outlined in the previous chapter and the political and economic changes that have been taking place in developing countries. The globalization of the world economy is causing firms to invest worldwide in order to assure their presence in every region of the world.

Another important trend is has been the rise of inflows into the US. The stock of foreign FDI in the US increased more rapidly than US FDI abroad.

The rapid increase in FDI growth into the US may be due to the attractiveness of the US market, the falling value of the dollar, and a belief by some foreign corporations that they could manage US assets and workers more efficiently than their American managers could.

It is difficult to say whether the increase in the FDI into the US is good for the country or not. To the extent that foreigners are making more productive use of US assets and workers, it is probably good for the country.

The management focus box details the techniques of Mexican cement manufacturer Cemex for its aggressive international expansion of cement manufacturing. Because cement is a product that is not easily exported due to its low ratio of value to weight, Cemex sought international expansion by acquisition.

Horizontal Foreign Direct Investment

Horizontal FDI is FDI in the same industry abroad as a firm operates in at home. A Japanese automobile manufacturer in Japan seeks to produce the same product in the USA. FDI would seem to be more expensive and risky than exporting or licensing, so there must be some other good reasons for firms to undertake FDI.

Transportation costs can make export infeasible, especially for products that have a low value/weight ratio (i.e. cement, soft drinks), or would require refrigeration or similar controlled environments. For items like electronics, software, and medical equipment, transportation costs may not be an impediment to exporting.

The most accepted reason for horizontal FDI relates to market imperfections. By imposing quotas, tariffs, or impediments, governments can make FDI and licensing more attractive than exporting.

Technological or managerial know-how can be difficult and dangerous to license, however, making it an infeasible alternative. A firm can lose control of critical competitive know-how, may not be able to optimize the flow and configuration of operations between countries, or simply may be unable to codify its knowledge in a way that would make licensing a practical option.

Firms may choose to undertake FDI simply to follow the lead of a competitor so as not be left behind or locked out of an opportunity.

FDI may be most likely to occur in certain stages of a product's lifecycle — when other countries have a large enough market to justify local production or when there is a need to locate production in a low cost location.

A firm may choose to undertake FDI in a particular country or region due to location specific advantages. An obvious example occurs with respect to natural resources, but it also applies to the ability to tap into a particular expertise (e.g. silicon valley) or be located near customers or suppliers with unique characteristics. Porter's diamond, as discussed in chapter 4, provides a partial explanation why firms in certain industries may find it attractive to invest in a particular country.

Vertical Foreign Direct Investment

Backward vertical FDI involves investment into an industry that provides inputs for a firm's domestic production processes. Forward vertical FDI involves investment in an industry that utilizes the outputs of a firm's domestic production processes.

The strategic behavior explanation for vertical FDI suggests that firms try to either create new entry barriers or erode competitors' entry barriers. While there certainly are some examples where the strategic behavior explanation seems to apply, the market imperfections explanation seems to present a more complete explanation.

Market imperfections can result from impediments to the sale of know-how and the need to invest in specialized assets.

Because specialized know-how can be difficult to sell or license, a firm may have to integrate vertically to be successful. The establishment of sales and services centers in high technology industries, or the investment in knowledge intensive extractive processes are two examples.

When specialized assets must be invested in (i.e. the aluminum smelter), companies may need to secure a supply of the needed inputs to assure that those assets can be used efficiently.

Implications for Business

The market imperfections theory suggests that exporting should be preferred to licensing and horizontal FDI as long as transport costs are minor and tariff barriers are trivial. If that is not the case, then firms should consider licensing and FDI.

FDI is more costly than licensing, but may be the most reasonable option. A decision tree suggesting when licensing, FDI, and exporting are most appropriate. Licensing tends not to be a good option in high technology industries where protecting firm specific know-how is critical, in industries where a firm must carefully coordinate and orchestrate its worldwide activities, or where there are intense cost pressures.

THE POLITICAL ECONOMY OF FOREIGN DIRECT INVESTMENT

The opening case on foreign investment in South Africa underlines the importance of political and social stability as a condition for the inflow of foreign capital. It also points out the futility and counter productiveness of the use of trade sanctions as an agent of economic change.

Home country governments can also affect ability of firms to take resources out of the country for investment elsewhere.

In addition to understanding the explicit rules laid out by home and host country governments, firms must evaluate their bargaining position and appropriate negotiating stances when they wish to alter established rules for FDI.

Political Ideology and FDI

The Radical/Marxist view of FDI suggested that FDI by MNEs from advanced capitalist nations keeps the less developed countries of the world relatively backward and dependent upon advanced capitalist nations for investment, jobs, and technology. According to this view, FDI is an instrument of economic domination — not economic development.

The radical view was popular from WWII into the 1980s, and practiced in Eastern Europe, India, China, and many socialist third world countries.

By the end of the 1980s, the radical position was generally disregarded, due to the collapse of communism, the abysmal economic performance of most of the countries that practiced the radical approach, and the contrasting strong economic performance of those developing countries that had embraced a freer market approach (i.e. Singapore, Hong Kong, South Korea).

The free market view sees the MNE as an instrument for dispersing the production and flow of goods and services in their most efficient manner. It is built on the philosophy of Smith and Ricardo and supported by the market imperfections explanation of FDI.

While the free market view is embraced by most advanced and developing nations, almost all countries impose some restrictions on FDI. Most countries have adopted a policy of "pragmatic nationalism," which lies somewhere between the radical and free market views.

The pragmatic approach suggests that governments should pursue policies designed to maximize the national benefits and minimize the national costs of FDI. Whereas in earlier years many countries discouraged FDI, or placed limits on the ownership level held by MNEs, many countries are now actively courting MNEs for FDI (as indicated in the opening case). That aggressiveness is also consistent with a pragmatic approach, as countries are offering inducements that would not be appropriate in a purely free market approach.

Examples of pragmatic policies are in Japan, the USA, and several EC countries.

The Benefits of FDI to Host Countries

- From a free market view, the best policy would be for all countries to stop intervening in the investment decisions of MNEs. In their view the benefits are generally so much greater than the costs that pragmatic nationalism will likely end up creating. These costs include both barriers and incentives from many countries, with the result that all countries are worse off than they would be under a free market approach.
- Due to MNEs large size and access to international capital markets, they may have resources available to them that smaller nationally based firms do not, and they may be able to bring resources into a country that would not be brought in otherwise.
- Technology is critical to economic growth, and MNEs may bring product and process technology into a country. Hence, not only is the technology valuable in itself, but also it may spur economic growth and the development of new technological capabilities.
- FDI may bring in managerial skills, increase the productive use of a country's resources, and spill over into improving the management talent in other firms that come into contact with the MNE.
- FDI can lead to increased employment and the creation of new jobs. Critics point out, however, that the reported number of jobs created do not often take into account the loss of jobs that may have occurred in other firms or regions of a country. Simply put, if Germany has gained jobs, has France lost jobs?
- FDI can have a beneficial effect on a country's balance of payments by (i) the initial capital investment, (ii) substituting for

imports that contribute to a current account deficit, and (iii) the current account surplus that results from exporting the products produced from a facility built with the initial FDI.

- FDI can also spur competition and economic growth in a country. Previously stodgy and protected firms may have to improve their product offerings and lower prices in order to compete on an international level. There can also be "follow the leader" effects, where the FDI of one firm will lead to subsequent FDI by other firms. This will also lead to increased competition and more choices for consumers.

The Costs of FDI to Host Countries

- MNEs operating in a particular country may have greater economic strength than domestic competitors and may subsidize operations in a country in order to drive out domestic competitors.
- Countries may want to restrict FDI in industries they wish to protect until their own "infant" firms have the strength to compete against established MNEs.
- When MNEs repatriate profits from FDI, these outflows show up as debits to a capital account.
- If MNEs import a great deal of components for assembly into the products produced in a host country, it will have an unfavorable impact the trade or current account balance.
- Some countries may feel that their national sovereignty is threatened by foreign MNEs that make decisions that affect the country from distant locations.

The Benefits and Costs of FDI to Home Countries

The benefits of FDI to the home country include an improvement in the balance of payments as a result of the inward flow of foreign earnings, positive employment effects when the foreign subsidiary creates demands for home country exports, and benefits from a reverse resource transfer effect.

The costs of FDI to the home country include adverse balance of payments effects that arise from the initial capital outflow, export substitution effects on the current account, and the potential loss of jobs to foreign operations. There is much political rhetoric in the US regarding lost jobs to Mexico by US firms that moved some assembly operations south of the border.

Even when there are negative short-term employment effects, in the long term these jobs would likely be lost in any case to foreign competitors. Moving production offshore can free up resources and people for other jobs where their value added is greater and may prove a net benefit to consumers that now have access to less expensive products.

Government Policy Instruments and FDI

Home countries can encourage FDI by offering insurance, making funds available, pressuring host governments to remove barriers, and initiating tax incentives.

Home countries can restrict FDI via explicit capital flow controls, punitive tax rules, or specific prohibitions for political concerns.

Host countries are increasingly encouraging FDI by offering tax incentives, low interest rate loans, or outright grants and subsidies. Countries, and regions of countries, compete with each other for new plants and facilities.

Host countries can restrict FDI by:

(1) imposing restraints on the ownership of domestic firms and assets and

(2) setting specific performance requirements relating to local content, export requirements, technology transfer, or local management participation.

Through the WTO there has been progress on liberalizing rules regarding FDI. That has occurred primarily in the areas of financial services and telecommunications. Work on a much more wide ranging pact on liberalizing FDI internationally has been stalled by a number of countries' hesitation to give up sovereignty over the control of investment in their country.

Implications for Business

A host government's attitude to FDI is a critical issue when considering whether to invest in a particular country.

There is both an art and a science to negotiating. The key to most negotiating is to allow the other part to believe they have "won."

A number of the issues discussed in the chapter relate to the bargaining power of both the host government and the investing firm. Issues like the potential for technology transfer, effects on the balance of payments, and possibility of job creation (among others) all can change the relative bargaining power of both parties.

Additional notes:

Is India Ready for Full Currency Convertibility?

India's political boldness in seeking peace with Pakistan in their half-century twilight struggle for Kashmir may soon be matched by economic moves equally as daring. Indeed, India is edging toward a truly bold reform: full international convertibility of the rupee. How it goes about this will not only effect India's economic development, but provide object lessons for China as it ponders convertibility in the years ahead.

Since 1991 India has been travelling on a path from rupee devaluation to full convertibility, with the Reserve Bank of India (RBI) relaxing a range of foreign-exchange controls. Resident Indians can now maintain a foreign-currency account and invest in shares of foreign companies, while non-resident Indians can repatriate legacy/inheritance assets. Indian companies listed abroad can buy property in foreign countries, and resident firms will be allowed to pre-pay external commercial debt up to US$100 million. Limits on exporters' foreign-currency accounts will be removed, and banks may invest in overseas money and debt markets.

Is India ready for full convertibility? The government is still lagging on its domestic economic reforms. Structural reform and privatization have slowed, eroding investors' confidence. But failure to address structural problems could expose the economy to external shocks in the long term. Hence it would be premature for India to open up its capital account immediately. Exchange rate stability is the key anchor when a country's reform process is underway. There is, however, little evidence that capital account convertibility has a meaningful impact on a country's growth rate.

With capital-account convertibility, the rupee's exchange rate will be determined more by capital flows than by inflation differentials, as

India's inflation rate remains broadly in line with the OECD average of around 3%. Because India is still running a trade deficit, there could be some pressure on the rupee following any negative shock. Although monetary growth is more than twice the rate of real GDP growth, the inflationary risk is probably low because substantial excess capacity exists. Indeed, throughout the 1990s, despite rising output, deflation occurred, which means that India's potential output is expanding.

The moves towards full capital-account convertibility have proceeded in step with impressive growth in India's foreign-currency reserves. Indeed, India's external liquidity position has strengthened dramatically in the past decade. As a result of a current-account surplus and an interest-rate differential of 3-4%, foreign reserves reached $70.3 billion by the end of 2002—enough to cover almost 15 months of imports—up from only US$4 billion in 1990.

Following the 1991 balance of payments crisis, the rupee's exchange rate was devalued around 20%. Exporters could exchange 30% of their earnings at the market rate. This was subsequently replaced with a two-tier exchange-rate system making the rupee partially convertible—60% of export earnings could be converted at the market exchange rate, and the rest at the RBI's fixed rate (used by the government to finance essential imports like petroleum, cooking oil, fertilizers, and life-saving drugs).

The two-tier exchange-rate system acted as an export tax, but it did not survive for long, giving way to a unified exchange rate on the trade account. Full convertibility on the current account followed in August 1994. The policy debate then turned to capital-account convertibility, with the IMF and the World Bank strongly in favor. In May 1997, the Tarapore Committee on Capital Account Convertibility charted a three-stage liberalization process to be completed by 1999-2000, with an accompanying emphasis on fiscal consolidation, a mandated inflation target, and a strong financial system.

Then the East Asian currency crisis put further action on hold and raised serious questions about when—and whether—to proceed. The sudden meltdown of apparently healthy economies served as a stark reminder that strong external liquidity should not be the driving force towards full convertibility. The downside risk of capital-account liberalization, after all, is higher exchange-rate volatility, and even countries with sound liquidity positions could not prevent a run on their reserves. The lesson for India is that, in the event of a domestic or external shock, full convertibility could prove to be a costly, short-lived experiment. The fundamental question is whether full convertibility will encourage higher net inflows or outflows of capital.

The downside risk of higher volatility for the rupee is aggravated by some serious problems, including a deficit running at 6% of GDP and the strategic stand-off with Pakistan. Short-term capital outflows—which might occur should either risk worsen—could create greater output volatility. So it is vital for India to increase the inward flow of long-term capital, regardless of whether the capital account is closed or open. In this context, it is noteworthy that China, with a closed capital account, has foreign-exchange reserves of US$286 billion, four times the size of India's, though China's economy is only double India's size. Nor is full convertibility the key to attracting higher inflows of foreign direct investment (FDI). China attracted FDI inflows of US$52.7 billion in 2002—the largest in the world.

India needs to attract higher FDI inflows to help soak up the economy's excess capacity. This underscores the importance for India's financial stability of successful management of the capital account (monitoring inflows and outflows) following any move toward full convertibility. But, in the near term, full capital account convertibility is not in India's interest.

Purchase Power Parity Additional Notes

What is Purchasing Power Parity?

Purchasing power parity (PPP) is a theory, which states that exchange rates between currencies are in equilibrium when their purchasing power is the same in each of the two countries. This means that the exchange rate between two countries should equal the ratio of the two countries' price level of a fixed basket of goods and services. When a country's domestic price level is increasing (i.e., a country experiences inflation), that country's exchange rate must depreciated in order to return to PPP.

Law of one Price

The basis for PPP is the "law of one price": In the absence of transportation and other transaction costs, competitive markets will equalize the price of an identical good in two countries when the prices are expressed in the same currency.

For example, a particular TV set that sells for 750 Canadian Dollars [CAD] in Vancouver should cost 500 US Dollars [USD] in Seattle when the exchange rate between Canada and the US is 1.50 CAD/USD. If the price of the TV in Vancouver was only 700 CAD, consumers in Seattle would prefer buying the TV set in Vancouver. If this process (called "arbitrage") is carried out at a large scale, the US consumers buying Canadian goods will bid up the value of the Canadian Dollar, thus making Canadian goods more costly to them. This process continues until the goods have again the same price. There are three caveats with this law of one price.

(1) As mentioned above, transportation costs, barriers to trade, and other transaction costs, can be significant.

(2) There must be competitive markets for the goods and services in both countries.

(3) The law of one price only applies to tradeable goods; immobile goods such as houses, and many services that are local, are of course not traded between countries.

Economists use two versions of Purchasing Power Parity: absolute PPP and relative PPP.

Absolute PPP was described in the previous paragraph; it refers to the equalization of price levels across countries. Put formally, the exchange rate between Canada and the United States $E_{CAD/USD}$ is equal to the price level in Canada P_{CAN} divided by the price level in the United States P_{USA}. Assume that the price level ratio P_{CAD}/P_{USD} implies a PPP exchange rate of 1.3 CAD per 1 USD. If today's exchange rate $E_{CAD/USD}$ is 1.5 CAD per 1 USD, PPP theory implies that the CAD will appreciate (get stronger) against the USD, and the USD will in turn depreciate (get weaker) against the CAD.

Relative PPP refers to rates of changes of price levels, that is, inflation rates. This proposition states that the rate of appreciation of a currency is equal to the difference in inflation rates between the foreign and the home country. For example, if Canada has an inflation rate of 1% and the US has an inflation rate of 3%, the US Dollar will depreciate against the Canadian Dollar by 2% per year. This proposition holds well empirically especially when the inflation differences are large.

Does PPP Determine Exchange Rates in the Short Term?

No. Exchange rate movements in the short term are news-driven. Announcements about interest rate changes, changes in perception of the growth path of economies and the like are all factors that drive exchange rates in the short run.

PPP, by comparison, describes the long run behaviour of exchange rates. The economic forces behind PPP will eventually equalize the purchasing power of currencies. This can take many years, however. A time horizon of 4-10 years would be typical.

How is PPP Calculated?

The simplest way to calculate purchasing power parity between two countries is to compare the price of a "standard" good that is in fact identical across countries.

Every year *The Economist* magazine publishes a light-hearted version of PPP: it's "Hamburger Index" that compares the price of a McDonald's hamburger around the world. More sophisticated versions of PPP look at a large number of goods and services. One of the key problems is that people in different countries consumer very different sets of goods and services, making it difficult to compare the purchasing power between countries.

According to PPP, by how Much are Currencies Overvalued or Undervalued?

The following chart compares the PPP of a currency with its actual exchange rate. The chart is updated periodically to reflect the current exchange rate. It is also updated about twice a year to reflect new estimates of PPP. The PPP estimates are taken from studies carried out by the Organization of Economic Cooperation and Development (OECD) and others; however, they should not be taken as "definitive". Different methods of calculation will arrive at different PPP rates.

The currencies listed below are compared to the US Dollar. A green bar indicated that the local currency is overvalued by the percentage figure shown on the axis; the currency is thus expected to depreciate against the US Dollar in the long run. A red bar indicates undervaluation of the local currency; the currency is thus expected to appreciate against the US Dollar in the long run.

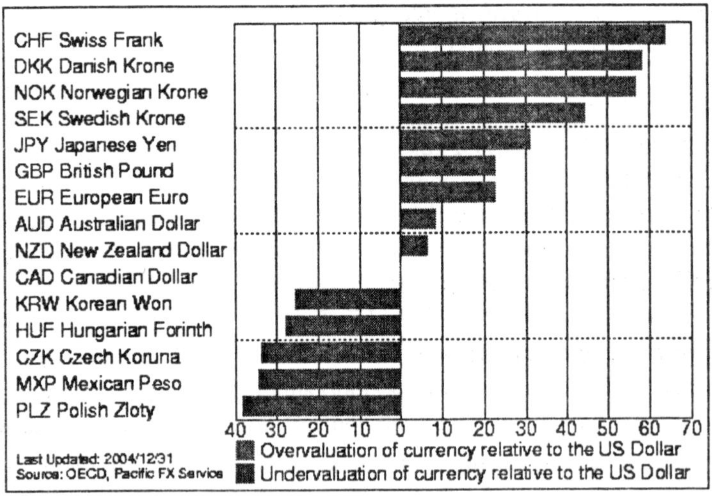

IMF(International Monetary Fund)

The International Monetary Fund (IMF) came into official existence on December 27, 1945, when 29 countries signed its Articles of Agreement at a conference held in Bretton Woods, New Hampshire, USA, from July 1-22, 1944. The IMF began financial operations on March 1, 1947.

- Current Membership: 182 countries
- Staff: Approximately 2,600 from 110 countries
- Managing Director: Michel Camdessus assumed office in 1987
- Governing Bodies: Board of Governors, Interim Committee, Executive Board
- Total Quotas: SDR 145 billion (US $195 billion)
- Accounting Unit: Special Drawing Right (SDR). As of September 10, 1998, SDR 1 equaled US $1.36163.

Statutory Purpose

The IMF was created to promote international monetary cooperation; to facilitate the expansion and balanced growth of international trade; to promote exchange stability; to assist in the establishment of a multilateral system of payments; to make its general resources temporarily available to its members experiencing balance of payments difficulties under adequate safeguards; and to shorten the duration and lessen the degree of disequilibrium in the international balances of payments of members.

How the IMF Came About

The International Monetary Fund (IMF or Fund) and the International Bank for Reconstruction and Development (IBRD or World Bank) were both established at the United Nations Monetary and Financial Conference, held at Bretton Woods, New Hampshire, on July 1-22, 1944.

The two were created to oversee stability in international monetary affairs and to facilitate the expansion of world trade. Membership in the World Bank requires membership in the IMF, and they are both specialized agencies of the United Nations. The World Bank was given domain over long-term financing for nations in need, while the IMF's mission was to monitor exchange rates, provide short-term financing for balance of payments adjustments, provide a forum for discussion about international monetary concerns, and give technical assistance to member countries. These functions are still generally true of both organizations, although the policies determining how they are carried out have been modified and amplified over time.

The Fund's legal authority is based on an international treaty called the Articles of Agreement (Articles or the Agreement) which came into force in December 1945. The first Article in the Agreement outlines the purposes of the Fund and, although the Articles have been amended three times in the course of the last 47 years prior to 1998, the first Article has never been altered.

The IMF started financial operations on March 1, 1947. Drawings on Fund reserves were made by 11 countries between 1947 and 1948, although there were no drawings in 1950 and very few in the following years. During this time the Fund worked on its drawings policies. One outcome was the stand-by arrangements, established in 1952, modified in 1956, and reviewed periodically since then. Stand-by arrangements provide a procedure for drawing on Fund resources with conditions based on a structural adjustment program for the borrower country. Stand-by arrangements became the model for other lending procedures designed by the Fund to meet the needs of its members.

By the mid-1970s, the Fund found itself becoming more of a lending institution than originally envisioned. The Fund's ability to meet the needs of its members was tested when the Organization of the Petroleum Exporting Countries (OPEC) quadrupled the price of crude oil in 1973-1974. Prices were increased again in 1979 and in 1980. This altered the international flow of funds as the OPEC countries' monetary reserves accumulated rapidly. At the same time, the industrial countries experienced strong inflationary pressures. These pressures were addressed by an increase in interest rates and a reduction of imports.

This resulted in balance of payments deficits for many of the developing countries, which were paying more for oil, paying higher interest rates on the loans from the industrial countries, and finding reduced markets for their exports. In response to this situation, the IMF created an Oil Facility in 1974, and enlarged it in 1975, to aid members in balance of payments difficulties. In addition, an Oil Facility Subsidy Account was established for the poorest countries to alleviate the cost of borrowing under the Oil Facility. During the 1970s, although the oil price shocks placed more countries in balance of payments difficulties and forced many of the developing countries to borrow not only against the Fund, but also against private banks which were receiving a surplus of OPEC petrodollars, it was generally perceived at the time that the debt cads would be short-lived.

It was not until Mexico threatened to default on its loans in 1982 that the world monetary community realized the extent and depth of the crisis. Throughout the 1980s the Fund played an increasingly larger role, not only as "lender-of-last-resort," but also as mediator with debtor countries in relation to creditor nations and private banks.

In the mid-1980s the Fund's lending operations increased dramatically. Stand-by arrangements are typically for one to three years, but the exigency of the debt crisis caused the Fund to devise programs for adjustment over longer periods. These are known as extended arrangements and, with other medium-term programs, can be arranged through the Structural Adjustment Facility or the Enhanced Structural Adjustment Facility. The terms of a structural adjustment program, or stabilization program, are known as conditionality. Programs include quantified targets or ceilings for bank credit, the budget deficit, foreign borrowing, external arrears, and international reserves.

They also include statements of policies that the member intends to follow. Conditionality came under detailed scrutiny during the 1980s as more and more developing countries adopted structural adjustment programs and later were unable to meet the terms of the agreement. The philosophy of the Fund was criticized as being too oriented to the industrial economies and not adapted to developing economies. During the late-1980s several plans were put forth, involving not only the Fund but the creditor nations and commercial banks as well, to reduce the debt and the debt service payments of the debtor nations. In 1989 the Fund developed new debt reduction guidelines, providing Fund support for commercial bank debt and debt service-reduction operations by member countries. The debt strategy is still being assessed and its success or failure has not been determined.

Training and Technical Assistance

Assistance is extended to members in the form of training and technical assistance. Beginning in 1950, the Fund offered training courses on balance of payments statistics and on international economics. In 1964 the IMF Institute was established fortify these training activities. The IMF Institute provides training courses for officials from member countries in such subjects as financial analysis and policy, balance of payments methodology, public finance, and government finance statistics.

The technical assistance program is operated through the Monetary and Exchange Affairs Department, the Fiscal Affairs Department, and the Bureau of Statistics. The Legal Department, the Bureau of Computing Services, and the area departments may also participate. Assistance is provided mainly through staff missions, field assignments by staff members or outside experts, and studies and recommendations prepared at headquarters. In providing technical assistance, the IMF emphasizes training government officials in macroeconomic management, reforming the tax system and tax administration developing central banking and financing systems, and improving statistical data. Advice is also provided on money and capital markets, central and general banking legislation, the structure of interest rates, regional cooperation among central banks, and the use of various instruments in monetary management. Technical assistance is most in evidence in the transformation of the centrally planned economies of Eastern Europe and the states of the former Soviet Union to market oriented economies. The IMF is assisting the new members in the choice of currency, developing import and export sectors, agreeing on ground rules for setting interest rates, reserve requirements, and credit guidelines, and in making structural reforms.

IMF Statistical Activities

Under Article VIII of the Agreement members are required to furnish the Fund such information as it deems necessary for its activities, including national data about their economic and financial condition. Article VIII also dates that the Fund shall act as a center for the collection and exchange of information on monetary and financial problems, thus facilitating the preparation of studies designed to assist members in developing policies which further the purposes of the Fund.

The Fund uses these statistics, in consultation with the member, as part of the fulfillment of the Fund's regulatory function, to assess the member's quota, and as part of the Fund's role in assessing the world economic outlook. In addition, the Fund has developed standards for the classification and presentation of balance of payments statistics and government finance statistics. It is concerned with maintaining the accuracy and consistency in the reporting of the data. The IMF compiles and publishes these statistics in a variety of publications.

12

Mistakes in Production

A great deal of attention has been focused recently on the service industries. They have certainly grown in importance so it is easy to overlook the significance of other industries-ones that actually produce physical products. The production of physical products, however, is a vital part of international business.

Companies which manufacture physical products encounter their own unique set of risks and make blunders that firms in the service industries avoid. These blunders can involve the location or layout of the production activity, the product, or its package.

LOCATION/LAYOUT

Many years ago, a well-known multinational fiber producer, Celanese, purchased a large tract of land containing eucalyptus trees in Sicily. It planned to build a pulp processing plant and then use the local trees as raw material. It was not until the plant was built and production was to begin that the company discovered that the local trees were too small, the supply was too limited, and the logs were unsuitable for use. The result: the firm was forced to import pulp at a cost so high the plant ended up losing over $55 million. This very expensive lesson occurred because the company tried to save a few dollars and minimize its costs by not sending a specialist to Sicily to check on the trees prior to purchase.

Ill-suited or inappropriate production sites have also left deep wounds in many other firms. One U.S. food processor built a pineapple cannery at the delta of a river in Mexico. Since the pineapple plantation was located upstream, the company planned to float the ripe fruit down to the cannery on barges. To its dismay, however, the firm soon discovered that at harvest time the river current was far too strong for barge traffic. Since no other feasible alternative method of transportation existed, the plant was closed. The new equipment was sold for a fraction of its original cost to a Mexican group that immediately relocated the cannery. This seemingly simple navigational oversight proved quite expensive to the firm.

The Hanna Mining Company experienced some logistical problems in Brazil. One of the basic strategies of the firm involved its ability to supply extract ore at increasing rates over time. Since a small-scale operation could not prove profitable, the company decided that by expanding every year it would become a profitable operation by the time the firm was able to export 2 million tons of ore. Few initial problems developed. The company, however, was unable to expand its operations as expected because local transportation facilities were inadequate. In this case, the firm's strategy failed because it had no way to transport the ore to market even though it maintained the capability to extract the required ore. (It should be noted that Hanna Mining reports that this was not a foreseeable problem, since the local railroad authorities failed to fulfill the contract's maximum delivery requirement.)

As another example, a French firm set up a timber mill in East Africa and was all set to open the mill when the French realized that usually there was not enough electrical power in the area to run the mill. Unfortunately, there may never be. The French had to dismantle this useless mill.

Sometimes it is not the plant location which is the problem, but the plant layout. An English pulp and paper company, for example, entered into a joint venture arrangement with another British firm, hoping to utilize the timber resources of British Columbia. They obtained a concession of enormous timberland acreage. The sawmill, however, was designed and set up by British engineers who were unfamiliar with the characteristics of British Colombian lumber. As a result, the mill was constructed with a setup which was not flexible enough to adjust to the numerous varieties and sizes of Canadian trees. Within three years the firms sold the mill at a substantial loss.

A large British shipment of U.S.-made textile machinery motors was returned because the British did not receive the motors that they thought they had ordered. Apparently, a right-handed motor in an English mill is considered to be a left-handed motor in the United States. Americans look at the production run from downstream and thus see the motor opposite to the British, who view things from the start of the production run.

PRODUCT

In developed countries, we often take for granted the vast array of products available for sale. In many countries, however, such product variety and selection do not exist. The assumption that the absence of a product from an economy automatically indicates a potentially good or profitable market has led a number of companies down a thorny path. More than one company has failed to consider that, even if the local consumers can afford the product, they may not really want it or may be interested in it only if it is substantially modified to fit their local tastes and preferences.

These modifications, known as adaptations, exist in two major forms: product and package. Product modification or the alteration of the physical product is occasionally required for the product to conform to local tastes or local conditions. Adaptation of the package is often necessary to attract the customer to the product or to maintain the product's integrity in a unique environment. Occasionally, a firm is forced to modify both the package and the product to create a suitable product for the new market.

PRODUCT ADAPTATION

Apple Computer entered the Japanese market before IBM, but it failed to take advantage of its head start. Apple tried to sell its U.S. models in Japan without modifying them. No efforts were made to even translate the user's manual into Japanese. Only after IBM entered the market using a customized approach did Apple realize its mistakes. Now that the company has translated its manual and has made some other changes, it is doing much better.

Similarly, Procter & Gamble encountered problems with the Japanese diaper market. After years of research, the company uncovered the problem: Japanese parents change diapers far more frequently than Americans but do not usually have the storage space of U.S. homes.

Thus, larger boxes of disposable diapers posed a storage problem for the average Japanese family. Once Procter & Gamble began producing thinner diapers sold in a smaller box, the popularity of the new diapers, "Ultra" Pampers, spread like a baby's rash and now it is the leading brand in Japan.

The Campbell Soup Company discovered that product modification could be an easier road to travel than consumer education when it tried to market its condensed soups in Great Britain. The company had used market-testing methods to confirm a British interest in its soups and had also priced the soup to be competitive. But initial sales were low: a result of the failure of the British to understand that the Campbell's soup was indeed priced competitively. The British were accustomed to buying canned soup but not in the condensed form. Therefore, it appeared to them that they were buying half as much soup for the same amount of money. Campbell Soup was faced with two choices: it could try to hurriedly mass educate the British buying public or it could alter the product. It wisely chose to modify its product by adding water so that its soups would be like the soups already accepted and found on the grocery shelves.

General Foods experienced similar difficulties when it tried to sell its U.S.-style "Jell-O" in Great Britain. Although the package of Jell-O contained the normal powdered substance Americans expect, the British simply were not interested. In Great Britain, the jellied form of such a product is the normal one to buy. To a Briton, if it does not jiggle and look good, then it simply is not "proper." By quickly changing its product to conform to the British norm, General Foods averted a possible disaster.

The sale of cigarettes outside the home country has been quite exasperating for several companies. The common presumption that all peoples enjoy identical products has often proven erroneous; in fact, some form of product modification has usually been necessary to gain market success. The failure to make the needed alteration, even though possibly a slight one, can radically hurt sales. More than one firm, for example, has encountered difficulties trying to sell filter-tipped cigarettes in the less developed countries. Consumers of wealthier nations, more aware of the health risks of smoking, are quite willing to pay a bit more for filtered cigarettes. In poor countries where life expectancy is often fewer than 30 years, the threat of death from lung cancer is lessened. Even if aware of the risks, the local smoker can usually neither afford the extra cost of the filtered cigarettes nor become too concerned about developing lung cancer at an advanced age. Consequently, the market for filter cigarettes in these countries is typically sluggish. Often the only modification needed to increase sales is the removal of the filter and the accompanying reduction in price.

Some products may require more technical modi-fication, however. Obviously, if the electrical current available in a potential market is different from the home country market, then electrical products require adaptation before introduction. Measurement systems vary between countries, and often components need to be modified to adhere to local standards. Product sizes must also be considered. A British firm, for example, experienced problems selling in Japan until it remodeled its product 1/16 in. to conform to Japanese specifications. Such small differences can easily cause major headaches for manufacturers. Fortunately, most companies quickly learn of these local standards and conditions and seldom introduce a totally inappropriate product. A much more difficult task is the detection of the subtle technical differences and the needed modifications.

Star Manufacturing Company of Japan quickly realized that it had introduced a printer that didn't arouse U.S. interests. The printer that had sold well in Japan did poorly in the United States because Americans wanted better graphics. The printer was soon modified and sales picked up immediately.

A duplicating machine manufacturer ran into serious problems in one country when it assumed that the quality paper required for its machines would be available. The local government owned its own paper company and, unfortunately, the paper size and quality were not highly standardized. Thus, the imported machines could not accommodate the varying characteristics. Because of the government's pride in its paper facilities, however, it would not allow the importation of the paper required. The machines sat idle, and the company's market was quickly closed. The company should have learned of this problem prior to its market entry. It then could have requested permission to import the correct paper, or it could have modified its machines to accommodate the local paper. Had neither been possible, the firm would have known not to market its products in that country. Similarly, Polaroid planned to introduce a slide copier as a central piece of its 1989 product line for both U.S. and European markets. Unfortunately, the engineers failed to realize that standard paper sizes vary. Therefore, the copier would not work using standard European paper. Hasty modifications were made, but not without extra costs.

Marketing its liquid detergents in Europe proved to be a challenge for Procter & Gamble as European washing machines dispense powdered detergents. Adapters to the machines were not a feasible option because each brand of machine required a different design. Procter & Gamble eventually came up with the solution: a plastic ball was supplied with each bottle of detergent. The "dosing ball" could be filled with detergent and placed in each load of laundry. Procter & Gamble now holds 50 percent of the liquid detergent market in Europe.

Refrigerator manufacturers from the Western nations initially encountered great difficulty in selling their products in Japan. The refrigerator motors were the major problem; they were simply too noisy for the typical Japanese home, which was often built with literally paper-thin walls. Sears is cited as one of the companies most successful in the sale of Western refrigerators in Japan. It achieved this status by designing a refrigerator specifically for use in the local conditions.

General Motors of Canada experienced major technical problems with one of its cars in Iraq. It shipped 13,500 Chevrolet "Malibu" automobiles there only to discover that the cars were mechanically unfit for the hot and dusty climate. Iraq refused delivery of the remaining 12,000 autos, which had been ordered, until GM modified the vehicles so that they performed more reliably. GM tripled its number of engineers and mechanics in Baghdad, but by the time the company figured out that supplementary air filters and different clutches would eliminate the mechanical failures, it began to encounter political problems. Thus 12,000 automobiles specially designed for desert driving collected snow in Canada while GM waited for the political dust to settle.

Unexpected major adjustments also had to be made by a U.S. tire producer after it opened a plant in France. Based on its previous success in France, the tire manufacturer built a new production facility without conducting any market research. Because of the changing driving habits of the French, however, new kinds of tires were required and adjustments were forced upon the manufacturer. The company learned its lesson, of course. It hired a market research executive before building its next plant.

The necessity for product adaptation has existed for hundreds of years. England's East India Company possibly lost control of India in 1857 because it failed to modify a product it provided. In those days bullets were often encased in pig wax, and the tops had to be bitten off before the bullets could be fired. The Asian Indian soldiers were furious when they discovered the pig wax, since it was against their religion to eat pork. The soldiers revolted and hundreds were killed on both sides before peace was restored. The bullets were modified, but the East India Company lost control of India to the British Crown.

Improper product modification can also lead to misery. China discovered this when it shipped shoes to Egypt. It had tried to make the shoes more appealing to the Egyptians by placing Arabic characters on the soles of the shoes. Unfortunately, the designers did not know Arabic and merely copied words from other material. The words they chose meant "God." It required China's ambassador to Egypt to soften the tension that resulted from this mistake.

Sometimes the modified product inadvertently reaches the wrong market. This too can cause problems. For example, one company received a great deal of unwanted attention from U.S. parents who purchased a talking doll they believed said, "Kill Mommy." These dolls, made in Hong Kong but shipped from Japan to many parts of the world, carried messages in the language of the country of destination. A packing error, however, caused some Spanish-speaking dolls to be sent to the United States. The Spanish message was "Quiero Mommy," which means "I love Mommy," but the rather poor-quality sound reproduction and the language difference altered the message and caused a media sensation.

TASTE/STYLE

One variable often requiring modification is taste. Both the food and tobacco industries can attest to this. Philip Morris encountered well-publicized problems when it tried to sell its U.S. blends in Canada. Many other companies have experienced similar difficulties in other countries. Most cigarette firms believe that "it is better to switch than fight," and cigarettes are now generally blended in deference to local taste preferences.

Vast numbers of food products have required taste adaptations in order to appeal to local consumers. General Foods experienced some problems and had to alter some of its coffees and foods to attract European and Japanese palates. Campbell Soup Company also was forced to change the flavor of some of its soups (notably the tomato soup) to suit European preferences. Many soft drinks have been modified to gain market acceptance in various parts of the world. Often all that is necessary is a subtle change, but without such variation, sales may slump. Both General Foods and Campbell Soup Company have enjoyed overseas successes because they realized this and acted accordingly. Nestlé has also successfully introduced dozens of blends of its Nescafé around the world.

Fast food chains have been especially quick to modify their offerings. McDonald's, for example, adjusts its menu for each foreign market. It has sold beer in Germany, wine in France, mutton pot pies in Australia, and "McSpaghetti" in the Philippines. Burger King in Venezuela does not use sesame seed buns, the milkshakes there are sweeter and creamier, and even the ketchup is much sweeter. Wendy's serves shrimp cake sandwiches in Japan. Shakey's sells chorizo in Mexico and squid in Japan. Arby's dropped its ham sandwiches from its menus in the Middle East. Kentucky Fried Chicken (KFC) serves "chips" rather than "fries" in England and has added rice and smoked chicken to its menus in Japan. KFC also initiated one of the more unique product modifications: in order to sell its chicken in Israel, it introduced kosher chicken.

"Pop-Tarts," which had proved to be quite a successful product in the United States, were unpopular in Britain. Not only was the taste considered too sweet there, but also most potential buyers at the time did not own toasters which could correctly warm the product. U.S. companies are not the only ones that have found that local tastes differ from those at home. European soups, for example, are considered too salty by most Americans and have not fared well on U.S. grocery shelves.

Food and tobacco manufacturers have not borne the effects of consumer preference alone. Style is another important ingredient in the product mix, and failure to reflect local style choices is also likely to cause financial losses for a company. Ford experienced well-publicized problems in Europe during the 1960s partially as a result of the amount of "Americanization" being introduced into the look of its European cars. Earlier style lines of Ford's European cars sold well in Europe because of their simple sleekness that was favored by the local people. When the more traditional aspects of the U.S. automobile (i.e., wideness, heaviness, and length) were incorporated into models of the 1960s, sales slumped. The sales resistance came to a halt when the cars produced once again reflected European tastes.

Cluett Peabody may have had similar problems, as its Belgian factory was closed after only three years. Cluett blames high costs for the closing, but Belgian retailers claim it was really due to a complaisant Belgian management which assented to U.S. styling, pricing, and sizing that were not in harmony with European tastes and budgets. Either cause for failure could have been eliminated through appropriate preliminary research and implementation of the indicated modifications.

PACKAGE

In many markets, the product may be quite acceptable but still may not sell well if housed in an inappropriate package. Packages play two key roles in marketing- they promote the product and they protect it. Packages that require long-distance shipping must be capable of withstanding the journey. Many companies have endeavored to export their products only to witness the return of crushed and partially empty containers.

Others have tried to ship perishable goods by means requiring months for delivery. Still others have placed the goods in packages unable to withstand moisture (or other unique conditions). In one such case, a firm in Taiwan shipped some drinking glasses to the Middle East. The company used wooden crates and padded the glasses with hay. Most of the glasses, however, were broken by the time they reached their destination. As the crates traveled into the drier Middle East, the moisture content of the hay dropped, and by the time the crates were delivered, the thin straw offered almost no protection. What works well in one part of the world doesn't neces-sarily work well everywhere!

Another Taiwanese firm encountered a similar problem. The Iranians refused payment on a shipment of wool because they claimed that the shipper lied about the weight of the shipment. After expensive delays, it was discovered that wool originating in humid countries (such as Taiwan) loses moisture when shipped to dry countries (such as Iran), and therefore weighs less after being shipped!

In some climates, packages must be specially designed to assure product survival. Quaker Oats, for example, uses special vacuum-sealed tins to protect its products sold in hot and humid countries.

Local storage conditions also vary, and the package must be an appropriate size and shape. Coca-Cola tried to introduce the two-liter plastic bottle in Spain, but market entry was difficult. The company soon discovered that few Spaniards had refrigerator doors with compartments large enough to accommodate the large-size bottle.

Detergents must be packaged differently to sell well in different countries. Americans, for example, are less concerned than Germans with such details as chemical actions and how the detergent actually works. The German package, therefore, must be modified to contain this extra information.

Seemingly harmless package labels have sometimes proven to be embarrassing to the company or even insulting to its potential consumers. One soft drink company inadvertently offended some of its customers in the Arab world because its labels incorporated six pointed stars. The stars were only considered to be a decoration by the firm, but the Arabs interpreted them as reflecting pro-Israeli sentiments. Naturally, the label had to be altered. Another company printed the label on its product in ten languages, including Hebrew, and then tried to market it in Arab countries.

Religious and cultural differences are constantly getting global companies into trouble. Even when a firm is well intentioned, its actions can backfire. McDonald's Corporation is a case in point. When the World Cup was being hosted in Britain, McDonald's decided to put the national flags of all 24 competitors on its hamburger bags.

The bags looked good and provided an international image appreciated by most people, but were considered offensive by many Muslims. It turned out that Saudi Arabia's team was in the competition and on their national flag is the Arabic passage, "There is no God but Allah, and Mohammed is his Prophet." Islamic leaders complained that these words should not be crumpled up and thrown into the trash. McDonald's ended up replacing 2 million bags. A well-known North American brewer encountered similar problems when it put those same flags on its bottles to highlight the same World Cup tournament. Not only was the Arabic passage vis-ible, it was on a product Islamic people should avoid- beer. The bottles had to be recalled.

Although many people do not realize it, the swastika symbol was not created by the Nazis. In fact, it has been used for centuries as a symbol of good luck in many countries. In India, M.P. Been Products has been using the symbol on many of its packages as a sort of company logo. However, when its managers decided to launch a new beer described as "German Pilsner," the combination of the beer name and the swastika on the same label was not well received.

Another example of offensive packaging is when a well-known rock band produced an album cover that portrayed two naked children sitting on a teeter-totter. This album cover was found to be so highly offensive to the Japanese community that it was banned from Japan.

U.S.-made medical containers drew a great deal of unwanted attention when they were used in Great Britain. The containers carried the instructions: "Take off top and push in bottom." This message, considered harmless in the United States, bore very sexual and humorous connotations to the British. Needless to say, the containers were soon modified.

In areas where many of the people are illiterate, the label usually displays a picture of what the package contains. This very logical practice proved to be quite perplexing to one big company. It tried to sell baby food in an African nation by using its regular label that showed a baby and stated the type of baby food in the jar. Unfortunately, the local population took one look at the labels and interpreted them to mean the jars contained ground-up babies! Sales, of course, were terrible.

Some European dry soup producers have solved their marketing problems in the United States by altering their labels. Rather than trying to change the product, they merely developed different uses for the product and stated this on the package label. U.S. and European dried soups are packaged identically but labeled differently. The U.S. package emphasizes the use of the product as a sauce or dip. As expected, U.S. sales were much better once the firms stressed the non-soup use.

Even something as innocuous as a wrapping can cause trouble. A New York exporter agreed to send some products to an Arab country and thoughtlessly wrapped the goods in local newspapers for shipment. The customer was arrested and his goods confiscated when the Arab customs inspectors opened up the packages and found that the wrappings used were Jewish newspapers.

Another U.S. firm also blundered in the Middle East. A carefully detailed business proposal that had required a great deal of preparation effort was sent to Saudi Arabia. The proposal, an excellent one, was bound with a pigskin cover and so was never even read! (Muslims are required to avoid pig products.)

The use of numbers provides another source of blunders. Each country has its own special lucky and unlucky numbers and using the wrong number can indeed be unlucky. A U.S. golf ball manufacturer, for example, tried to sell golf balls, packaged in groups of four, to the Japanese. Problems arose because the pronunciation of the word "four" in Japanese also sounds like the Japanese word for "death". The number four, therefore, is considered undesirable, and items grouped into fours simply don't sell well. (The number seven is a particularly tricky number. It is considered good luck in many countries, but bad luck in others. It even has magical connotations in parts of Africa.)

U.S. airlines with routes between Japan and Hawaii initially experienced very erratic success. Some days the flights were fully booked while other days the planes flew nearly empty. It took some time, but the airlines eventually figured out the problem. Apparently, the Japanese have traditional days that are considered good for weddings. These "lucky days" are naturally followed by honeymoons, and Hawaii is a favored destination. In order to even out the flying load, the airlines began offering discounts for the days when the honeymooners were not flying.

COLOR

The choice of package and product coloring can be tricky. Sometimes companies have failed to sell their products overseas and have never known why. Often the reason was a simple one: the product or its container was merely an inappropriate color.

Green, for instance, is often associated with disease in countries that have dense, green jungles but is associated with cosmetics by the French, Dutch, and Swedes.

Various colors represent death. Black signifies death to Americans and many Europeans, while in Japan and many other Asian countries, white represents death.

Latin Americans generally associate purple with death, but dark red is the appropriate mourning color along the Ivory Coast. And even though white is the color repres-enting death to some; it expresses joy to those living in Ghana.

In many countries, bright colors such as yellow and orange express joy. To most of the world, blue is thought to be a masculine color, but it is not as manly as red in the United Kingdom or France and in Iran blue represents an undesirable color. Although pink is believed to be the foremost feminine color by Americans, most of the rest of the world considers yellow to be the most feminine color.

Red is felt to be blasphemous in some African countries but is generally considered to be a color reflecting wealth or luxury elsewhere. A red circle has been successfully used on many packages sold in Latin America, but it is unpopular in some parts of Asia, where it conjures up images of the Japanese flag.

Pictures of flowers can be found on many package labels, but there, too, caution is required. Certain flowers and their colors can convey hidden messages. In France and many countries that have experienced a British influence, the white lily is often used for funerals. Mexicans, though, use lilies to lift superstitious spells. A purple flower symbolizes death to a Brazilian while yellow flowers represent death or disrespect in Mexico. In France and the Soviet Union, however, the yellow flower signifies infidelity.

United Airlines had start-up problems with its initial flights from Hong Kong. It seems that the company handed out white carnations without realizing that, to many Asians, such flowers represent death and bad luck. Thus, they soon switched to red carnations.

SUMMARY

Product and package modifications are often required to enhance a product's appeal to the foreign consumer. Sometimes the alterations are minor; other times they are more complex. Market testing can help a firm avoid the entry of an inappropriate product; the failure to initiate such studies or develop thorough ones has led a number of com-panies to blunder.

In all fairness to multinational firms, however, market tests can be quite tricky to initiate and conduct. It is difficult indeed to "cover all the bases," and one of the hardest tasks is the identification of the proper testing locations. Since firms cannot always afford to test each product everywhere: sample areas are normally identified as being representative of a country or region. Some companies have used an area of France for their west European test market; others have used Belgium. Each firm must determine the region most appropriate for its product. This is no easy task. In fact, a com-bination of locations may be necessary. Wherever these places are, though, they must be found, because market testing is essential.

13

Immitations of Names

Shakespeare once queried, "What's in a name?" A number of business people, after a bit of international marketing, might appropriately respond, "More than you might think." Many companies have discovered that even something as seemingly innocuous as a name can prove to be insulting and embarrassing. Both product and company names can fall prey to such troubles.

PRODUCT NAMES

Product names often take on various unintended and hidden meanings. The experience of a major soap maker serves as a classic example. When this company was considering a name for a new soap powder it wished to market internationally, it wisely ran a translation test of the proposed name in 50 major languages. In English and most of the major European languages, the name meant "dainty." In other tongues, however, it did not translate so appropriately. In Gaelic, it became "song," in Flemish it meant "aloof," and it said "horse" in the language of one African tribe. In Persia, the name was translated as "hazy" or "dim-witted," and to the Koreans the name sounded like a person out of his mind. Finally, in all of the Slavic languages the name was considered obscene and offensive. Naturally, the proposed name was hastily abandoned. This experience, though, demonstrates the importance of a name and how carefully it should be considered prior to the introduction of a product.

UNUSUAL PROBLEMS

"Golden Harp Superior Pilsner" is hard enough to say in English, but it is even more difficult to say if English is not your mother tongue.

In Malaysia (where they do not even have harps), the words are very difficult to pronounce and certainly do not sound like the name of a beer. Therefore, Ogilvy & Mather shortened the product's name to "Goldie" and used a sexy blonde to promote the brew. The problem was that the label still read "Golden Harp Superior Pilsner" so, when Malaysians ordered a Goldie, all they usually got from the bartender was a blank stare. The product was eventually withdrawn.

Today, more and more firms are seeking assistance in the hope of avoiding costly and embarrassing mistakes. Even the largest and most sophisticated firms are not immune to the difficulties of product-name interpretation. For example, when the Coca-Cola Company was planning its strategy for marketing in China in the 1920s, it wanted to introduce its product with the English pronunciation of "Coca-Cola." A translator developed a group of Chinese characters which, when pronounced, sounded like the product name. These characters were placed on the cola bottles and marketed. Was it any wonder that sales levels were low? The characters actually translated to "a wax-flattened mare" or "bite the wax tadpole." Since the product was new, sound was unimportant to the consumers; meaning was vital. Today Coca-Cola is again marketing its cola in China. The new characters used on the bottle translate to "happiness in the mouth." From its first marketing attempts Coca-Cola learned a valuable lesson in international marketing.

Olympia reportedly tried to introduce a photocopier in Chile under the name "Roto". The copiers, however, did not sell well. Why? Two possible explanations: (1) roto is the Spanish word for "broken", and (2) roto is the word used to delineate the lowest class in Chile.

One of Japan's largest tourist agencies suffered the perils of a misinterpreted name problem. The confusion occurred when it first entered the English-speaking markets and began receiving requests for unusual sex tours. It finally discovered the reason was its name, Kinki Nippon Tourist Company. The owners changed the name.

Some car manufacturers have experienced comparable situations. In fact, problems often develop with the names used in international automobile promotions. For example, difficulties arose during the translation of the name of the U.S. car "Randan." Apparently this name was interpreted by some Japanese to mean "idiot." The American Motors Corporation's "Matador" usually conjures up images of virility and strength, but in Puerto Rico it means "killer"-not a favorable connotation in a place with high traffic fatality rates.

Toyota has been a very successful international company, but it too has had some problems. Its rather popular MR2, for example, has sold well in several countries, but has had troubles in France because the name MR2 is often pronounced as merde, meaning human waste.

"Apache" pickup trucks do not sell well to most American Indians-that is, except to Apaches. This type of problem is not unique to Chevy, nor is it new. Studebaker introduced the "Dictator" back in 1927 but had to discontinue the line in 1936 when politics in Italy and Germany drew world attention.

Initial sales of Nissan's sports car, the "Fair Lady", were so disappointing in the United States that management decided to investigate the cause. The conclusion: the name Fair Lady was not sporty enough. Thus, the name was changed to "240 Z" and the car became one of the most successful Nissan has ever launched.

In 2003, General Motors decided to rename its Buick "LaCrosse" in Canada. Why? Well, in Quebec, la crosse is slang for masturbation.

Ford encountered problems with some of its cars as well. It introduced a low-cost truck, the "Fiera," into some of the less developed countries. Unfortunately the name meant "ugly old woman" in Spanish. Needless to say, this name did not encourage sales. Ford also experienced slow sales when it introduced a top-of-the-line automobile, the "Comet," in Mexico under the name "Caliente." The puzzlingly low sales levels were finally understood when Ford discovered that caliente is slang for a streetwalker. Additional headaches were reportedly experienced when Ford's "Pinto" was briefly introduced in Brazil under its English name. The name was speedily changed to "Corcel" (which means "horse" in Portuguese) after Ford discovered that the Portuguese slang translation of pinto is a "small male appendage."

The naming of a new automobile model to be marketed in Germany by Rolls-Royce was a difficult undertaking. The company felt that the English name "Silver Mist" was very appealing but discovered that the name would undoubtedly not capture the German market as hoped. In German, the translated meaning of "mist" is actually "excrement," and the Germans could not possibly have found such a name attractive.

Unfortunately, the Sunbeam Corporation did not learn of this particular translation problem in time and attempted to enter the German market advertising its new mist-producing hair curling iron, the "Mist-Stick." As should have been expected, the Germans had no interest in a "dung" or "manure" wand.

When Sharwood's launched its latest product range in the United Kingdom, it promised that the "deliciously rich" sauces based on a traditional northern Indian method of cooking would "change the way consumers make curry." Sharwood's was so confident that its new "Bundh" sauces would be a hit that it backed the launch with a huge $14.2 million television advertising campaign. Unfortunately, bundh in Punjabi has an altogether less savoury meaning-the nearest English translation is "ass".

Jolly Green Giant products were incorrectly translated into Arabic to say that they were products from the "intimidating Green Ogre".

Bacardi developed and launched a fruity drink and named it "Pavian," thinking this sounded exotic and desirable. It wasn't popular in Germany, though, because Pavian means "baboon" there.

In the early 1980s, a German beer company launched a new brand in West Africa and named it "Eku." Sales were uneven, and it took the firm two years to figure out the cause. Foreigners and some local tribe members purchased the beer, but one important tribe totally avoided it. Apparently eku was the local slang word in that tribe for excrement. As word spread, members of other tribes and even the foreigners started drinking it less. In the meantime, however, more than a few natives enjoyed watching outsiders consume Eku. Naturally, the name was eventually dropped.

Firms occasionally try to enter the foreign market promoting a product bearing an untranslated name. Sometimes this tactic works, but other times it does not work as well as expected. At least one global firm can attest to this. The company consistently marketed one of its pieces of equipment under the name "Grab Bucket." To its chagrin, the firm learned that in Germany it was actually advertising the sale of cemetery plot flowers. In German, the word Grab is interpreted as grave, and bucket is pronounced like bouquet. So, because of these linguistic anomalies, the company did not appear to be selling what it thought at all.

When Vicks cough drops were first introduced to the German market, the company was upset to learn that the German pronunciation of "v" is "f," which results in the guttural equivalent of "sexual penetration." "Puff" tissues did not do well in Germany, either. Puff, in German, is a colloquial term for a house of prostitution. (In fact, most British weren't impressed with the name, either, since "puff" is a very derogatory term in England for a homosexual.) Ford Motor Company introduced the "Probe" in Germany, where Probe translates as a "test" or "rehearsal," which caused customers to think they were buying a test car, instead of the real thing.

The most ironic part of this example is that Ford has a fully staffed German subsidiary, again emphasizing the need for checking and double-checking names as thoroughly as possible before introduction, to avoid blunders.

Many other companies have suffered similar pitfalls. A U.S. company was taken by surprise when it introduced its product in Latin America and learned that the name of the product meant "jackass oil" in Spanish. Another well-intentioned firm sold shampoo in Brazil under the name "Evitol." Little did it realize that it was claiming to be selling a "dandruff contraceptive." A manufacturing company sold its machines in the Soviet Union under the name "Bardak"-a word that signifies a brothel in Russian.

One U.S. product failed to capture the Swedish market when the product name was translated to "enema," which the product was not. Kellogg has done fairly well with its sales of cereals overseas, but even it had to rename its "Bran Buds" cereal in Sweden when the company discovered that the name translates roughly as "burned farmer." Parker Pen sells a pen in most countries under the name "Jotter." However, it wisely uses other names in some Latin American markets, because "Jotter" sometimes means a jockstrap.

A Finnish brewery introduced two new beverages in the United States-"Koff" beer and "Siff" beer. Is it any wonder that sales were sluggish? Another name, unappealing to Americans, can be found on the package of a delicious chocolate and fruit product sold in the European deli. The chocolate concoction has the undesirable English name "Zit!" "Sic" (a French soft drink), "Super Piss" (a Finnish product for unfreezing car doors), and "Bum" (a Spanish potato chip) will probably not be sold in the United States either.

Other product names that would prove to be a problem in the United States are "Polio," a Czech laundry detergent; "Cat Wetty," a Japanese moistened hand towel; "Homo," an Asian fish sausage; "Swine," Chinese chocolates; "Ass Glue," a Chinese glue; "Last Climax," Japanese paper tissues; and "Creap Creamy Powder," a Japanese coffee creamer.

The Chinese attempted to introduce products to the U.S. market using brand names such as "White Elephant" brand batteries; "Sea Cucumber" brand shirts; "Maxipuke" playing cards (which in Chinese, pu ke, is pronounced in two syllables and means poker); as well as "Pansy" brand men's underwear.

A Japanese company tried to sell its baby powder in the United States under the name "Skinababe." Not surprisingly, sales were very low.

An Australian brewer sells a popular beer in Australia by the name of "XXXX" which is pronounced "Four X." The company planned to export this beer to the United States until it learned that the Americans were already familiar with "Fourex"-a brand of condoms.

The reported troubles of a U.S. company that markets "Pet" milk serves as another example. This firm reportedly experienced difficulties introducing its product in French-speaking areas. It seems that the word pet in French means, among other things, "to break wind." And had Colgate-Palmolive attempted to gain market entry with its "Cue" toothpaste in French-speaking regions, it too would have encountered comparable problems. Cue is a pornographic word in French.

An American woman will long remember her international experience with Coca-Cola. She was dispensing sample tasters of "Fresca" soda pop when she unintentionally elicited a great deal of laughter from passersby. She only later realized the cause when she discovered that in Mexican slang the word fresca means "lesbian."

Close examination of foreign markets and language differences are necessary and should be required before a product's domestically successful name is introduced abroad. Unfortunately, this simple warning is sometimes neglected in a company's enthusiasm to plunge into overseas marketing operations.

Manufacturers often assume that products that have enjoyed domestic success will naturally receive the same reception overseas. However, this is not always the case, as the following examples demonstrate.

Princess Housewares, a large U.S. appliance manufacturer, introduced a line of electric housewares in the German market. The company's brand name, well known and highly regarded in the United States, was relatively unknown in Germany. Its name, though, which had a definite American sound, turned out to be a real drawback to sales, as the German consumers disliked the American association.

Name adaptations sometimes prove to be winners; other times they do not. The Johnson Wax Company successfully introduced its product "Pledge" in Germany under the name of "Pronto," but problems arose when the product entered the market in the Netherlands as "Pliz." In Dutch, the pronunciation of Pliz sounds like "piss." Understandably, it was rather difficult for the customer of the conventional Dutch grocery store to ask for the product.

Sometimes the required change in the product name is a rather simple one. Wrigley, for example, merely altered the spelling of its "Spearmint" chewing gum to "Speermint" to aid in the German pronunciation of the flavor. "Maxwell House" proved slightly more difficult. The name was changed to "Maxwell Kaffee" in Germany, "Legal" in France, and "Monky" in Spain.

As evidenced, firms have blundered by changing product names and by failing to alter names. This is not to say, however, that one is "damned if you do and damned if you do not." Adequate name assessments prior to market introduction can reduce potential name blunders.

OBSCENE MEANINGS

Inappropriate product names sometimes prove to be quite humorous, but in a number of cases, the names have actually borne fairly obscene implications and connotations. A few illustrations of this type of blunder are cited below.

Bird's Eye considered itself quite fortunate when it discovered that a proposed name for one of its fish food products was inappropriate. Wisely, the company decided against the name when it uncovered that the name translated to "genitals." Not all firms have been so lucky, however. A well-known oil company was caught in an embarrassing situation when it learned of the "indecent" name it had chosen for its products. The company established operations in Indonesia and manufactured machinery displaying the name "Nonox." One can imagine the firm's discomfort when it was informed that Nonox sounded similar to the Javanese slang word nonok-a word comparable to the U.S. idiom for female "private parts."

Obviously the employees who proposed the name "Joni" for a new facial cream which was to be marketed in India had never read the erotic Indian classic Kama Sutra. If they had, they would surely have known that the Hindu word joni represents the most intimate areas of the female body.

The example of a vitamin product introduced in South America serves as a final illustration of how product names can unintentionally become obscenities. In this case, a company introduced its vitamins as "Fundavit" and boasted that they satisfied the fundamental vitamin requirements. The name had to be modified when the firm learned that fundola in Spanish stands for the rear end of an attractive young female.

OTHER OFFENSIVE NAMES

As illustrated, certain product name choices can create embarrassing situations for companies when the names are interpreted as indecencies. On occasion, a company chooses a name which, although not obscene, turns out to be in poor taste and offensive to certain groups of people. One example is the name "Black Nikka" chosen for a brand of Japanese whisky sold in the United States and found to be demeaning by some black Americans.

Consider also the bold experiment in international marketing that brought together the state-controlled tobacco monopolies of five countries (France, Italy, Portugal, Austria, and Japan) to launch a major promotion of a new brand of cigarettes, "Champagne." This venture proved to be an embarrassment to the French government, and the case wound up in the international law courts with the French champagne producers in a fury. These producers claimed that the use of "Champagne" as a brand name "is deplorable, and the connection with health hazards may permanently damage our image."1

Reebok unveiled a new women's sneaker named "Incubus." In medieval folklore Incubus was a demon who ravished women in their sleep. Reebok was forced to discontinue the shoe.

COMPANY NAMES

Product names are not the only ones that can generate company blunders. If a firm name is misinterpreted or incorrectly translated, it too can cause humorous, obscene, offensive, or unexpected situations. A number of examples are described in the following paragraphs.

Colonel Sanders (KFC) experienced resistance marketing its chicken in Germany because some folks connected the word "Colonel" with the U.S. military that is not popular with all Germans. And because Brazilians have trouble pronouncing "Kentucky Fried Chicken," the name "Sanders" was used there.

A private Egyptian airline, Misair, proved to be rather unpopular with the French nationals. Could the fact that the name, which when pronounced meant "misery" in French, have contributed to the airline's plight? Another airline trying to gain acceptance in Australia only complicated matters when it chose the firm name "Emu." The emu is an Australian bird that is incapable of flying. But Emu was not the only company to run into snags while conducting business in Australia. The AMF Cor-poration was forced to change its name. Why? Because AMF is the official designation for the Australian military forces. Similarly, Sears (originally Sears Roebuck & Co.) was forbidden to use its name in Spain. The company commanded respect and enjoyed a good reputation there, but since the Castillian Spanish pronunciation of Sears sounded much like "Seat" (the name of Spain's largest car manufacturer), Seat forced Sears to incorporate the name Roebuck on all its products.

As a final illustration, consider the trade magazine that promoted giftware and launched a worldwide circulation effort. The magazine used the word gift in its title and as part of its name. When it was later revealed that Gift is the German word for "poison," a red-faced publishing executive supposedly retorted that the Germans should simply find a new word for poison!

Of course, not all companies have been forced to change their names. In fact, some of them have traveled quite well. Kodak may be the most famous example. A research team deliberately "developed" this name after carefully searching for a word which was pronounceable everywhere but had no specific meaning anywhere. Exxon is another such name that was reportedly accepted only after a lengthy and expensive computer-assisted search.

SUMMARY

Multinational corporations have experienced many unexpected troubles concerning company or product names, and even attempts to alter names have led to blunders. It should be evident that careful planning and study of the potential market are necessary, as name adaptation can be every bit as important as product or package modification.

14

Marketing Strategy

The field of marketing has probably experienced the most corporate headaches. The old adage, "if something can go wrong, it will," seems especially true for marketing managers; they have undoubtedly blundered every single marketing task imaginable.

Early blunders often occurred because people forgot that cultures vary from country to country. Unfortunately, this error continues to be made. A print advertisement for men's cologne, for example, pictured a man and his dog in an American rural setting. The picture was well accepted in America but was not effective when used in northern Africa. The advertiser simply assumed that the American "man's best friend" was loved everywhere when, in fact, Muslims usually consider dogs to be either signs of bad luck or symbols of uncleanliness. Neither interpretation helped sales of the cologne.

Procter & Gamble blundered in Japan when trying to sell "Camay" soap. It seems that it aired a popular European television advertisement showing a woman bathing. In the ad, her husband enters the bathroom and touches her approvingly. The Japanese, however, considered this behavior to be inappropriate and in poor taste for television. Such ads are no longer used in Japan and P&G is now doing much better there.

A well-known American designer tried to launch a new fragrance in Latin America. The advertising message emphasized the perfume's fresh camellia scent. Naturally, sales were slow there because camellias are flowers used for funerals in most of Latin America.

Procter & Gamble's original Japanese promotion of "Cheer" laundry detergent boasted that the detergent was effective at "all water temperatures." The slogan proved successful in the United States because

Americans wash their laundry in many different temperatures depending on the preference of the consumer. However, the Japanese wash most clothes in cold water, so the promotion was almost meaningless to them. Procter & Gamble changed its approach and ran ads touting Cheer's superior cleaning in cold water. Now Cheer sells much better in Japan.

Not all blunders, of course, are due to the erroneous assumption that what works at home will always work abroad also. Sometimes, the promotional campaign is just launched at the wrong time.

Timing is one of the most critical elements in the launching of a new product. Most firms understand this and also recognize that various cultures perceive time differently. Since some nationalities are more conscious of time factors than others, extra time must often be allocated and care given to assure that everything is completed as scheduled. One firm aware of these constraints properly timed everything, or so it thought. Various types of promotional activities were arranged for its product's market entries, but one thing was overlooked- the product. Because someone forgot to assure its availability, all of the expensive, well-planned promotions became meaningless.

The Israel Government Tourist Office wisely suspended an ad campaign in the Netherlands that proclaimed that Tel Aviv and Jerusalem were only "a stone's throw" apart. The timing of the ad was unfortunate, as real stone throwing was actually occurring in the country at the time.

PROMOTIONS

Promotional efforts often misfire; some downfalls, though, are more predictable than others. A cosmetics firm attempted to sell its lipstick in Japan using a television ad that depicted Nero coming to life just as a pretty woman wearing the lipstick strolled by. This was a hard sell because the Japanese women did not know of Nero. If a firm decides to use historical figures in promotional campaigns, it is well advised to first consider using locally known historical figures.

Hoover vacuum cleaners could not "sweep up the mess" from a recent sales promotion blunder considered one of the biggest in corporate history. The costly and embarrassing blunder was an offer by Hoover Europe for two free overseas airline tickets to anybody in Britain or Ireland who bought one of its vacuum cleaners. The problem was that the tickets were worth more than the cost of the cleaner. This promotion turned into a court battle when disgruntled customers never received their flights. Hoover tried to attach conditions to the deal, in an effort to recover from the error. After spending $72 million on flying 220,000 people they hoped to end the case. But over 365,000 other customers still had not flown. As a result three top European executives were fired.

In a different type of case, a company formed a joint venture with an Asian firm. Both companies believed everything to be in order. Their plan included a large production run and a simultaneous, large promotional effort. The production process ran smoothly, but the expected promotional efforts never materialized. Each company had assumed that the other would coordinate and pay for all promotional activities. In fact, each firm simply assumed the customs of its own country's business practices and was not prepared to accept the other country's norm. Neither company would have agreed to the venture had it thought that it would be responsible for promotion costs. The promotion was never undertaken, and the joint venture eventually broke up.

Potential problems of ill-thought campaigns by global brand managers and advertisers who advertise in the United States can still have potential negative global ramifications. The U.S. cosmetics firm Clinique had to stop running a print ad for its "Elixir" perfume when Thailand's government sent a letter of protest to the company complaining the ad was an insult to Buddhists. The perfume ad, which ran in Vogue and other U.S. fashion magazines, depicts a snake crawling over the head of an image of the lord Buddha. Clinique reportedly pulled the ad and sent a letter of apology to the Thai ambassador in Washington, expressed its shock to hear about any possible negative perceptions presented by the picture.

One of United's promotional campaigns used the slogan, "We know the Orient." In the ads, the names of Far Eastern countries were printed below the pictures of foreign coins. Sadly, the slogan was not very convincing-the coins and countries did not match up.

A company must be especially careful when entering a new market with a new product or service. The old saying, "you only get a chance to make a first impression once," has never been truer. A blunder at the start is hard to recover from. America-on-line (AOL) learned this lesson. In fact, AOL reportedly had several problems while launching a new promotional campaign in Brazil. Hundreds of would-be new users were mistakenly given music CDs rather than the intended CD-ROMs needed to start up AOL's service. However, as unlikely as this may seem, they may have been the lucky ones. It turned out that those new subscribers receiving the "correct" CD-ROMs discovered that some of their computer programs were changed without warning. Web browsers were altered and home pages were replaced. AOL certainly did not make a good first impression with these people.

Another U.S. corporation believed it had developed a good promotional plan when it decided to distribute simulated old coins displaying the company logo. To make the coins appear a bit more realistic, the company placed a monetary value on them and, to avoid any chance of claims of counterfeiting, it used the obviously phony value of $1 billion. The coins were passed out at a trade show in West Germany but, to the company's surprise, the coins seemed to anger the locals. Apparently the Germans felt that the company was trying to show off American wealth, and they resented this impression. The coins would have been more effective if they had displayed some denomination of the German mark.

As the women's movement continues to gain mo-mentum, more and more firms are realizing they must scrutinize all promotional efforts carefully to make sure that their advertisements are not offensive to women. Failure to recognize potential problems can cause later difficulties (such as product boycotts). Quebec, for example, now has a review board that monitors possibly offensive advertisements. In 1981, it presented its first "awards" for sexism. One "award" was conferred for a Sony and La Place stereo shop ad. This ad portrayed a big-busted woman, her nipples showing through her T-shirt, roller-skating while holding her Sony tape deck.

The review jury found the promotion offensive, as there was no connection between the woman and the product being advertised. Another "award" went to Procter & Gamble for its 30-second "Mr. Clean" television commercial. In this ad, a little girl is shown cleaning up her brother's mess as he watches. The jury felt the company was reinforcing the old sex role stereotypes that housecleaning is women's work and the women should serve the men.

An advertising campaign for Fiat's "Cinquecento" automobile backfired in Spain when they sent anonymous love letters to women in an attempt to attract the "independent, modern, working woman." Instead, El Mundo newspaper reported that the letters made women feel threatened, as if they were being stalked by a psychopath, and created jealous scenes between spouses. The letters were printed on pink paper, personally addressed, complimented and invited the recipient to indulge in "a little adventure" after noticing "how [you] glanced interestedly in my direction."

BMW reportedly experienced some awkward moments a few years ago while launching its new 3-series models in Great Britain. It wanted to remind the television viewers of its proud heritage. It wanted to say that the new models are based on BMW's great tradition and experience with its previous models. BMW tried to do this by depicting the sporty car with DNA-type strings attached, but it used DNA symbols without bothering to find out much about them. For most viewers this advertisement was fine, until someone pointed out that the DNA depicted actually belonged to a slow-moving 10,000-year-old woolly mammoth (now extinct, of course). Not exactly the image desired.

Nike experienced some awkward moments in the United States when one of its television advertisements included people from various countries reportedly stating Nike's slogan-"Just do it"-in their native languages.

However, one man, a Samburu tribesman, was really saying, "I don't want these, give me big shoes." Naturally, Nike's competition made sure people learned of the error. Nike admitted that their people did not really know what the natives were saying, but one suspects that Nike will be more careful in the future.

Most people wealthy enough to afford to stay at New York's Helmsley Palace Hotel know enough about the world to know that the Taj Mahal is a mausoleum. However, that did not stop Leona Helmsley from approving a promotion that compared her hotel with the Taj Mahal. The headline stated, "In India it's the Taj Mahal. In New York it's the Helmsley Palace." It went on to proclaim, "Service and appointments fit for royalty-you-our guests."

In Chapter 2, the problem of using inappropriate product and package colors was discussed. Colors can create promotional difficulties as well. The Singer Company, for example, found it necessary to halt an elaborate outdoor ad campaign when, just prior to the campaign's introduction, the company discovered that the background color, blue, was the local color representing death. Singer was fortunate that the error was discovered when it was. Because Singer had hired local people to implement its promotional plan, the potential blunder was averted.

The McDonnell Douglas Corporation experienced unexpected difficulties with a brochure that it planned to distribute to potential aircraft customers in India. The promotional material depicted turbaned men, but the photos were not well received. The company had used old National Geographic pictures and had overlooked the fact that Pakistani men, not Indians, were wearing the turbans!

The "Marlboro" man projects a strong masculine image in the United States and in Europe. Attempts to use it were unsuccessful in Hong Kong, where the totally urban people did not identify at all with horseback riding in the countryside. So Philip Morris quickly changed its ad to reflect a Hong Kong-style Marlboro man. He is still a virile cowboy, but he is younger, better dressed, and owns a truck and the land he's standing on.

Conducting business in a communist country is especially tricky. A slip of the tongue or pen can prove fatal. Even the name of the country can cause trouble, since the names given to some countries by the West are usually different than those used by the countries themselves. The failure to use the proper country name is often considered an insensitive or offensive act. For instance, the English-language catalog of a Swedish firm had to be changed because the catalog cited "North Korea" instead of the "People's Republic of Korea."

A geographical blunder occurred when France introduced a new postage stamp in 1991, bearing a picture of Easter Island and claiming it to be a French territory; the Chilean government protested, since it is part of Chile. Blunders like this really weaken relations between countries, especially with Latin America, where relationships are of vital importance.

United Airlines finally received permission in 1982 to initiate flights to Japan only to have its introductory campaign crash. United's public relations people in the United States tried to show customers the company's new route. Unfortunately, the map they used failed to include a major Japanese island. The Japanese are extremely sensitive about their territorial claims (and losses), and were highly offended by such a map. To them it showed ignorance or, perhaps worse, insensitivity. Although only a few copies of the map ever existed, the blunder made headline news in the second largest Japanese newspaper, and drew a hasty apology from United. As United admitted, the mistake would never have happened if its staff in Tokyo had a chance to look at the map before its release.

Americans are not the only managers who face the challenges of marketing internationally. In one edition of Newsweek an image ad from STET, the Italian telephone company, was shown promoting itself as global. It showed a picture of a Chinese temple on a lakeshore, with a reflection in the water of a Roman arch. The effect was somewhat lost, however, because the image of the temple was flipped from left to right, and therefore all the Chinese writing on the temple was in mirror-image characters. This did not impress those who could read Chinese.

Several firms have tried to use old, reliable promotional methods in countries where they simply do not work. Billboard advertisements are perfectly legal in most parts of the Middle East, for example, but this does not mean they should be used. Many companies have tried to employ billboards, but instead of advertising their product, they have merely exposed their lack of awareness of local weather conditions. In the Middle East environment, billboards often last less than two weeks.

Companies have even been known to promote their products using the wrong language. In Dubai, for example, only 10 percent of the population speak Arabic. The remaining 90 percent of the people originate from Pakistan, India, Iran, or elsewhere. Several European and U.S. firms, however, have assumed that all Middle Eastern countries are primarily populated with Arabic-speaking people and so have promoted their products only in Arabic. Time magazine ran a Spanish-language ad in its Brazilian edition. Someone must have forgotten that they speak Portuguese in Brazil, not Spanish!

MISUNDERSTANDINGS

In many cases, the language of the promotional effort is correct but the message is simply not effective. It is one thing to use the right language, but it is quite another to use it so that the intended message is properly communicated. As a classic illustration, consider the company that rented space on a wall beside the main road leading from the airport into Buenos Aires. The following message was placed on the wall; "With [brand name] you'd be there already." Just one slight problem existed: The message was misunderstood because it was placed on the wall of a cemetery.

Isuzu reflected a cultural gap of knowledge when it used a line in a television advertisement for its "Trooper" utility vehicle that said, "You don't have to buy the farm to get one." This phrase was, unfortunately, an old aviation expression implying that owners of the trucks might "crash and burn."

It may be easy to place a message in a slightly wrong location, but Amalie Refining was off by quite a few miles. One of its Spanish-language billboards somehow landed along the roadside in Knoxville, Tennessee.

Arabic writing is very sacred to the Islamic community. Several blunders are prime examples. One such example was Arabic writing printed on bathroom products. Croscill Home Fashions, in New York, had no idea that the pattern contained words at all. The company spent between $10,000 to $20,000 to change the design when it found out from the Council on American-Islamic Relations that it was considered undignified. Specific bath items were printed with writing recognizable as a common Islamic phrase, "There is no victor but God." It was considered in poor taste on bath towels and wash cloths because they are items used to wipe the body.

The fashion industry learned a lesson in an unfortunate error that was not intended as an insult when Lagerfeld introduced a new fashion collection in 1994 that borrowed Arabic script to decorate some low-cut evening gowns. When the Muslim leaders saw a photo of one of the Chanel dance dresses they commented that the patterns on the dresses were incidental examples of a "new Occidental crusade against Muslims in order to annihilate them." Lagerfeld was forced to remove the dresses from the Chanel collection.

Nike attempted to use Arabic script on athletic shoes. The script resembled the word "Allah," the word for God. Muslims hold holy symbols as sacred and not to be represented on shoes that will be covered in dirt, walked on and then disposed of. The logo was meant to look like flames displayed on the shoes and sold during the summer, with names like "Air Bakin'," "Air Melt," "Air Grill," and "Air B-Que." The blunder was discovered by the Council on American-Islamic Relations who demanded that Nike apologize for the use of the logo. The company admitted to recognizing the error prior to the release of the shoes and regretted any misunderstanding. In addition, a member of the Muslim organization wanted Nike to also participate in sensitivity-training programs about Islamic culture.

A firm at an international trade fair committed a different type of location error. In order to keep people out of a restricted area of its booth, the company displayed a sign depicting an open, flat hand with all fingers pointing up on a swinging door. To the company's surprise, the idea backfired. The local people interpreted the symbol to mean they should place their hands there and push the door open.

Symbols or logos have caused troubles for other companies as well. A U.S. firm marketing in Brazil found itself a bit embarrassed when it used a large deer as a sign for masculinity. The word deer is a Brazilian street name for a homosexual. Another company blundered in India when it used an owl in its promotional efforts. To an Indian, the owl is a symbol for bad luck, and indeed it proved to be just that for the firm.

Muslims in Dhaka, Bangladesh went on a rampage, ransacking shoe stores because they mistook the Thom McAn logo on some sandals for the Arabic characters for "Allah." They thought the Western company was denigrating their religion. Police were called in to stop the rioting, but at least one person was killed and 50 people were wounded before it was over.

Several companies have gotten into trouble by using the traditional U.S. sign showing a hand giving the "OK" signal. It communicates the message well in the United States, but is a very vulgar sign in many countries. It's best to simply avoid using it overseas in any promotional activities or other forms of communication.

A few years ago a Japanese steel firm, Sumitomo, introduced its specialty steel pipe into the U.S. market. Sumitomo used a Tokyo-based, Japanese agency to help develop its advertisements. The steel was named "Sumitomo High Toughness," and the name was promoted by the acronym SHT in bold letters. So bold, in fact, that the full-page ads run in trade journal were three-fourths filled with SHT. Located at the bottom of the page was a short message that ended with the claim that the product "was made to match its name." The importance of local input simply cannot be overemphasized!

One laundry detergent company certainly wishes now that it had contacted a few locals before it initiated its promotional campaign in the Middle East. All of the company's advertisements pictured soiled clothes on the left, its box of soap in the middle, and clean clothes on the right. But because in that area of the world people tend to read from the right to the left, many potential customers interpreted the message to indicate the soap actually soiled the clothes.

In Seoul, senior executives at Samsung Group re-portedly did not notice that a wall calendar's model for July, holding Samsung products, was wearing a see-through blouse. The wall calendar, portraying international models, was sent overseas to customers and partners as a gift. The group was informed that the calendar photo offended some Americans. The group's manager of the personnel department responded by admitting that they were unaware of the potential problem.

Even if the correct shots and words are used, problems can crop up because of incorrect intonation. Missionaries in Africa discovered this when someone finally informed them that the messages in their songs were being misunderstood. The words were correctly translated, but the tones and pitches used were not. For example, the Igbo people of Nigeria learned to sing the second verse of "Oh, come, all ye faithful." They were thought to be singing "Very God, begotten, not created," but the actual meaning was "God's pig, which is never shared." Another hymn with words of "There is no sorrow in heaven" came out "There is no egg on the bicycle."

Care must be taken even when the consumers of a foreign market speak the same language. A British and U.S. joint venture proposal ran into serious difficulties, for example, when the U.S. firm requested that certain key points be "tabled." The British firm agreed and both parties prepared for negotiations. When the British team brought up for discussion those topics that had been "tabled," both parties became highly irritated. In the United States "to table a motion" means to delay discussion of it, but in England the same phrase often means to bring the topic to the table for discussion. The Americans had requested the exact opposite of what they had really wanted.

Similar problems were encountered by another U.S. company attempting to conduct business in Britain. The firm had effectively used the phrase "You can use no finer napkin at your dinner table" in the United States and because of economies of scale, etc., decided to use the same commercials in England. After all, Britons do speak English. To a Briton, however, an American does not speak English, but speaks "American" and uses different phrases and word meanings. Since the British word "napkin" or "nappy" actually means "diaper," the American firm was unknowingly advertising that "You could use no finer diaper at your dinner table." The ad was entertaining, but could hardly be expected to boost sales greatly.

American troubles with the English language are not limited to England, of course. One U.S. banker in Australia discovered this when he attended an important dinner given in his honor. He was invited to speak after the meal, but he certainly started off on the wrong foot when he indicated that he was "full." The subsequent nervous laughter of the other diners suggested something was wrong, so he tried to clarify the situation by saying that he was "stuffed." One can imagine his astonishment when he learned that "full" implied being drunk and that "stuffed" suggested involvement in sexual intercourse.

STRATEGY

Often it is the promotional strategy that runs amuck and creates the promotional blunders. Whereas some companies have appeared culturally insensitive, others have actually blundered by going to the opposite extreme.

They have tried to fake being local or have tried to play up to local nationalist pride. Dow Breweries, for instance, introduced a new beer in Quebec, Canada, called "Kebec." The promotion incorporated the Canadian flag and attempted to evoke nationalistic pride. Dow's strategy backfired, however, when major local groups protested the "profane" use of "sacred" symbols. The campaign was halted within 15 days.

In an eager effort to get out "good news" fast, Thunderbird blundered in a press release in 1997 by saying it was the oldest management school in the world in a release handed to the Academy of International

Business members in Mexico for its annual meeting. The problem was it wasn't true-as most readers knew. People were offended because of the missing word "international" as it should have said it was the oldest international management school.

Similarly, when McDonald's used an illustration of Mexico's national flag on its place mats in 1988, the company drew the ire of local authorities. The Mexicans simply did not approve of catsup being splattered all over one of its national symbols, so the place mats were confiscated. The offense, of course, was unintentional, but McDonald's apologized anyway.

Alka-Seltzer suffered a drastic downturn in its market share and profits when its new German owner, Bayer, decided to abandon Alka-Seltzer's traditional identity as a cure for blue-collar hangovers and tried to pitch the product as a remedy for young professional stress. Bayer eventually realized that it misunderstood the U.S. market so it switched back and recovered.

A French beer company experienced difficulty trying to enter the U.S. market when it projected itself as American. Its decision to portray its imported beer as locally brewed was not a wise one because the U.S. market was already flooded with local beers. The company, realizing its error, now does well promoting its beer as an import.

Products sell better when the promotions emphasize what the consumer considers important. Tires can be used as an example. Tire safety is stressed in Britain, durability and mileage are emphasized in the United States and agile performance is considered important in Germany. Goodyear learned this lesson early and has been successful selling the same tire in all three markets using different messages.

General Mills, producer of "Betty Crocker" brand cakes, tried to introduce cake mixes to the Japanese. They found out that most Japanese households did not have an oven, and preferred to buy cakes. Market research revealed that almost every household did have a rice cooker so General Mills developed a product called "Cakeron," a cake mix to be cooked in the rice cooker. Sales went well during the introduction of Cakeron. But when sales dwindled, market research revealed that since rice was often left over and saved in the rice cooker, baking cakes was inconvenient. What was important to the Japanese household was the consumption of rice. In addition, the cake mixes often left an aftertaste in the rice cooker. The comparison was drawn that a Japanese cook who makes cakes in a rice cooker is like an English housewife making coffee in her teapot. This just does not happen.

Multinationals, therefore, must consider varying promotional tactics. Volvo has applied this concept quite successfully. The company has emphasized economy, durability, and safety in the United States; status and leisure in France; performance in Germany; and safety in Switzerland. Price is considered to be a critical variable to Mexican consumers, but quality is of more importance to Venezuelans.

Test markets can be used to evaluate promotional campaigns, but results are not necessarily fail-safe. U.S. companies often use Puerto Rico as a typical Latin American test market. Although Puerto Rico is a convenient, almost barrier-free, Spanish-speaking market and thus an appealing test market, the people of each Latin American country have their own unique tastes and preferences. Therefore, firms must realize that the success of a promotional strategy in Puerto Rico does not necessarily assure success in all Latin American countries. All that should be gleaned with confidence from a positive result in Puerto Rico is that the strategy is worth testing in the country under consideration. Major blunders have occurred when this second testing procedure was skipped. The managers of one company, for example, were so excited by the impressive results experienced in Puerto Rico that they shipped large quantities of their product, a hair fixer, to Argentina. Sales were practically nonexistent even though the commercials so successful in Puerto Rico were used. Sales improved only after the local sales manager convinced the company to alter the ads and direct them towards a more European-type customer.

Unilever experienced a somewhat unique type of promotional problem. The company marketed a popular detergent, "Radion," in Germany. It also sold the same basic product in Austria but marketed it under a different brand name. Because Germans and Austrians both speak German and are often exposed to each other's media, consumers in each country were being introduced to what they thought were competitive products. Since the promotional campaigns developed for one country easily reached the consumers in the other country, a more efficient and effective marketing strategy would have been to use the same brand name in both countries. Had this occurred, the promotional overlap would have reinforced their efforts and helped sales.

Avon Products blundered in its approach to marketing cosmetics when it tried to employ housewives to sell door to door in their neighborhoods. What Avon didn't realize is that Japanese housewives are very hesitant to sell any products to people they don't know. The concept of inviting strangers into the home, like it is done in the West, is a completely unusual concept to Japanese women.

One fairly common U.S. practice is that of utilizing the same promotional strategy for all domestic subsidiaries. Promotional budgets often are based on a fixed-percentage-of-sales basis. This strategy often works well with domestic ventures but usually proves foolish when it is attempted for overseas subsidiaries as well. U.S. companies that try to force such standardization are often asking their foreign managers to do the impossible. For one thing, some types of media are not legally available. In many countries, no television advertisements are permitted. This alone makes a U.S.-style promotional budget infeasible. A second problem is one of scale. The use of a standard percentage of sales may be appropriate for large domestic subsidiaries, but for small foreign subsidiaries, 10 percent may not support a single promotional campaign. Several companies have attempted standardized promotional budgets, but most have now realized that each market provides different opportunities and challenges at different cost structures. A better strategy is to standardize the methods used to analyze opportunities and the methods used to develop local promotional budgets. Subsidiaries can then be urged to follow these established methods during the development of their own promotional budgets.

Cultural Differences

Firms that failed to study local customs carefully have made dozens of blunders. As one example, consider the public display of physical contact between members of opposite sexes. In many countries, this is totally unacceptable and offensive. Thailand is one of these countries. A firm trying to introduce its mouthwash there, however, was not aware of this norm and promoted its product through an ad that displayed a young couple holding hands. By changing the advertisement to feature two women, the commercials were deemed acceptable and no longer offensive to the Thais. The Asian Indians found a BiNoca Talc ad disturbing even though the woman in the advertisement was wearing a body stocking. The promotion, appearing in many of the major local newspapers, featured an attractive but apparently nude young woman lavishly splashing herself with BiNoca's talcum powder. Strategic portions of her body were carefully covered with the slogan "Don't go wild-just enough is all you need of BiNoca talc." The public, however, was not prepared for the ad's use of the female form and found the ads extremely indecent.

In other countries, such exposure is not deemed as offensive. In fact, the French, more than many nationalities, accept commercials that feature a great deal of the female body.

To some groups, the display of certain seemingly innocent parts of the body proves to be offensive. One U.S. shoe manufacturer promoted its product through photos of bare feet. Although considered a harmless advertisement by many, the photos were introduced in Southeast Asia where exposure of the foot is considered an insult.

Mountain Bell experienced a similar problem when one of its promotional photos depicted an executive talking on the telephone with his feet propped up on his desk. The photos, seen by Middle and Far Easterners, were considered to be in poor taste. To them, the display of the sole of the foot or shoe is a terrible insult.

Another U.S. firm trying to do business in Saudi Arabia ran into problems with some advertising artwork. The ad pictured a man's fist clenching a rock. This design was intended to symbolize the company's solid position as a manufacturer of rock-crushing equipment. Unfortunately, the upward position of the hand symbolized a motion considered very offensive by the Saudis. As pointed out previously, local input can be vital in avoiding blunders. Many promotional errors could have been averted had this warning been heeded.

Pepsodent reportedly tried to sell its toothpaste in regions of Southeast Asia through a promotion that stressed that the toothpaste helped enhance white teeth. In this area, where some local people deliberately chewed betel nut in order to achieve the social prestige of darkly stained teeth, such an ad was understandably less than effective. The slogan "You'll wonder where the yellow went" was also viewed by many as a racial slur.

A marketer of eyeglasses promoted his spectacles in Thailand using commercials that featured animals wearing glasses. This was an unfortunate decision, however, since animals there are considered a low life form, and it is beneath humans to wear anything worn by an animal.

The failure of firms to consider specialized aspects of local religions has created a number of difficulties. Companies have encountered problems in Asia when they incorporated pictures of Buddha in their promotions. Religious ties are strong in this area, and the use of local religious symbols in advertising is strongly resented -especially when words are deliberately or even accidentally printed across the picture of Buddha. One company was nearly burned to the ground when it ignorantly tried such a strategy. The seemingly minor incident led to a major international political conflict remembered for years.

Another religious-type blunder occurred when a refrigerator manufacturer ran an ad picturing a refrigerator containing a centrally placed chunk of ham. The typical refrigerator advertisement often features a refrigerator full of delicious food, and because these photos are difficult to take, the photos are generally used in as many places as possible. This company used its stock photo one place too many, though, when it was used in the Middle East where Muslims do not eat ham. Locals considered the ad to be both insensitive and unappealing.

An entertainment promoter also encountered difficulties when he failed to recognize one of the Muslim mores. He had booked Anita Sarawak in Singapore, and during her performance, encouraged her to hold her pet dog while singing "Me and you and a dog named Boo." This gimmick had worked well in other countries but caused a major commotion in Singapore. Plans for subsequent taped broadcasts of the show were cancelled, all because of the dog. According to Islamic beliefs, dogs are dirty and should not be shown or kept as pets.

Doubletree Hotels Corporation committed a costly blunder when it announced a national marketing campaign with a 30-second spot that was part of a $31 million campaign to convey employee personal warmth and quality of caring about the guests at the hotel. Instead, it found out from the Council on American- Islamic Relations, an Islamic advocacy group in Washington D.C., that the television ad was offensive. The ad portrayed three hotel employees dressed in Arab-style clothing bowing to guests. The complaint was that the employees appeared to be "praying" to guests, the way in which Muslims pray to God. This was interpreted as poking fun at another religion's prayer rituals. The Austin, Texas staff was completely unaware that the ad could be interpreted offensive to the Islamic community.

Saudi Arabia nearly restricted an airline from ini-tiating flights when the company authorized "normal" newspaper advertisements. The ads featured attractive hostesses serving champagne to the happy airline passengers. Because in Saudi Arabia alcohol is illegal and unveiled women are not permitted to mix with men, the photo was viewed as an attempt to alter religious customs.

As stated earlier, successful advertisements usually involve cultural assumptions, so using the same commercial in more than one country can be dangerous. Cosmetics firms in the United States, for example, often pitch their messages to flatter the American woman's ego by telling her how attractive she is or will be if she uses their products. Similar commercials have been introduced in France and have failed. French women do not identify themselves as being ultra-glamorous nor do they believe that they can be. Often they do not even realize that the commercial is aimed at them, and so they simply assume that the message must be intended for a rare few.

Acceptable methods of information presentation also vary from culture to culture. In the Orient, for example, a person should not try to make the other "lose face." But to be taken seriously in Italy, a person must try to win the argument. A person speaking precisely will be taken literally in Switzerland. The British prefer a much "softer sell" than the Germans.

As mentioned previously, the choosing of a color is another important task. At least two different firms encountered problems in their Hong Kong marketing efforts when they decided to use green hats in commercials. One company attempted to sell its beer using the message that the beer was so good that even the Irish like it. The Irishman, of course, wore a green hat while drinking his beer. The other firm marketed cleaning agents and in its commercial featured individuals tossing hats at a male model. A green hat eventually landed on the man. In both cases, the color chosen was not appropriate; the green hat is a Chinese symbol used to identify a man as a cuckold. Understandably, both products were avoided.

As Guinness Stout can attest, Hong Kong has been the site of more than one unexpected turn of events. This firm's thick brew, considered especially well suited for the virile men of the British Empire, had somehow achieved a reputation in Hong Kong as being an excellent drink for women during pregnancy or menstrual periods. Consequently, when the drink was promoted in Hong Kong as one for men, it elicited much laughter. Any man ordering it was likely to be asked if it was his "time of the month!"

Another unusual problem occurred in Peru when a laundry detergent containing stain-removing enzymes was introduced through a cartoon depicting large-mouthed enzymes eating the dirt off of clothes. Although sales levels were initially good, they quickly dropped off. A local Peruvian custom was at the bottom of the company's problem. Peruvian women believed that they must boil their clothes to kill the germs, and the voracious cartoon creatures in the ad reinforced this belief. However, because the boiling destroyed the enzymes, the detergent did not perform as advertised.

As a result, since the product was not as effective as expected, the women only tried it once.

Not all companies find that their products are being used correctly, but sometimes unusual uses do not hurt sales. Gervais Danone, for example, was able to turn the tables on a potential problem. The company, finding that the Mexicans had little interest in its products, decided to alter its promotional strategy. It found that it was eventually able to interest the adults in using its cheeses for butter and its "Petite Suisse," a creamy whipped cheese, as a good snack for the children.

The Latin Market in the United States

Not all cultural problems occur outside the multinational company's home country. For example, a significant Latin market exists in the United States, and it is becoming increasingly obvious that companies need to be aware of Latin culture. Sometimes it is even worthwhile to develop separate and special promotional campaigns aimed at this market. Colgate-Palmolive, for example, has been able to promote its toothpaste effectively within the Hispanic community through ads that place less emphasis on health and more emphasis on appearance. Not all companies are so successful, however. Several examples of misses or near misses in promotional efforts are cited in the following paragraphs. Braniff Airlines produced one infamous advertise-ment that was broadcast in Spanish over several U.S. radio stations. Unfortunately, the speaker unintentionally encouraged travelers to "fly naked" when the message actually was intended to describe the leather seats in Braniff airplanes. Someone had written the message correctly, using "en cuero" for "in leather". But en cueros means "naked" in Spanish, and the "s" is not pronounced.

Therefore, both words sound the same. So while the message was technically correctly translated, had a native Spanish-speaking person looked over the ad first, the problem would not have arisen.

Coors commercials promoting the slogan "Taste the high country" featured people enjoying Coors beer and life in the Rocky Mountains. This approach, very effective with Anglo-Americans, did not appeal to Mexican-Americans, who could not identify with mountain life. Therefore, the Spanish language ads were modified. The mountains were identified as a good source of beer, but one did not necessarily need to live in the mountains to enjoy the beer or to be happy. The new slogan, in its English version, became "Take the beer from the high country and bring it to your high country-wherever it may be."

McDonald's has used "Hispanic ads" in several Spanish-speaking markets within the United States. However, these same ads proved unsuccessful when introduced into Puerto Rico. Apparently they were deemed as "too Mexican" so separate ads were developed.

In another McDonald's blunder that promoted Big Macs with a picture of a French master chef, the chef discovered that the publicity campaign was going on in the Netherlands. When the chef found out, he demanded $2.7 million in damages. The chef commented, "I have licensed my face and my name in all the countries of the world. This confusion between the art that we practice and the sandwich making they do cannot be tolerated." McDonald's settled with the chef, who donated the money to the Ecole des Arts Culinaires d'Ecully, where they train top-flight French chefs.

Johnson & Johnson was fortunate and discovered a potential cultural blunder in time to correct it. The firm was all set to promote its disposable diapers through advertisements that contained references to a mother's wet lap and a father's being dry when it was uncovered that such phrases bore indelicate sexual references to Hispanic consumers. This discovery was fortunate since such an ad would have created a great deal of embarrassment for the company.

Pedro Domecq wines also averted a mishap when it was about to use the slogan "the art of simpatico drinking" to promote Spanish wines. A U.S. advertising agency had created the slogan, which was intended to tie together the Spanish wine and the favorable U.S. translation and use of the word simpatico.

However, the Spanish do not use the word with the same connotation. The correct Spanish usage is "El es muy simpatico" (he is very likable, agreeable, genial). Since, in Spanish, simpa-tico always refers to a person and never to drinking, the promotional campaign would have seemed foolish to the Spanish-speaking community. Fortunately, some Spanish-speaking managers from Pedro Domecq revealed this error in time.

PRODUCT PRICING

Setting an appropriate price for a product is often much more difficult than it appears. If only one insignificant detail of the pricing procedure is overlooked or misjudged, major troubles can develop for the firm.

Consider the experience of a company trying to market cans of luncheon meat. In order to beat the prices of its competitors, the firm slightly cut its prices by rounding them off to easy-to-record, even numbers. The customary prices of the competitors' products were a bit higher, and to the disappointment of the company, customers seemed quite willing to pay the minor extra charge. A local business practice was actually involved in this mishap. Local retail outlets usually operated on very small profit margins. These retailers found, their customers would not request the small change owed when purchasing the fractionally higher priced can of meat. Naturally, in order to keep their "tip," the retailers heavily promoted the competition. It took the firm over six months to readjust its price and begin selling its product again.

The "Delacre" line of luxury biscuits promoted under the Pepperidge Farm label encountered problems when it was introduced into the United States. The biscuits did not sell well until the British firm Peek

Frean introduced them at a much lower price. Products are not prized in all countries, so what some may be willing to pay highly for, others may not. In a foreign environment, any assumption concerning a product's "special value" is dangerous. Unless the market is clearly established, the implementation of a high pricing strategy is not likely to achieve high sales volumes.

Price negotiation can also prove to be a tricky undertaking. If the company negotiators are unaware of local customs, inappropriate prices are quite likely to result. This risk is best illustrated by examining the negotiation process involving Americans and Japanese. American managers are accustomed to pressure decision making and are often given the authority to make final decisions.

Japanese managers, on the other hand, prefer to negotiate more slowly, tend to make decisions by group consensus, and always politely listen to everyone in their group before reaching an official decision. Because Americans are generally unaware of these tendencies, they have often created problems for themselves. A typical situation involves an American negotiating with Japanese managers in order to buy or sell some product or service.

The American, often anxious to complete the deal, tends (in the eyes of the Japanese) to rush the negotiation process. All too often, when the time for price discussion arrives, the American will quickly suggest a price. Being used to the give-and-take of negotiating, the American usually does not make the best possible offer at the start nor necessarily expects it to be accepted. Here is where the troubles arise. When people hesitate, an American tends to assume that the price mentioned is an unacceptable one.

Therefore, an American will sometimes hastily improve the offer even before it is rejected or the process is unsuccessfully terminated. But the American negotiating with Japanese managers may commit a blunder by quickly altering the price. This has happened on numerous occasions, but in at least one reported case, an American raised the price he was willing to pay three times after the Japanese were prepared to accept. Unaware of Japanese customs, he did not realize that the hesitation and discussion between the Japanese (in Japanese, of course) were not a result of unhappiness over the price quoted. With each higher price offer, the Japanese negotiators expressed amazement (in Japanese) but then proceeded to check out their colleagues' opinions. This delay only unwittingly encouraged the American to offer even more.

Many companies have been able to buy or sell merchandise at the right prices but have quoted the prices forgetting that exchange rates fluctuate. Because totally accurate exchange rate forecasting is not possible, some mistakes have been made. The direction of currency movement is fairly predictable, though, and should be considered when a company prices a contract for future payment.

Similarly, in most countries, inflation is fairly predictable. The failure to analyze inflationary factors has hurt a number of companies. A German company, for example, agreed to a $163 million Algerian construction contract. The price set was fair enough at the time of the commitment, but costs rose dramatically during the life of the contract. Unfortunately, the firm had failed to include protective price escalators in the original contract. Additionally, it soon discovered that payments were made in the local Algerian currency that had also declined in value. This double-edged sword cut out all the company's expected profits and cost the firm millions of dollars.

Credit, another price-related variable, is often critical to the marketing strategy. Although the product might be appropriately priced, it may not sell if credit terms are unacceptable. Consider a multinational firm that had carefully test-marketed its specially modified washing machines and concluded that they would sell well in Latin America. Sales were slow even though a large shipment had been made available. Eventually the firm discovered the trouble: local competitors were making their sales on credit.

Apparently those participating in the market test had assumed that credit would be made available since it was the local business practice. So, when asked during the test if they would buy, they replied "yes." Only after they discovered that no credit would be provided did they change their minds and decide not to purchase the product. As evidenced, all aspects of pricing and selling strategies must be considered carefully.

SUMMARY

This chapter has introduced a number of problems encountered when companies attempted to promote products in international markets. Blunders have been made in all types of media and for a wide variety of reasons. Both simple and complex misunderstandings have led to difficulties. Sometimes mistakes arose from human error or the use of culturally insensitive persons. On occasion, an entire promotional strategy has proved foolish. In many cases, the blunders were simply the result of the company's failure to understand cultural differences, some basic but some more subtle. A few problems encountered were based upon pricing errors. With so many different kinds of potential blunders, it is easy to believe that every promotional task imaginable has been bungled at one time or another by someone, someplace.

15

Care in Translation

Translation errors are the cause of the greatest number and variety of blunders in international business. There are three basic categories of translation errors: simple carelessness, multiple-meaning words, and idioms. All three types are described and discussed in this chapter.

CARELESSNESS

The most prevalent type of translation blunder is merely the careless rendering of a promotional message into another language. Obviously, these mistakes can often result in an embarrassing or damaging situation and thus directly injure sales.

Consider the case of the Doutor Coffee Company, a Tokyo retailer. It was trying to promote coffee as relaxing and wanted to convey "it takes a load off your chest." But the phrase came out as "ease your bosoms," a rough translation of the English slogan.

A food company did indeed make a "big mistake" when it advertised its giant burrito as a "burrada." The colloquial meaning of the word burrada is "big mistake." Spanish language translations seem to be treacherous for some companies. One Spanish ad promoted Budweiser as the "Queen of Beers"-just a bit off their usual "King of Beers" slogan. Another Spanish-language blunder was made when an advertisement for "Bud Lite" beer was translated into Spanish as "Filling, less delicious" rather than "Delicious, less filling."

In an advertisement that ran in New York, Acura proudly proclaimed, "The Legend and Integra, cars that break tradition, now your bank account." Obviously Acura intended to say "not" rather than "now," but to some consumers the error may have an accidental ring of truth to it. An American in Michigan got so upset with the success of Japanese auto makers that he decided to make and sell T-shirts displaying a message that was supposed to say in both English and Japanese "Buy American made". Naturally, he had no trouble with the English, but the Japanese translation came out as "Buy an American maid." Close!

A toy bear, made in Taiwan, "sang" Christmas carols in English. One song, though, didn't quite come out correctly: it was "Oh, little town of Birmingham." It helps to know the story!

One company in Taiwan tried to sell diet food to expatriates living there. The company urged consumers to buy its product to add "roughage" to their systems. How much "roughage" should a person consume? Well, the instructions claimed that one should eat it until "your tool floats." Do you suppose they meant "stool?"

An automobile manufacturer promoted its product in an English-speaking market by declaring that its product "topped them all." This may have been so, but the French Canadians would not have known. When the product was introduced, the phrase was mistranslated in French. The result: the company actually boasted that its cars were "topped by them all." Another U.S. manufacturer in the auto industry advertised its auto battery as "highly rated." Unfortunately, when the company introduced its product in Venezuela, the battery was described as "highly overrated." Here again the company had used a thoughtless translation of a key promotional phrase. Needless to say, sales did not boom in either case.

Translation blunders are easy to make-especially if you are speaking in a difficult language you do not have experience in. Finnish is widely recognized as a difficult language, but some organizations try to bring their messages to Finland in Finnish anyway. Usually, it is worth while, but every so often the results have been "awkward." The Church of Jesus Christ of Latter-day Saints (the "Mormon Church") is one of the organizations that has had some problems in Finland. It regularly sends some of its members there to learn Finnish and talk with the people about the Church. These missionaries are so well intended and sincere-sounding, however, that it is usually quite amusing to the local Finnish listener to hear the missionary say, "We are American missionaries and we go around killing people." Apparently this happens frequently because the Finnish word for "meeting" is tappamaan, but that word is often mispronounced by foreigners as "tapamaan," which means "killing". Kentucky Fried Chicken has done very well overseas, as many can attest. However, even a good company can make mistakes. KFC experienced real problems when the phrase "finger lickin' good" came out in Chinese as "eat your fingers off." Eastern Airlines translated its "We earn our wings daily" message into Spanish in such a way that the translated message implied that the airline's passengers often ended up dead. This, naturally, did not help Eastern's struggle to avoid bankruptcy. And the Olfa Corporation, a Japanese manufacturer, sold knives in the United States with a very interesting warning on the package, "Caution: blade extremely sharp! Keep out of children."

A Canadian importer of Turkish shirts destined for Quebec used a dictionary to help him translate the label "Made in Turkey". Unfortunately, his translated message, "Fabriqué en Dinde," reflected his knowledge of French-dinde is the bird, Turquie is the country.

Some years ago, the prestigious prep school, Phillips-Exeter, established its own "School Year Abroad" (SYA) program in Barcelona, Spain. As Thanksgiving rolled around, the director called in his young, bilingual, Spanish secretary and instructed her to get a half-dozen turkeys for this important American holiday. She immediately called the Turkish Consulate General. Not much was going on, so they were thrilled to accept the invitation. Still on the phone, the secretary informed the director of SYA that she had the six Turkeys and asked how they should come dressed. The director replied, "Make sure they're cleaned."

An interesting, but unimpressive, warning label was displayed on the irons made by the German company Rowenta. It said, "Do not iron clothes on body." The label did not inspire confidence in the product or its manufacturer.

Careless translations can prove to be humorous to the consumer and/or embarrassing to the firm. Consider, for example, the experience of the Otis Engineering Corporation when it participated in an exhibition held in Moscow. Initially, the company's representatives could not discern why its display won Soviet snickers as well as praise. Much to their disappointment and embarrassment, it was discovered that a careless translator had rendered a sign that identified "completion equipment" as "equipment for orgasms." On the opposite side of the globe, another firm was experiencing the headaches caused by a poor translator. In this case, a Mexican magazine promotion for an American-brand shirt carried a message stating the exact opposite of what had originally been intended. The advertisement, instead of declaring "When I used this shirt, I felt good," read "Until I used this shirt, I felt good."

There is an old saying, "The world is paved with good intentions." This certainly holds true for many international business endeavours. However, effort alone just is not enough sometimes. This might be best illustrated with the experiences of one Japanese firm trying to do business in China. In order to present itself in a better light, it decided to have English-language labels on its products. It thought this would add prestige to its products, but the Japanese messages were so poorly translated into English that the results were quite negative. After all, who would be interested in meat called "liver putty," a toilet paper named "My Fanny Brand," ready-to-eat pancakes identified as "strawberry crap dessert"; an antifreeze spray claimed to be a "hot piss brand," or a health product that was recommended by a pediatrician (doctor for children) who was called a "specialist in deceased children"?

Public signs translated from foreign languages and designed to assist English-speaking visitors are sources of lost meaning in the translation. In Zurich the notice said, "Because of the impropriety of entertaining guests of the opposite sex in the bedroom, it is suggested that the lobby be used for this purpose." In an Acapulco hotel when trying to promote quality control, "the manager has personally passed all the water served here."

International business people often encounter some interesting signs in their hotels while travelling abroad. Try to guess where these were found:

"Please leave your values at the front desk" (Paris).

"The flattening of underwear with pleasure is the job of the chambermaid" (Zagreb).

"The lift is being fixed for the next day. During that time we regret that you will be unbearable" (Bucharest).

Of course people have poorly translated English into other languages as well. "Violators will be fined" was translated into Spanish to say, "Rapists will be killed" (Phoenix). Posters and advertisements were also printed in Phoenix which were supposed to say "Hear the concert of the year" in Spanish, but the curly tilde over the letter "n" in one word was omitted. This resulted in the message actually saying, "Hear the concert of the anus." It is not clear how many people attended this concert.

A sign in a cocktail lounge in Norway read "Ladies are requested not to have children at the bar." In Moscow a sign in a hotel welcomes you to "visit the cemetery where famous Russian and Soviet composers, artists and writers are buried daily except Thursday." Participants at a conference must have smiled when they read a sign which said, "For anyone who has children and doesn't know it, there is a day care on the first floor."

The zoo in Budapest tells visitors, "Please do not feed the animals. If you have any suitable food, give it to the guard on duty." An airline office in Copenhagen promises to "take your bags and send them in all directions." Some clothing signs advertised more than they bargained for when they said, "fur coats made for ladies from their own skin." Even the dry cleaners' ads may convey some peculiar offerings such as "Drop your trousers here for best results" in Bangkok or "Ladies, leave your clothes here and spend the afternoon having a good time" in Rome.

Restaurants seem to have the same kind of loss in translation problems. A Polish menu advertised "roasted duck let loose" while a Swiss diner sent a warning message, "Our wines leave you nothing to hope for," and a bathroom sign in Finland suggests, "To stop the drip, turn cock to right."

The Frank Perdue Company is well known for its catchy messages promoting its chicken products. At least one of its popular slogans, though, was not translated very well. The message, declaring approximately "It takes a tough man to make a tender chicken," somehow came out closer to "It takes a sexually excited man to make a chick affectionate."

Many a small business has thwarted its own efforts through the use of poor translation. For example, one businessperson, trying to save a bit of money, hired an Indonesian exchange student to translate the instruction manual of a computer destined for Jakarta. Not surprisingly, the student did not understand computer terminology, so the computer "software" was translated as "underwear." The manual must have provided interesting reading! In efforts to attract tourists and foreign business people, some small businesses have created rather funny situations. For instance, public signs translated from foreign languages, and designed to assist English-speaking visitors, are sometimes sources of confusion in the translation. A department store in Thailand posted a sign that read "Visit our bargain basement one flight up." Another misguided individual in Thailand tried to attract business with a sign that asked, "Would you like to ride on your ass?" And in Japan, an interesting but misleading translation showed up on a sign in a Japanese garden. The posted sign read, "Japanese garden is the mental home of the Japanese."

English translations around the world carry lost meanings in translation. In a Belgrade hotel elevator: "To move the cabin, push button for wishing floor. If the cabin should enter more persons, each one should press a number of wishing floor. Driving is then going alphabetically by national order." A hotel in Athens wants visitors to "complain at the office between the hours of 9 a.m. and 11 a.m. daily." In Tokyo at the bar you can order "special cocktails for the ladies with nuts."

A car rental firm in Tokyo printed a brochure to assist drivers that read, "When passenger of foot heave in sight, tootle the horn. Trumpet him melodiously at first, but if he still obstacles your passage then tootle him with vigor." Or in a Leipzig elevator the sign read, "Do not enter lift backwards, and only when lit up."

The frequency of these sorts of amusing translations is amazing. In an Austrian ski resort hotel, guests were told "Not to perambulate the corridors in the hours of repose in the boots of ascension." Two different signs above a shop entrance convincingly state "English well talking" and "Here speeching American." In Akko, Israel, a restaurant featured "lamp chops". In a Polish hotel the menu offers "Salad a firm's own make: limpid red beet soup with cheesy dumplings in the form of a finger; roasted duck let loose; and beef rashers beaten up in the country people's fashion."

In fact, menus seem to be the most interesting place to find these entertaining translations. They seem to be everywhere. A restaurant in China offered "cold shredded children" and "dreaded veal cutlet." A restaurant in Vietnam offered "pork with fresh garbage," while one in Los Angeles offered "French creeps." It is possible, of course, that these menus were not printed in error at all, but one hopes so.

A number of years ago U.S. businessmen reported seeing a sign in a Tokyo hotel which read "You are respectfully requested to take advantage of the chambermaids." The translation is probably misleading, but not as costly as the faulty translations of some equipment-handling instructions that have led to the injury and death of several construction employees in the Middle East.

An interesting sign in Czechoslovakia read, "Take one of our horse-driven tours. We guarantee no miscarriages." That, however, probably didn't generate as much interest as the sign in a French shop window that read, "We sell dresses for street walking." It is probably best to assume that both signs were the result of translation errors.

One dentist in Hong Kong apparently advertises "Teeth extracted by the latest Methodists." A more startling sign, however, showed up in the window of a tailor in Jordan. The sign advised: "Order you summers suit. Because if big rush we will execute customers in strict rotation."

A company in Taiwan wished to help foreigners communicate more effectively, so it advertised its expertise in a brochure. The text read, in part, that "communication was a new challenge," and that the firm could "translet [sic] your idea clearly . . . to people who have no lot of time to sit or listen." Obviously, the firm needed to hire someone to help it improve its own communication skills!

A Chinese restaurant in Virginia ran an ad in a local newspaper with a line of Chinese characters printed upside down. That is an understandable mistake, but the restaurant compounded this mistake in its subsequent ad that tried to explain the error. The characters were the correct way up in the second ad, but in reverse order. There is no report as to how the third version looked.

A firm in the Middle East was able to attract attention, but not exactly the kind it had hoped. It seems that a Saudi Arabian laundry had posted, in English, a list of its cleaning prices. It was not its prices, though, that were attracting people. The company had used a poor translator, and among the many spelling errors on the poster was the omission of the letter "r" in lady's shirt." One can imagine the customers' reactions! It is easy to understand the importance of an accurate translation and the negative results possible if this work is not done carefully.

One of the more unusual errors made by a small business occurred in Kowloon. A sign in the hotel read, "It is forbidden to steal hotel towels, please if you are not person to do such is please not to read notice." What one can assume from this is that someone tried to communicate in another language, but with a bit of difficulty.

Poorly translated signs in business windows and establishments seem to be very common. In fact, as of this writing, a well established and frequently updated website is reporting hundreds of recently discovered incidents-each documented with photos of the frequently humorous blunders. (Some sections of the website may be offensive or at least too graphic for some people, but these sections can easily be avoided.)

Translation blunders seem to occur everywhere but for now consider only one area of the world-Quebec. Quebec has been the site of a number of corporate blunders, most of them due to simple carelessness. There is no reason, for example, for a firm to have used the words lavement d'auto (car enema) instead of the correct lavage d'auto (car wash), but one firm did. Another company boasted of "lait frais usage" (used fresh milk) when it meant to brag of "lait frais employé" (fresh milk used). The "terrific" pens of one firm were promoted as "terrifiantes" (terrifying) instead. Indeed, such a poor translation is terrifying! One company, intending to report that its appliance would use any kind of electrical current, actually stated that the appliance wore out any kind of liquid. And imagine how one company felt when its product to reduce heartburn was advertised as one that reduced warmth of heart. Another unfortunate firm claimed that its product was a stumbling block to success when it really wanted to claim that its product provided a stepping stone to success.

The omission of an accent mark created difficulties for at least one company. An American firm hoped to surprise its Mexican-based employees with a New Year's Eve party. Preparations were complete, including balloons with printed slogans (in Spanish) declaring "Happy New Year." However, the tilde accent mark over the "n" in año was left off. Without the mark, the word read "ano" ("anus" in Spanish). Happy New Anus? Needless to say, the balloons came down before midnight! All of these blunders point out that even the smallest translation error can greatly affect the intended message and the market's reaction to that message. Occasionally it may only be one seemingly insignificant letter that can change the entire context of the copy. Consider one unfortunate international corporation that had its annual report translated into Spanish. In the sentence "Our vast enterprise achieved record sales . . ." the word "vast" was translated into basto. The actual Spanish word is vasto, but people often become confused because the letters "b" and "v" are pronounced similarly. Due to this error in translation, however, the entire meaning of the sentence was modified to "our crude and uncultured enterprise achieved record sales . . ."

Poor translations get companies into trouble more often than anything else. Usually, these translations are only embarrassing, but sometimes they can be much more serious. Mead Johnson Nutritionals found this out the hard way. It had to recall two different baby food products because the instructions on how the products were to be prepared had been incorrectly translated from English to Spanish. Both the 16 oz powder infant formula and the 32 oz ready-to-use infant formula had dangerous preparation instructions, according to the U.S. Food and Drug Administration. It reported that, if the baby food were prepared according to the incorrect Spanish instructions, the formula could cause seizures, irregular heartbeat, renal failure and death. Obviously, no company wants to make this kind of blunder.

While selling products in Mexico, Microsoft Corporation committed a blunder when the Word 6.0 program suggested a series of synonyms in the thesaurus that were offensive. Examples included words such as "man-eater," "cannibal" or "barbarian" that were replaced by the Spanish term for black people. The thesaurus recommended in place of "indians" to use the term "man-eating savages." The term "lesbian" suggested substituting the word "vicious" or "perverse." "Occidental" was more positively portrayed, with synonyms such as "white," "civilized" and "cultured."

MULTIPLE MEANINGS

The second category of translation blunders involves translated messages that can convey more than one meaning. The trials and tribulations experienced by the Parker Pen Company serve as an excellent illustration of how an innocent translation of a multiple-meaning word or phrase can create complex problems. In its advertisements destined for Latin America, Parker had hoped to use the word bola to describe its ballpoint pen. However, it was discovered that the word conveys different meanings in different Latin countries. To some, bola conveys the intended meaning of "ball," while in another country, the translation means "revolution." Bola represents an obscenity in a third country, and in yet another, it means a "lie" or "fabrication." Luckily, the firm was able to uncover this translation problem before it could ever become a blunder.

The company, however, was not so fortunate when it tried to introduce its fountain pens in some parts of Latin America. The Parker Pen Company had developed and promoted in the United States one of the first truly reliable fountain pens. The pen could be carried in a person's shirt without the person worrying about the possibility of embarrassing ink stains.

The advertisements (and the pens) performed so well that the Parker pen became quite well known. Eventually, the promotion was shortened to convey that Parker pens avoid embarrassment. Because this condensed version of the promotional slogan was so successful over time, the older expanded message was taken for granted and basically forgotten. Later, when the firm decided to enter the Latin American market, it merely translated the same condensed promotional slogan then being used in the United States: "Avoid embarrassment-use Parker pens." The company even posted metal signs featuring this short message on the buildings in which its pens were sold, but the results of the company's promotional efforts were not as anticipated. What had gone wrong? The com-pany had promoted a slogan that contained a multiple-meaning word. The Spanish word for "embarrassment" was also used to indicate pregnancy, so the Parker Pen Company was unknowingly promoting its pens as contraceptives!

An American toothpaste manufacturer also experienced pains with its "pregnancy." The company promised its customers that they would be more "interesting" if they used the firm's toothpaste. What the advertising coordinators did not realize, however, was that in some Latin American countries "interesting" is another euphem-ism for "pregnant."

Continuing with problems of pregnancy, consider the case of a freelance Arabic translator who translated an American computer manual into his native language.

When confronted with the terms "dummy" and "load," specialized electronics terms, he consulted his dictionary and found the equivalents of "dummy" and "load." When he put these two together, he produced the Arabic term for "false pregnancy."

The Dairy Association's huge success with the campaign "Got milk?" prompted them to expand advertising to Mexico. However, it was soon brought to their attention that the Spanish translation read "Are you lactating?"

A clothing store in Tokyo claimed that "Our nylons cost more than common, but you'll find they are the best in the long run."

Wendy's was saved from committing two separate blunders in Germany by advertising agency staff members. In one case, Wendy's wanted to promote its "old-fashioned" qualities. A literal translation, however, would have resulted in the company promoting itself as "outdated". In another example, Wendy's wanted to emphasize that its hamburgers could be prepared 256 ways. The problem? The German word Wendy's wanted to use for "ways" usually meant "roads" or "highways." Although such errors may sometimes entertain the public, it is certainly preferable to catch these mistakes before they confuse the consumer or embarrass the company.

The Spanish certainly enjoyed a good laugh when Chrysler Corporation tried to promote its successful U.S. slogan, "Dart is power." It seems that the translated version of this message implied that drivers of the car needed sexual vigor!

The well-known vacuum cleaner manufacturer, Electrolux, is a Swedish-owned company. New ads were developed for the U.S. market proclaiming "Electrolux sucks better." Obviously, the firm was not attuned to some common American slang! In Thailand, a bar located nearby some trees and buildings that blocked out the hot sun innocently advertised itself as "the shadiest bar in Bangkok."

These double-meaning translation errors embarrass the firms involved. One company caught in this situation was granted the dubious distinction of winning Playboy magazine's annual "Booby-Boo-Boo

Award." Apparently when Hunt-Wesson introduced the "Big John" family brand in Canada it experienced a bit of difficulty with the French translation. The name, translated as "Gros Jos," also turned out to be a colloquial French expression that denoted a woman with large breasts. In this case the company was fortunate. Its sales were not badly hurt, for a number of men wanted to order the "Gros Jos"!

Hunt-Wesson has not been the only company to find itself in such a humorous position. A U.S. airline that proudly advertised swank "rendezvous lounges" aboard its Boeing 747 jets may have wished that its promotion had never reached Brazil. After advertising these accommodations, the company belatedly learned that "rendezvous" in Portuguese represents a room that is rented out for prostitution. Although the promotion was successful in attracting attention, sales did not increase. No Brazilian wanted to be seen getting on or off the airline's plane. Here again a company's failure to understand all of the meanings and implications of the translated message was responsible for its subsequent difficulties.

Several major tobacco companies have also experienced the pitfall of a double meaning. These firms advertised "low-tar" cigarettes in Spanish-speaking countries but misused the word brea. Brea literally translates to "tar," but it is the type of tar used for paving streets. Care for a "low-asphalt" cigarette, anyone?

A sign in a Japanese museum advised patrons in English to "Please refrain from taking photographs and reproducing." Literal translations are risky. It is probably just as well that most people in English-speaking countries do not know that the motto of Tokyo Gas & Electric is "My life, my gas."

Translated words may often mean about the same thing, but they may not elicit the same feelings. As an example, "As smooth as a baby's bottom" was translated into Japanese to "As smooth as a baby's ass." Translators must be encouraged to convey the intended mood even if this means that they must forgo a literal translation and use some alternative wording instead.

American cooks understand what is meant by tomato "paste", but how does one translate this into Arabic? The closest translation is something like "tomato glue." Thus, translators have had to use the

Arabic words for "tomato puree." Sounds a bit more appetizing, doesn't it? Sometimes someone in a company simply forgets that words have well-known double meanings. One firm, for example, experienced trouble conducting market research. It requested information regarding the annual German production of washers. The firm was actually seeking data on washing machines but, instead, received material on the production of flat metal discs (also known as washers). Here the translation problem was not so much with the translated word or the translator but with the original word. Adolph Coors Company hired an agency to develop promotional material for its Coors Light beer that would appeal to Hispanics in the United States. The copywriter tried to translate the phrase "Turn it loose" into Spanish, but unfortunately used words which meant "Drink Coors and get diarrhea." The commercial received a lot of attention but not the kind Coors had hoped for!

Tropicana tried to sell its orange juice in Miami, claiming that it was "jugo de China." "China" means "orange" to Puerto Ricans, but not to the Cubans in Miami. Thus, the Cubans thought that it was "juice from China" and were not very interested in the product. Miami is frequently the location for linguistic problems. Several different cultures coexist there, with people speaking different languages-or sometimes the same one with different meanings. Take the word bichos, for example. It means "bugs" to Mexicans, but the word denotes a man's private parts to Puerto Ricans. Therefore, the insecticide company's posters guaranteeing that its products would kill all "bichos" was not very successful in some parts of Miami!

One final example of the troublesome multiple-meaning word involves the banking industry. An American bank was given a 30-day option on the purchase of a Middle Eastern bank. During the final negotiations, an unfortunate buyer proposed in French that the loans be put into an escrow account. The local sellers, quite humiliated and shocked, quickly left the room shouting, "A reserve for cheating? Never!" The misunderstanding stemmed from the word escrow which when translated into French means a cheat. Quite upset, the sellers decided to find another interested party willing to purchase the bank. Translations play a key role in all aspects of international business, and accuracy is of utmost importance. A company can be hurt greatly by one simple faulty translation.

IDIOMS

Having discussed not only those errors resulting from careless translation but also those due to multiple meanings, consider now the third type of blunder: those made during the translation of idioms and expressions. Because of the unique aspect of the idiomatic expressions that characterize every language, this is often the most difficult area. The following examples have been chosen as illustrations.

Most firms realize it takes more than a bilingual dictionary to translate commercial messages and their intended meanings. However, a few firms have used the simplest, most literal translations for their promotions and as a result have found themselves promoting something other than what they had thought. An American company, for instance, advertised its product to a Spanish audience, exclaiming that anyone who didn't wear its brand of hosiery just "wouldn't have a leg to stand on." But when the copy was translated the firm actually declared that the wearer would "only have one leg."

Another case of a troublesome literal translation occurred in French-speaking Quebec. The point-of-sale campaign of a laundry soap company stressed the extra-strong cleaning powers of its product and how great it was for the especially dirty parts of the wash, "les parts de sale." When the soap sales declined, the company investigated and discovered that this phrase is comparable to the American slang phrase "private parts."

The American expression "touch-toe" was responsible for a blunder made by a manufacturer of dental equipment. In a brochure written for the Soviet market, the company featured the "touch-toe" control of its dental chair movement. The translator, however, rendered the description of this feature in such a way that the Russians thought that the dentist had to be barefooted in order to operate the equipment. What a unique feature, indeed!

Several other brief examples of mistranslated English idioms or expressions can be cited to illustrate how often these blunders have been made. One European firm certainly missed the point when it translated the expression "out of sight, out of mind" as "invisible things are insane" in Thailand. There is also the story of the phrase "the spirit is willing, but the flesh is weak" being translated to "the liquor is holding out all right, but the meat has spoiled." And consider, finally, a translation of "Schweppes Tonic Water" to the Italian il water. The copy was speedily dehydrated to "Schweppes Tonica" because il water idiomatically indicates a bathroom.

If anything is to be learned from these examples, it is the necessity for caution in the translation and interpretation of intended messages. Exact wording should not always be translated literally. This can be most appropriately demonstrated by citing ten idioms used in the United States. If any of these were to be used in Quebec, for example, the French translation should not be a literal one but should approximate the local phrase or idiom commonly used there. The U.S. version is mentioned first and is followed by the comparable French Canadian expression.

"To murder the King's English" should be translated as "to speak French like a Spanish cow."

"Nothing to sneeze at" should become "nothing to spit on."

"Welcome as a bull in a china shop" should become "welcome as a dog in a bowling alley."

"A little birdie told me so" should become "my little finger told it to me."

"To be sitting on the fence" should become "to swim between two streams."

"I have a hangover" should become "I have a sore hair."

"To cry in one's beer" should become "to have the sad wine."

"Unable to make head or tail of it" should become "to lose one's Latin."

"To make a mountain out of a molehill" should become "to drown in a glass of water."

"You can't teach an old dog new tricks" should become "one does not teach an old monkey to make faces."

It need not be an entire phrase that needs rewording, but only one simple word. What the people of one country take for granted as the only correct word or sound might be totally inappropriate to others. Take, for example, the words used for animal sounds. In reality, an animal makes the same noise in every country, but humans interpret the sound differently from country to country. Companies that sell pet food and supplies and those taking the risky approach of featuring animals in promotions need to take extra precautions when speaking for animals. If the messages are to be effective, then the firms must be sure that they are communicating in languages that can be understood.

SUMMARY

Faulty translations have caused the most blunders in international business. These translation mistakes have hindered not only marketing efforts and negotiations but also many other aspects of business. They are usually due to carelessness, but language subtleties, words with multiple meanings, and difficult-to-translate idioms also cause problems. Fortunately, translation blunders are some of the easiest to avoid.

16

Organisation Management

"Management"-the act, manner, or practice of managing, handling, or controlling something. Certainly a dictionary's basic definition of this word helps us understand why so many blunders can occur in this area of business.

An American executive's mishandling of a presentation prepared for a small Caribbean country serves as a simple example of a management blunder. The meeting was held in the Prime Minister's conference room, and the executive began his presentation with, "Honorable Mr. Tollis and esteemed members of the cabinet." The Prime Minister interrupted him several times, asking him to start over. Eventually, someone advised the bewildered and then embarrassed businessman that Mr. Tollis had been deposed six months earlier!

Unfortunately, people sometimes get careless. Thoughtless conversations, however, can prove costly. When in a foreign-speaking country, it is easy to forget that some people may understand many languages. All too often, speakers learn too late that others understand what they are saying. In fact, visitors to the United States often assume no one understands their native tongue and then promptly say something they quickly regret. An Italian businessman, for example, reportedly flew to Los Angeles to talk with a potential American investor.

The driver of the American picked up the Italian at the airport. Believing that the driver did not understand Italian, the visitor, speaking in Italian, apparently made some very negative remarks about the potential investor to his accompanying business associate. These remarks were reported by the driver, who did indeed understand what was being said, and the business deal collapsed.

There are many facets of management. Consider Renault, which, like many firms, has tried to use various barter plans but has experienced mixed success. Trading cars for other products can be profitable but only if the traded products are correctly marketed. In order to sell its cars in South America, Renault agreed to accept coffee beans in payment. The plan seemed safe, as coffee beans are easily traded on world commodity markets. Renault's problems began when the company decided to use the beans to produce instant coffee rather than simply sell the coffee beans wholesale. Without carefully checking the credentials of a fast-talking businessman, Renault agreed to build two plants employing his "miracle new process" for the production of instant coffee. Renault later learned that its new associate had earlier run into legal problems with some of his other international business schemes, but not before it discovered that the "miracle process" failed to work properly and that its new associate had disappeared. Renault lost about $120 million but learned a valuable lesson.

Imperial-Eastman Corporation encountered numerous problems in the operations of its various overseas enterprises. In at least one instance, the company experienced unexpected difficulties when it failed to retain its overseas U.S. personnel for a long enough period of time. Before the operation's critical start-up period was completely over, the company relieved its U.S. personnel and relied solely on its locally hired staff to continue running the operation. However, as critical problems developed, Imperial-Eastman discovered that the local staff was not sufficiently experienced to handle the difficult problems resulting from the new operation. In other ventures, the company suffered from poor estimates of initial inventory needs that created production/delivery disruptions. Losses were incurred when the firm did not allow for delayed delivery and subcontractors failed to deliver on time.

A precarious balance seems to exist between the number of foreign managers and the number of U.S. managers needed for a successful operation. Imperial-Eastman experienced problems by relying too heavily on inexperienced local managers, but General Electric encountered troubles by its placement and retention of U.S. employees in most managerial positions. In some cases, because the U.S. employees were unfamiliar with the local business practices, they unknowingly nullified the firm's ability to compete with local business people.

General Electric encountered more culturally oriented management problems in France. Its French employees were upset when they were ordered to wear GE T-shirts to a function (too American), post English-language posters, and in general behave as if the subsidiary was an extension of the United States. Eventually, compromises were made on both sides, but morale already had been badly damaged.

The cases cited above are typical of the types of management blunders that have plagued multinational corporations. Management problems are most often caused by cultural differences that outside managers do not understand and by labor practices with which they are unfamiliar.

CULTURAL DIFFERENCES

A Korean firm, Kunja Industrial Company, which owns the Kunja Knitting Mills plant in South Carolina, made the news when an American employee innocently "crooked" his "pointing finger" trying to catch the attention of his Korean boss and bring him closer. The employee succeeded in getting attention all right. However, he certainly didn't succeed in getting his boss physically or emotionally any closer. In fact, he was almost fired. The U.S. finger-moving gesture for asking someone to come closer is considered a vulgar gesture in Korea!

A similar blunder was made by former President George Bush. The President was visiting Australia. As he walked up the stairs to his plane, he turned and gave a thumbs up signal, thinking he was indicating that things had gone well. Perhaps they had-at least to that point -but the thumbs-up gesture in Australia is essentially the equivalent of the raised middle finger in the United States. Unknowingly, he had correctly indicated that things ended badly.

Culture includes how different people dress and what is considered acceptable business attire. A notable blunder occurred when Spanish businessmen arrived in Saudi Arabia with a full delegation, confident that they had prepared to encourage the Saudis to spend some of their oil money on Spanish products. The entourage included a number of young, intelligent, bilingual (Spanish/English) women dressed in the height of current style. The blunder occurred when the Saudi police took one look at the miniskirts of the female delegates and immediately shipped the entire group home on the next plane to Spain. Traditionally, women do not show their bare legs in Saudi Arabian culture. When doing business in another country, it is often easy to assume that things there are the same as in your country. Sometimes they are, but sometimes they are different. One U.S. firm with a subsidiary in a small island state learned this the hard way when it hired a local manager to run the subsidiary. One person was highly recommended by local contacts, was intelligent, well spoken, and related well to the local workers. She was interviewed by a representative from headquarters and seemed to be the best choice for the position. Initially, operations seemed to go quite well, but it soon became evident that there was a problem. Major discrepancies surfaced in terms of inventory levels and in the reports of parts shipped. The cause of these problems was finally uncovered. The manager could not do the basic arithmetic of adding or subtracting-skills critical to the job. No one had thought to ask about these skills because they were simply assumed.

It is also wise to know the proper way to dismiss an employee when working with other cultures. This is a difficult task to perform in familiar territory but it is especially tricky when one is in a foreign country and does not always fully understand the local culture. An American manager stationed in Indonesia reportedly discovered this when he tried to fire an oilrig employee. Rather than notifying the employee privately of his dismissal, the manager publicly told the timekeeper to send the man "packing." In Indonesia, this public dismissal was considered an unacceptable "loss of face" which offended both the dismissed man and his friends. So, rather than leave quietly, the man grabbed fire axes and ran after the American manager. Reportedly, the American was barely rescued in time. Obviously, it is dangerous to ignore local management practices and customs!

In an attempt to offer U.S. Southern hospitality, an American businessman was saying goodbye to a Saudi Arabian businessman at the airport after a successful meeting and finished with, "Y'all come and visit." Apparently the Saudi businessman was mortally offended because it was inconceivable to the Saudi that he and his chauffeur should be invited to the United States.

Another American manager was sent to Malaysia to close a major deal. While there he was introduced to someone he thought was named Roger so he pro-ceeded to call him "Rog" several times during the negotiations. Unfortunately, this important potential client was a "rajah," which is an important Malaysian title of nobility. The U.S. tendency to use first names, and even more familiar abbreviated names, was the cause of a serious error in this case. Rather than showing respect, the American appeared disrespectful and insensitive. When the error was discovered, the damage had been done. It is always best to know whom you are dealing with in advance and how that person prefers to be addressed.

A Brazilian executive created major problems for his firm when he treated his secretaries in the United States as personal servants. Not only did he ask them to do his personal shopping, he even asked them to mend his clothes!

The acquisition of the Firestone tire company by Japan's Bridgestone did not proceed as smoothly as hoped. In fact, John Nevin, a crusty former chairman of Firestone, admitted that his style appeared abrupt and abrasive at times to the Japanese, whose manner is much more subtle. He needed to be less direct and forceful with them and they had to become more aware of American-style directness. Both sides tried to adjust, but it did not work out, so new managers had to be brought in.

Milwaukee-based Manpower chairman, Mitchell From-stein, reports that Blue Arrow, a British employment firm, took over Manpower in 1987 but put little effort into understanding how the U.S. labor market differed from the British market. Even the company newsletter directed to the U.S. market ignored U.S. interests. American managers began to openly rebel. Eventually, the Americans wound up in control of the combined company.

In Las Vegas, the Japanese owners of the casinos reportedly ran into problems when they tried to use Japanese management techniques. Among other things, they tried to make decisions the typical Japanese way- by consensus. The approach works well in Japan for many firms but was deemed as too slow and cumbersome in the fast-moving casino environment.

An American company went to a great deal of expense to carefully plan a massive layoff of employees in one of its European subsidiaries. Just before the plan was implemented, however, the firm learned that such layoffs were illegal. Time and money could easily have been saved had managers known of the local labor laws. In a wave of ethnocentrism the new American owners of a Spanish company changed the firm's previous prestigious Spanish name to that of the U.S. parent, flew the American flag from the company flagpole, and widely announced the sophisticated and superb technology being introduced. The company even suggested that those who had managed the company prior to the takeover by the Americans were incompetent. Then, in a special interview with a prominent U.S. business publication, the new management elaborated on its revamping of the whole Spanish company, boasting that its efforts had succeeded in rejuvenating the floundering Spanish operation. Naturally, the article found its way back to the Spanish public and greatly angered the Spanish who were associated with the company. In fact, the blunder was so serious that it resulted in a general slowdown of work. (Strikes were then officially banned.)

The Spanish press released an extremely damaging attack, and local authorities made the conduct of the company's business very difficult. The result: the newly acquired subsidiary lost a great deal of its previous business.

POOR PERSONNEL CHOICES

Just as in any domestic employment position, if a firm places an inappropriate person in an international job, the results can prove disastrous. Several companies have blundered by placing culturally insensitive individuals in sensitive management and sales positions overseas.

A friend of mine reports that he was involved in negotiations with Saudis to sell them material to clean up oil spills. As the deal was about to be closed, a U.S. bank was invited to send some of its people to a closing meeting in Switzerland. The senior banker attending the meeting was well informed of the details of the proposed deal, but it became painfully obvious that at least one of his assistants needed more careful briefing and training when the subject of financing the deal came up. The assistant was asked how he wanted it done and he replied, "It does not matter unless the buyers are Arabs. You can't trust those Arabs."

Interestingly enough, the Saudis were mature enough to realize that one person does not necessarily represent the attitude of the entire bank. When the senior banker immediately apologized, the Saudis simply said they needed time to think things over. They then privately told the senior banker that they would still use his bank and could work with him, but would not under any circumstances work with his anti-Arab assistant. The point was not lost on anyone-including the assistant (who is no longer working for that bank).

In one case, a firm introduced a technical product into a market relatively free of competition. Believing that market entry would pose no problem, the company did not pay enough attention to the personal characteristics of the man it chose as its European sales manager. This was unfortunate. The individual chosen disliked the French and made no effort to ingratiate himself or learn their culture or language. His dislike even spilled over to his abrupt treatment of the sales force. A competitor soon came along and was able to take over much of the market and most of the man's original sales force.

Similarly, an executive from Lucerne, Switzerland, negotiating a business venture with a Japanese firm failed to recognize the importance of personal sentiment to the Japanese and he paid the price. The president of the Japanese company sponsored a party in Tokyo and exclaimed, "I will not do business with a man who does not like us!" The Lucerne executive believed he had concealed his dislike for the Japanese during his stay, but the president of the Japanese company had seen through his mask. The Japanese executive, therefore, refused to proceed with the business deal even though the partnership would undoubtedly have proven mutually profitable.

An employee's attitude, however, is not the only variable of importance. A person may be well intended but simply not be qualified for the job. Several such cases can be cited. A major U.S. appliance manufacturer, for instance, experiencing difficulties in Spain, sent three troubleshooters to investigate. The company overlooked one important fact: the individuals could not speak Spanish. After repeated efforts to communicate failed, the Spaniards eventually lost respect for the three spe-cialists. The problems worsened until a Spanish-speaking manager was sent to help. A similar situation occurred in Germany. A U.S. manager who understood only a little German was sent to Germany to discuss marketing plans with the local subsidiary managers. The local managers, however, spoke little English. Both sides tried to understand each other, but neither nationality did very well. Eventually they parted, thinking that they were in agreement. It was later discovered that during the meeting many important points were overlooked, and the company subsequently lost numerous sales opportunities.

Even though a manager maintains the right attitude and speaks the language, a successful performance is not assured. Raytheon hired Italian-Americans to manage operations in Sicily but found that the strategy was not as effective as hoped. In this case the trouble lay in the origins of the managers. Because their family ties were with the mainland and not Sicilian, these men were not trusted or accepted.

An effective expatriate manager must possess special abilities and traits if he or she is to avoid blundering. Among the most important characteristics are:

- An ability to get along well with people.
- An awareness of cultural differences.
- Open-mindedness.
- Tolerance of foreign cultures.
- Adaptability to new cultures, ideas, and challenges.
- The ability to adjust quickly to new conditions.
- An interest in facts, not blind assumptions.
- Previous business experience.
- Previous experience with foreign cultures.
- The ability to learn foreign languages.

This list is by no means complete. With so many necessary characteristics, it is no wonder that business people sometimes make mistakes.

LABOR RELATIONS

Many non-American companies have experienced difficulties adjusting to U.S. labor practices when they acquire U.S. firms. The Japanese have received the most attention concerning this, but Europeans have also run up against their share of troubles. Britain's Grand Met, for example, angered Pillsbury's minority employees when, as the new owner, it fired several black middle managers (including the head of its affirmative action program). In another case, a European firm lost a talented employee when it purchased a company and expected a female executive to start serving coffee at the board meetings.

Because of cultural similarities, a Japanese company doing business in Indonesia consistently hired Bataks, members of an ethnic group with characteristics similar to the Japanese. Other Indonesians, however, resented this hiring practice, viewed it as discriminatory, and forced the company to change its policy.

A U.S. tin mining firm had problems retaining employees in Bolivia even though it paid the employees more than the local competition did. It seems that the problem lay with the method of payment. The U.S. company paid on time every week, but the Bolivians preferred to be paid by the hour. Thus, they could take a few hours off from time to time and not risk the loss of an entire week's wages.

Americans ran into trouble in Iran long before the Iranian revolution. One problem encountered by business people was the widespread belief that foreigners discriminated against Iranians. A U.S. company cemented this belief when it promised local employees that U.S. workers would not be treated preferentially but then provided better health benefits for the U.S. employees. Verbal promises are taken very seriously in Iran, so the firm's failure to keep its promise was viewed as a major breach of trust and further evidence that foreigners discriminate against Iranians.

Many companies have faced labor troubles in Europe, where governments tend to protect employees and often make layoffs difficult. Some of the most sensationalized cases have occurred in France. Shortly after World War II ended, many U.S. companies rushed into France, hired people, and enjoyed the ensuing business boom. However, the good times didn't last for ever and more than a few firms made the mistake of trying to reduce employment levels. General Motors, Remington Rand, General Electric, and other firms soon found themselves in trouble and were forced to reverse layoff decisions.

Italy has also been the scene of many unpleasant labor disputes with U.S. firms. Raytheon's layoff attempts eventually forced it to close its plant in Sicily at a loss of many millions of dollars.

Another U.S. firm experienced a different kind of problem. The company had a tradition of holding picnics where management and workers mingled with ease in a comfortable environment, so the firm tried to export its company picnic to Spain. To highlight management's "democratic" beliefs, the U.S. executives even dressed as chefs and served the food. However, the picnic failed to help develop the desired rapport between the U.S. managers and the Spanish workers. In fact, it was a very awkward event, as the lower-level staff clung together and did not want to be served by their superiors. When an executive approached the picnic table, everyone stood up. The company quickly learned that Spanish attitudes of class distinction and social groups make casual mixing and socializing of workers with executives very difficult.

The United Kingdom has been the home for some of the best-known labor problems of U.S. companies. Ford Motor Company, for example, ran into hard times in England because the British managers and laborers felt that the U.S. managers there were treated better and were given more power. Many employees openly resented this apparent favoritism. Several key British executives even quit. The company lowered the number of Americans there and this reduced the problem, but decisions from headquarters were still resented. At one point, British newspapers ran such headlines as "Local Ford plants can't even build a bathroom without permission from Detroit." Actually, this was not far from the truth at the time. Now, much more power is delegated to the local managers (who are more likely now to be British) and Ford's labor relations are much better. The Roberts Arundel textile machinery plant in Stockport, England had to close down after managers tried to impose U.S. labor practices. Mr. Arundel later admitted that it was a mistake to try to change worker habits, but they had thought that production line work would go better if those famous tea breaks were dropped. Employees thought otherwise! It is usually easier to change management practices than radically alter local work habits.

SUMMARY

Obviously, management practices that work domestically do not necessarily work overseas. Different cultures require that companies take different approaches. Managers need to understand local business procedures, governmental expectations, and labor practices. A minor misunderstanding can easily lead to a major blunder and the wrong person on the job can lead to disaster.

17

Strategic Management

Companies have committed a wide variety of strategic mistakes over the years. Many have been related to their choice of how to enter the foreign market. Supply decisions, though, have also caused a surprising number of problems. Some of the strategic errors have involved fairly complex issues. Naturally, all of these blunders were regretted.

ENTRY MODE

A company which is "going international" has a variety of entry methods available to it. Acquiring an existing firm, starting up a new operation, forming a joint venture with a local company, and signing licensing agreements are some of the most popular modes of entry. Each method offers advantages and disadvantages.

It might seem that the creation of a joint venture, for example, would eliminate all of the problems encountered by a company "going overseas." With the combined expertise and efforts of both local and foreign firms, major problems or possible blunders would surely be eliminated. However, although certain types of errors are definitely less likely, a multitude of other problems can arise and pose serious threats to the venture's success.

More than a few firms have experienced unexpected problems with joint ventures. One U.S. firm that entered into a joint venture with some South American capitalists did not fully comprehend its initial errors until some five years later. At the time of the company's commitment, its South American partners were temporarily in favor with those in the local government. However, the joint venture began to gradually experience various forms of host government harassment and, consequently, profits slowly declined. The U.S. partner lost investment money, effort, and time. What had happened? They had failed to analyze the situation thoroughly. Early analyses should have revealed both the existence of a volatile political scene and the high degree of political involvement in local business practices.

Dow Chemical Company's joint venture in Korea failed for many reasons, but one important cause was poor communication. Misunderstandings were everywhere and communication seemed to get nowhere. The situation became so bad that Dow Chemical decided to go public with complaints about its partner. This, of course, infuriated the Koreans. Asians tend to keep problems very private, so Dow's strategy of applying public pressure backfired. The Koreans, in fact, felt that they had no choice but to withdraw from the joint venture, as anything else would be viewed as a further loss of face.

A company should create a joint venture only after giving the idea careful consideration. Although another firm may be "willing and waiting" to become a partner, its eagerness does not necessarily assure success. One U.S. manager found this to be especially true. During an inspection of his company's European operations, he met with a number of Belgian pump manufacturing executives. Because one particular company exhibited a great deal of interest in forming a partnership, a joint enterprise was quickly formed. A Belgian was established as the president of the new company, and the U.S. firm's manager in Belgium became the vice-president for manufacturing and engineering. However, friction between these two men and company losses precipitated a crisis. The partnership was dissolved, and the U.S. company bought up all of the Belgian shares at book value. The result: it was many years before the operation became profitable. Undoubtedly, the U.S. firm's unfortunate choice of a partner hindered this venture's success. Partners must be selected with caution, and employee personalities should be considered.

A bakery products firm contracted to sell its entire line of baked goods through a sole distributor in a developing country. The distributor had really only been interested in carrying a few items and found the tie-in arrangement disagreeable. Therefore, relations between the manufacturer and distributor quickly degenerated to the point where little communication existed between them. A serious decline in sales subsequently occurred. Unfortunately, this information did not reach the manufacturer very quickly and large quantities of baked goods spoiled.

Although blunders are often caused by a company's failure to thoroughly investigate potential partners, sometimes a firm's failure to take advantage of a possible joint venture or licensing agreement also results in a suboptimal situation. For instance, parts "specifically for use in" equipment manufactured by the Caterpillar Tractor Company began surfacing for sale in various markets. These products had neither been approved nor manufactured by the Caterpillar Company. The firm, however, was unable to establish any legal claims. If the company had initially sought out a local partner, the demand for these similar parts most assuredly would have benefited Caterpillar. As it turned out, the local manufacturers saw no reason to avoid competing with the totally foreign-owned Caterpillar Tractor Company.

Licensing decisions are as difficult to analyze as those decisions involving the creation of a joint venture. Failure to make the correct decision at the right time can result in the loss of substantial long-range business prospects and potential profits. In one case, a U.S. manufacturer not only licensed the manufacture and sale of its products to an English firm but also granted the firm the exclusive right to sublicense the U.S. expertise to other countries.

At the time the decision was made, the company was not interested in expanding overseas. The firm believed that it was best to simply collect the royalties and thus eliminate its need to provide additional investment money. Within a few years, worldwide markets for the firm's products developed. Naturally, the company greatly regretted its earlier decision to permit exclusive licensing.

A similar case involved a U.S. pharmaceutical firm which licensed its manufacturing techniques to an Asian company. The Asian company, heavily promoting the products, enjoyed great success. As a result of the licensing terms, however, the Asian company reaped almost all of the tremendous profits. Having never realized the product's potential, the U.S. company had permitted the licensing. If the U.S. firm had committed to a more direct form of involvement, such as equity participation, it could have earned greater profits. In this instance, the company's failure to carefully study the market and product opportunities eventually resulted in a lost opportunity.

Sometimes the licensee, although pleased to have been granted the license, is not as enthusiastic about the product as the licensor. One U.S. firm discovered this when it granted an exclusive license to a Japanese company. The Japanese company was given the right to manufacture and sell one of the U.S. firm's specialty products for a period of 20 years. Market studies had indicated that the product, which had been extremely successful in the United States, was destined to replace some of the more conventional materials currently in use in Japan. The U.S. firm had carefully studied its potential licensees and had chosen the Japanese company because of its strength of distribution, size, and record of profit performance. However, the Japanese firm, continuing to push the more conventional materials, failed to promote the new product actively. Since the contract included no agreement concerning minimum royalties, the U.S. company earned no income for the first 10 years. Having failed to recognize the Japanese company's marketing initiatives and lack of interest, the U.S. firm was forced to accept the fact that it could not enter the market itself until the expiration of the 20-year license.

The natural tendency for any company is to "get in while the going is good." One U.S. firm particularly eager to begin operations in India quickly negotiated terms and completed arrangements with its local partners. Certain required documents, however, such as the industrial license, foreign collaboration agreements, capital issues permit, import licenses for machinery and equipment, etc., were slow in being issued. Trying to expedite governmental approval of these items, the U.S. firm agreed to accept a lower royalty fee than originally stipulated. Despite all of this extra effort, the project was not greatly expedited, and the lower royalty fee reduced the firm's profit by approximately half of a million dollars over the life of the agreement.

Warner-Lambert ran into major problems trying to sell "Trident," "Chiclets," and other brands of chewing gum to the Japanese. Because its local wholesalers were not promoting the products to the extent Warner-Lambert desired, the firm decided to change its strategy. The company tried to bypass its wholesalers but quickly realized its mistake. Not only did this move upset the wholesalers; it also created suspicions among the retailers who often consider companies unreliable if they switch business tactics. To recover, the company asked its sales force to collect the retail sales orders for the wholesalers.

Heinz also experienced difficulties with the Japanese market. Attempting to enter the market quickly, Heinz gained a minority interest in a company called Nichiro Fisheries. Not only did the fishery name imply that all the products were fish-oriented, but the partnership simply was not appropriate. Nichiro Fisheries did not hold enough capital nor did it maintain the broad distribution channels necessary to market Heinz's products adequately.

Failing to consider the values or reliability of a potential partner can also prove disastrous. In some countries, it is normal for a company to take whatever it can from its partner. When both parties expect this, reasonable safeguards can be established. When one company is not aware of this practice, though, blunders can certainly result. For example, a U.S. chemical manufacturer agreed to a partnership after being visited by some overseas managers. The strategy developed involved the export of raw materials by the U.S. firm and the manufacture of products by the foreign company. All of the details were carefully stipulated in the contract, but within six months of the first large shipment of raw materials, the partnership broke up. What had gone wrong? Credit terms had not been met, earnings were disputed, and payments had not been sent. The well-known and "respected" local partner had gained part of his visibility through his ability to delay or avoid paying his obligations-a common local practice. The U.S. company should have been aware of this local custom. It then would have known to require payment in advance (the locally accepted practice) or could have established some other financially safe arrangement. To the local courts, the U.S. firm appeared foolish and deserved the loss-after all, the company had failed to follow sound, normal, business practices.

SUPPLY PROBLEMS

Most companies try to save money by purchasing supplies in large quantities. There are, however, logical limits governing this strategy. One example of excessive purchasing occurred in Chile. The Chilean government used to have high tariffs on automobile imports. Over time, this policy created a large pent-up demand for cars. In the late 1970s the government began to radically reduce tariffs and, consequently, demand quickly outstripped supply. By 1981 these tariffs had dropped so low that large numbers of Chileans could afford new autos. Because dealers were unable to fill the vast number of orders, a five-month waiting period for most automobile models was not unusual. Believing that this demand might be unlimited, dealers ordered up to ten times their normal number of cars for 1982 even though the economy began experiencing a recession and the new models were higher-priced. A flooded market resulted. Most of the demand for autos had already been satisfied, and few of the fairly new cars needed to be replaced. Economic uncertainty and higher prices also kept customers away. The result was that inventories grew so high that dealers had no room to store the cars. Many loads (more than a year's supply) were left on board ships lying offshore, incurring high storage costs. The lesson: optimistic, straight-line projections of sales figures are obviously dangerous. Temporary causes of demand should be analyzed and estimates made to determine the amount of pent-up demand still remaining.

Nigeria, though, probably experienced the largest purchasing blunder. Due to increased oil revenues that resulted from the sharp rise of oil prices in the mid-1970s, Nigeria began to initiate major modernization programs. An economically minded bureaucrat decided to purchase, mostly from other countries, the total amount of cement needed to construct all of the new buildings being planned. Soon the cement began to arrive by the shipload. The dockworkers were unable to unload the cement as fast as it arrived, so the ships were forced to await their turn for unloading. Within weeks, there were so many shiploads of unloaded cement that someone computed the length of time required to unload all of the ships. Even with an expanded dock in Lagos, it was calculated that the 20 million tons of cement could not be fully unloaded for 40 years! Much of the cement had to be dumped overboard. The cost to hold the ships until unloading was greater than the cost of reordering the cement.

EverReady, of England, encountered supply problems of a different nature. Hoping to introduce its product to the Nigerians, the company chose a strategy that stressed broad market penetration. The EverReady name and battery were heavily promoted, and a large production run was shipped to Lagos. No problems occurred during the unloading, but the firm probably wished that some had. Apparently a defective chemical had been used during the production of the batteries, and those shipped to Lagos were worthless. Unfortunately, someone had forgotten to test them prior to shipment. Although the first batteries appearing on the heavily promoted Nigerian market sold quickly, word soon spread that the product was not dependable. Since no backup supply of good batteries was available, the promotional effort was wasted, and the firm developed a reputation in Nigeria as being an unreliable company which produced poor goods. Later, when normal batteries reached the Nigerian market, consumers avoided them. It took years for EverReady to overcome its initial reputation there.

Large department stores often purchase stock from many sources, including foreign countries. It is especially important for the buyers of these goods to be familiar with local foreign customs. They should also be fluent in the required language or have translation assistance. One overconfident buyer created quite a problem for her Italian firm. Believing that she knew English fairly well, she was sent to Britain to purchase clothing. When she found some appropriate sweaters at Bourne & Hollingsworth, she attempted to request "four to five thousand pounds' worth." It became quite obvious, however, that there had been a "misunderstanding" when she returned to Italy and the delivery trucks began arriving. They were carrying the "forty-five" thousand pounds' worth (approximately U.S.$90,000) that she had actually ordered!

Often a company is initially successful overseas but later experiences major difficulties. This occurred to one company that was located in Africa. The firm began purchasing huge supplies of old, used inner tubes discarded by the U.S. Army during World War II. These inexpensive discards were easily cut to form rubber bands, and soon the company had captured the entire local rubber band market. After making over $1 million on the venture, the owners felt extremely clever and successful until someone pointed out that the supply of old inner tubes had dried up. The war was over, the army had left, and the newer tires of the few vehicles still in use were tubeless. Awash with money and confidence, the managers decided to "go big league" and buy modern equipment. The machinery and supplies, of course, were expensive and quite difficult to maintain. The company, unskilled in the new process, and failing to realize how different the new system would be, was unable to produce rubber bands at affordable prices. The strategy failed, and all of the former profits were lost.

Supply difficulties have hindered a number of companies. As was mentioned in the second chapter, one U.S. pineapple firm was unable to transport its fruit down the river to its processing plant because it had failed to analyze the typical river conditions. Similarly, the Soviet Union built a large, expensive steel mill for India only to discover that the mill had been located in an area without adequate transportation facilities. The steel mill, intended as a showplace for Soviet propaganda purposes, became an embarrassment instead.

Another firm developed problems when it tried to buy steel plates from Japanese manufacturers. At the root of this blunder was the company's failure to understand the Japanese tendency to answer "yes." By inviting all of the Japanese plate producers to bid, the company felt that it would attain the lowest price. The low bidder offered to sell at such an appealing price that the firm decided to order all of the needed galvanized steel plates from that particular Japanese company. The Japanese firm was first contacted, however, to assure product availability, since the quantity required was so large. "Yes" the company responded; it would fulfill the large order. The U.S. corporation confidently awaited the shipment. Eventually a small, partial shipment arrived containing plates that had obviously been hand dipped. Since, during the normal production process, machines do all of the dipping, the U.S. firm became suspicious. Upon visiting the Japanese plant, its suspicions were confirmed. The plant was quite small and simply could not supply the necessary quantities. Although the Japanese managers knew this would be the case, they did not want to lose face by admitting that their company was so small. They had simply hoped that all would work out.

COMPLEX PROBLEMS

Although some of the strategic errors committed by multinational corporations are fairly easy to understand, others are complex and involve several components. Simmons, Ford, Raytheon, and General Electric have all experienced complex problems within their foreign operations.

The Simmons Company, a marketer of quality beds, might never have taken the plunge to expand to Japan if it had known the magnitude of the problems it would encounter. With numerous successful overseas ventures under its belt and confident of its product, the Simmons Company set out in the early 1960s to manufacture mattresses in Japan. Four years later, the company was still experiencing substantial losses in Japan. Several complex problems plagued its operation. Although aware of many of the difficulties surrounding the Japanese market, the company had underestimated the degree of complexity present in the Japanese environment.

Simmons had realized that it would face several obstacles. Not only did most Japanese still sleep on futons (a type of floor mat), but the company also recognized that the complex and unusual Japanese distribution system could be quite confusing. The fact that an oligopolistic group of local manufacturers vied for control of the limited market only complicated matters further.

However, because the firm strongly believed in its product and know-how, Simmons Tokyo (later, Simmons Japan) was organized in October 1964. Entry into the market had been timed to coincide with the Tokyo Olympic Games when the demand for beds would sharply rise over a short period of time. Early production progressed smoothly, but problems developed later.

Among the difficulties the company encountered was its choice of a sales force. Because of the existence of social class differences and subtle language styles, the salespeople were most effective if they and the client were of the same class. Therefore, the initial eight-man sales force had to be rigorously screened. Even after an appropriate personnel choice, a problem ensued. None of the salesmen had ever slept on a bed! How could they be expected to sincerely endorse Simmons's product?

Simmons also learned that it had priced its beds by as much as $60 above domestic prices. Even the distribution system proved baffling-everyday conduct and favors were often intertwined. A customer might engage in business with a supplier to whom he owed a favor regardless of the price difference, and this behavior produced a tangled distribution network with complex relationships. Since no Japanese wished to lose face, Simmons also discovered that trying to operate outside of this established system was quite difficult.

And finally, Simmons made an unfortunate decision regarding advertising media. The company chose print media and concentrated its distribution in the Tokyo area instead of using television, the most effective and penetrating advertising medium in Japan.

Another U.S. firm encountered other types of problems in its efforts to "go international." A foreign firm interested in creating a joint venture in Asia approached an electronics firm. Because the product potential appeared so high, the company wished to establish the venture fully before any competition could be enticed into the market. So an agreement was quickly arranged. In its haste, however, the U.S. firm failed to investigate completely such important marketing factors as competitive environment, market maturity, distribution requirements, marketing costs, penetration strategy, promotional programs, etc. Also, the U.S. company did not carefully evaluate its partner's experience, general know-how, and operational procedures. As a result, problems that should have been considered and resolved during the initial planning stages of the venture were still cropping up years later.

Ford Motor Company has established a very successful record in international business. In fact, it has been the most successful U.S. automotive company to engage in business outside of North America. Even Ford, however, has encountered its share of troubles. In 1973, for instance, after experiencing great success in the Philippines with the Fiera, Ford introduced the vehicle in Thailand. It sold poorly, however. Ford had overestimated its reputation and had incorrectly assumed that Thai consumers would prefer a Ford to other cars. The company had also assumed that the Fiera's low price would attract customers, but it was not prepared to offer the credit terms extended by its competitors. Furthermore, the Fiera frequently experienced breakdowns because vehicles in Thailand were usually loaded two or three times beyond normally designed capacities. By the time a sturdier model was introduced, the Fiera had already earned a reputation for being unreliable.

When Raytheon's local partner withdrew from its Sicilian joint venture due to declining profits, Raytheon was unable to find a replacement partner for its television tube-producing plant. The plant needed modernization, but the needed modifications required substantial capital investment. Thus, Raytheon tried to continue selling out-of-date tubes. Not only were the tubes outdated, but the market was saturated. The company failed to develop any export markets even though sales dropped significantly in Italy. Losses continued to mount, so the firm fired one-quarter of its employees. The dismissal of Sicilian employees without prior governmental approval and without major payments to those involved, however, was an extremely unacceptable business practice. The result: the local governmental officials took control of the plant, and Raytheon lost over $25 million.

In a different part of Europe, another large U.S. corporation came very close to committing a similar error. To realize substantial cost savings, the company planned a massive cost reduction program that involved the layoff of a significant number of employees. It was fortunate for the company that prior to the initiation of the program it learned that layoffs based on these grounds were highly unacceptable in the host country. Since much of the firm's business was with agencies of the host government, this action surely would have evoked great unhappiness and the government agencies would have been pressured to place their orders with other suppliers. Sales undoubtedly would have dropped, but even more damaging and far-reaching would have been the company's loss of reputation. Indeed the blunder was avoided, but the company had needlessly allocated time and money to develop a plan that never could have worked. Much waste could have been eliminated had the corporation been aware of this local business practice.

General Electric also experienced overseas troubles. The company was initially so optimistic and enthusiastic about some of its foreign ventures that its original projections and timetables were unrealistic and consequently led to disappointment. Because of these early letdowns, management tended to be wary of complete ownership or majority interest in its overseas operations. And in some South American projects the company tried too long to maintain the distribution channels it had developed over the years. By doing so, it became particularly vulnerable to the rise of innovative competition during a period of rapidly changing environments and thus failed to aggressively seek out and adopt new methods of distribution.

ADDITIONAL MISTAKES

Embarrassing and expensive slip-ups can result when firms cut back. During strategic moves, such as downsizing, some of the employees who remain may not have received proper training in order to handle international transactions appropriately. Such was the case for the Carlson Travel Network when one client, a manufacturing executive, was traveling from Japan to Taiwan. Upon arrival in Taiwan the executive arrived without the proper visa. Through the fault of the employee at the travel network, the executive spent 18 hours on a return trip to his home office, unable to finish his business trip. The expense to the network was a second ticket, upgraded to first class, and incidental expenses of the first trip.

Sometimes a company finds that its golden touch is not golden everywhere. The Tengelmann group of West Germany discovered this when it bought a U.S. supermarket chain, the A&P. The firm's normal strategy of offering a limited line of low-cost, store brand groceries worked well for Tengelmann in Europe. However, its attempts to use this same strategy in the United States failed and resulted in a $75 million loss over a two-year period. As the chairman, James Wood, reported, "The mistake we foreigners often make is to judge the U.S. on the basis of what we know about Europe. Americans want a fuller range of products from a supermarket than people on the other side of the water."

Foreign firms often get tripped up in the United States because they fail to develop clear strategies unique to their U.S. operations. Extensions of home strategies often are inappropriate, but foreign-owned firms seem determined to learn this the hard way. The purchase of the A.B. Dick Company by General Electric of Britain is a case in point. Because the British firm did well in the United Kingdom advertising and selling its "modern" office products, it promoted this theme when marketing A.B. Dick products in the United States. The problem? Eighty percent of the A.B. Dick products were not modern, and so the company's strategy was ineffective.

Europeans, of course, are not the only ones who sometimes assume that what works at home will also work abroad. A highly successful U.S. supermarket chain experienced difficulties in its overseas venture. The U.S. company and a renowned Japanese company, Sumitomo Shoji Kaisha, formed a supermarket joint venture in Japan. Small Japanese retailers, however, strongly objected to the bond created by these two giants, so Sumitomo Shoji helped set up a dummy company and permitted the U.S. firm to manage it. The U.S. company employed the techniques proven successful in U.S. supermarket management but could not produce profitable financial statements in Japan. After studying the Japanese distribution system, the Japanese traditional ways of doing business, and the characteristics of the Japanese customers, the U.S. management decided that it was necessary to convert the operations to a "Japanese mode." The Japanese customers found the new system acceptable, and the venture began to thrive.

Parker Pen decided to streamline its product line and "globalize" its operations. Parker reduced its global product line from 500 styles in about 150 countries to 100 pen styles and decided to use a single international campaign. The concept sounded fine and certainly permitted real production and marketing savings, but it created serious morale problems for Parker's managers. Overseas managers resented the U.S. mandated plan. Profits sank, management rebelled, and the strategy was eventually discontinued. Parker Pen now lets local managers determine promotional plans.

In another case, a U.S. consumer products firm developed a plan to create a world structure of subsidiaries through the acquisition of similar companies located in both developed and developing countries. Through these subsidiaries, it hoped to form a worldwide market for its products. Therefore, small and medium-sized companies in Europe, Latin America, and Japan were purchased within a three-year period. Special efforts were made to add the U.S. products to the existing lines of the acquired companies, since the consumer goods available through these foreign companies were different from those in the parent's line.

However, the U.S. company ran into several problems using this strategy. Not only had it failed to consider the tastes of its potential customers, in most cases the U.S. products did not even meet foreign requirements. Furthermore, the marketing, advertising, and promotional techniques that had produced such a long record of company success in the United States were not appropriate for the foreign environments. Because of the lack of supermarkets and retail chain outlets, lower stand-ards of living, limited television advertising exposure, and lower levels of literacy, the U.S. techniques proved ineffective in these new markets.

Many cases can be cited to illustrate the importance of conducting a thorough preliminary market study. Consider, for example, the U.S. company that discovered its failure to understand its Japanese partner's distribution network greatly hindered the venture's success. Hoping to achieve optimum market penetration for its product, that was relatively new to the Japanese, the U.S. firm selected the best distribution networks of its Japanese partner and set up a single-level system of wholesalers. Even though the product sold well through the selected distribution channels, market penetration fell short of expectation because the product did not receive the needed national coverage. The original decision to use the partner's best distribution networks appeared wise, but the firm failed to fully realize how numerous and diffuse the Japanese retail outlet networks can be and overestimated the effectiveness of its planned network.

Distribution problems do not only occur within the Japanese system. Having received encouraging results from a preliminary market study, a major U.S. manufacturer of mixed feed for poultry decided to establish a market in Spain. Although local business people advised the firm against forming a subsidiary that was wholly owned, the company went ahead with its plans.

A factory was built, technical staff was brought in, and operations were set up. However, once production began, the firm discovered that it could not sell its products. Why? The Spanish poultry growers and feed producers comprised a closely knit group, and new-comers were not welcome. To overcome this obstacle, the firm bought a series of chicken farms. To its dismay, the company discovered that no one would buy its chickens either! Had the company heeded the local advice and understood the local business practices, these difficulties could have been avoided.

Many other companies have suffered from similar pitfalls. For instance, one U.S. cosmetics manufacturer experienced difficulties when it tried to sell its products in France solely through a chain store. By utilizing this method, the firm felt it could achieve maximum market exposure while still holding down marketing and distribution costs. In some countries, this system might have worked. In France, however, "perfumers" (small local retailers specializing in cosmetics) are traditionally con-sidered the opinion makers, and most manufacturers give exclusive franchise to two or three local perfumers. Word-of-mouth promotion is vital, and the public relies heavily on the opinions of these perfumers. When it bypassed them, the U.S. company angered the perfumers to the point that they discredited the U.S. product and damaged the manufacturer's reputation in France.

A clear, consistent strategy is required if a company is to succeed in the international marketplace. Asuag A6, a Swiss watchmaker, realized this too late. The firm needed to acquire technology and decided to do so by purchasing a dozen different U.S. firms. Although some of the companies proved useful to the watchmaker, they did not seem to fit together well. Many were not even compatible with others in the acquisition package. Trying to work them together only made matters worse. All 12 were eventually sold-at a loss of over $25 million.

Fujitec, a Japanese elevator manufacturer, came to the United States with high aspirations-too high, as it turned out. Rather than concentrate on one geographical area, the firm simultaneously sought out large projects all over the country. However, it apparently failed to recognize the regional preferences of U.S. consumers and tried to approach the market as if none existed. As a con-sequence, the company did not consider important cultural subtleties and lost money. Japan may be a fairly homogeneous market, but the U.S. market is not. Few companies have the ability to enter all regions at the same time. Most find that they need business experience in one or two regions of the United States before they can attempt a national campaign.

Companies have experienced many difficulties as a result of poor strategy decisions. As an illustration, consider the aerospace division of Ling-Temco-Vought (LTV), which tried to create a mechanical substitute for the water buffalo. Because the company's research and development facilities were located in the United States, the firm developed the machine there. Unfortunately this was not a wise decision. The machines produced by the company were eventually exposed to the unique Asian weather conditions and experienced numerous problems.

An unfortunate decision made by Gillette nearly cost the company the razor blade market. The firm had developed a superior stainless steel blade, but because the new blade was so outstanding and would require fewer replacements, the company preferred not to market it. So Gillette sold the technology to a British garden tool manufacturer, Wilkinson. Because Gillette had assumed that Wilkinson would only use the new technology in the production of its garden tools, it failed to restrict Wilkinson from competing in the razor blade market. However, Wilkinson Sword blades were promptly introduced and sold as fast as they could be produced. Gillette's superior marketing skills and experience in the razor blade market enabled it to eventually recover, but the challenge was unwelcome and expensive.

SUMMARY

False assumptions frequently cause expensive blunders. One of the most common assumptions is that conditions that exist at home also exist abroad. Another frequently assumed idea is that what works well at home will also work well overseas. It should be abundantly clear that these are two of the most dangerous assumptions that can be made by managers. Few things are the same everywhere, and almost no strategy works well everywhere.

Strategic blunders are generally not as entertaining to read about as some of the other international business mistakes, but they are usually more critical to the firm and thus more important to avoid. Although some mistakes can be quickly corrected, logistical problems can be very difficult to overcome. A few strategic blunders have even resulted in millions of lost dollars. There are no simple short cuts to avoid strategic errors. The development of a strategy requires care and attention to detail.

18

Other Areas of International Business Problems

The previous chapters have contained numerous examples of blunders made in the areas of production, translation, name choices, marketing, management, and strategy. These types of blunders are frequently committed and often quite visible. Once made, these mistakes can be rather difficult to conceal. Blunders occurring in the other areas of business, such as law, finance, and market research, are either less frequently committed or easier to hide. They certainly are not reported as often, but they can be just as costly or critical to the success of the business venture.

LEGAL

The legal details involved in any transaction certainly can seem confusing and boring. However, a lack of awareness or understanding of these technicalities can prove to be disastrous, as illustrated in the plight of a U.S. person transacting business in Saudi Arabia. A Californian is reported to have found himself trapped in Saudi Arabia as a result of a dispute he was having with his Saudi partner. The Saudi, an associate in a janitorial supplies venture, had sponsored his Californian partner's entry into Saudi Arabia, but refused to sponsor the man's departure unless he was paid the $100,000 he claimed was due him. Under Saudi law, a foreigner can not leave the country without the endorsement of the person who sponsored his entry! The American settled by paying $55,000. "It was the only way I could get out," he said. The problem might have been avoided if he had insisted in advance on a written agreement with the Saudi.

A U.S. firm discovered the value of using clear and concise contractual language when one of its West African contract clauses cost the company about $100,000. The troublesome clause read, "The monies paid by the Ministry to the Consultant shall constitute full payment to the Consultant including all local income taxes on the Consultant." The firm understood this to mean that payments were tax-free. The government ruled otherwise. And since another clause in the contract said that disagreements were to be settled by the local government, the firm lost.

One large firm went to China with a 50-plus page legal document to license pollution control technology. The Chinese laughed at them, tossed it out, and the proposed deal would have fallen through, but because good personal relations had been established, they allowed the firm to start over. A 10-page document was then developed and accepted.

A big firm in China wanted a contract and agreed to two versions: one in English and the other in Chinese. "Both versions shall have equal force." This later led to many problems and costly debates.

A Columbus, Ohio company committed a "minor" error in filling out a form in Brazil. Unfortunately, this mistake resulted in the firm being unable to withdraw $200,000 in profits it eventually earned there. What was the "minor" error? Someone had failed to place a check in a box on the document that would have allowed the company to withdraw profits at a reasonable rate.

AT&T experienced troubles in Thailand in 1989 trying to obtain a major phone equipment contract. After a great deal of effort, AT&T submitted a proposal but it was promptly rejected. Apparently, Thailand had specified that a 10-year warranty was required, but the AT&T lawyers working out of the United States proposed a five-year warranty. The company's employees and contacts in Thailand understood the requirement, but the contract had been drawn up by lawyers thousands of miles away. In fact, AT&T has had such relatively little on-the-scene overseas experience that as late as 1989, when an emergency meeting was called in Italy, several of its U.S.-based "international" managers had to reveal that they did not even own a passport.

Most countries have now established regulations dealing with advertising. As many companies can avow, failure to follow these guidelines almost always results in a legal dispute. Singapore's airline can attest to this. The company placed advertisements in local Norwegian magazines featuring a photo of a girl's face on a pillow. The message essentially said "Bring me a pillow and brandy for a tired father." The Norwegians were upset with the ad, and eventually the promotion was ruled misleading and sexually discriminating.

Similarly, the use of a commercial featuring a bikini-clad woman created difficulties for Goodyear. The advertisement was apparently shown in several countries where the skimpy attire was not locally permitted. The company was forced to alter the commercial and so replaced the young beauty with fully dressed people having a good time. The message, "Get where the fun is," remained unchanged, but the "new" commercial was considered more acceptable and effective.

Goodyear Tire also experienced legal problems with an advertisement it tried to export to Germany. The ad, successfully used in the United States, highlighted the strength of Goodyear's tire cord by showing that it could break a steel chain. Goodyear discovered, however, that in Germany it was illegal to imply that another product was inferior. Because Goodyear's promotion was interpreted to be disparaging to the German steel chain manufacturers, the government halted the promotional campaign.

Toyota learned that they need to be aware of the claims they make with an ad, especially when adapting to the Chinese culture. The Chinese are well known for their high standards for truth in advertising. This applies to foreign companies who enter the Chinese market. The case of Toyota's advertising campaign is based on an old Chinese proverb that read, "When you get to the foot of the mountain, a road will appear." The Toyota ad read, "Wherever there is a road, there is a Toyota." It was one year after all the slogans appeared on billboards, on television, and in newspapers when the Chinese authorities claimed that Toyota was guilty of false advertising. The reasons given by the Chinese officials included that "China has roads but there are not necessarily Toyotas on them. The roads in other countries do not necessarily have them either." As a result, Toyota learned the difference between standards in a strict socialist advertising society verses a more lax capitalistic society.

Claridge cigarettes advertised its product in Australia using a campaign that featured Robin Hood and Friar Tuck. Australians, believing that their children might find the ad appealing, felt that the orientation was inappropriate and they forced Claridge to alter its advertisements.

Ford experienced a similar problem with one of its ads distributed in Norway. The advertisement featured children talking to a car salesman, with the caption "Is it true that there is a waiting period for Fords?" Local groups complained that it was improper to use the children in the promotion because they were not directly connected to the product. While such use could easily be considered harmless and enjoyable by many, a firm must consider potential legal expenses should it find itself defending its ads.

A novel twist occurred in France, where Philip Morris and the R.J. Reynolds Tobacco Company were enjoying much financial success. The companies, in fact, were so successful that a local company, SEITA, tried to sell its cigarettes as if they, too, were foreign imports. Their packages bore the name "News" and were printed totally in English. Not even the well-known French name of the parent company was listed. French law, however, prohibited this omission, and so, in this case, it was the local company that experienced the legal difficulties in its effort to thwart foreign competition.

The complexities of foreign investment laws have also been frequent sources of problems. The 3M Company, for example, submitted an application to the Japanese government to establish a joint venture with 15 firms of the Sumitomo industrial group. The company's failure to consider all of the applicable Japanese investment laws delayed the governmental approval required. By the time the approval was obtained-four years later- domestic manufacturers such as Sony and Tokyo Denki Kagaka had succeeded in streamlining the production of magnetic tape products and, unfortunately, Sumitomo-3M's share of the market was held to a very small percentage of the total Japanese market.

False assumptions regarding the level of host government support have led to many problems. Massey-Ferguson, for example, believed it had won Turkish support to establish a tractor-producing plant. The company heavily relied on that support to help with sales. Unfortunately, the support never materialized and the venture eventually died.

Sometimes companies win governmental support when perhaps they should not. It is, for example, possible at times to gain legal approval to do (or not do) things which should not (or should) be done. This legal support offers a business protection but it can prove to be temporary or controversial. Several firms have found all too suddenly that, as times change, the definition of what is acceptable can change.

Consider a company in Spain that obtained permission from the Spanish government to use badly outdated technology which polluted the atmosphere. A sudden change in weather created a dangerous health situation, however. Several people died, the local population rioted, the government withdrew its approval, and the company paid the price for hiding behind the legal protection of the government.

Several U.S. firms have encountered legal problems either at home or abroad because they were affiliated in some way with overseas business operations which "traded with the enemy." U.S. law sometimes forbids U.S. firms to sell certain products to certain countries. Special problems can arise when overseas joint ventures or even licensed firms start trading with these outlawed countries. If the U.S. parent or partner company does not restrict business activity, the U.S. government takes legal action. But, if the U.S. parent or partner discontinues the business overseas, the host government may take legal action of its own. Just because the U.S. government restricts business activities in a country does not mean that all countries curtail business operations there. This can be an awkward, Catch 22-type situation-one that is best avoided by anticipating the potential problem and clarifying everything before formalizing any joint venture or signing any agreement.

For example, Fruehauf, a U.S. truck manufacturer, sold truck bodies to a French firm through its French subsidiary. The French firm then finished the trucks and sold them to the People's Republic of China. The U.S. government took action against Fruehauf for selling trucks to China (an outlawed destination at the time). Consequently, this U.S. behavior caused the French government to seize control of Fruehauf's French subsidiary.

France believed that Fruehauf had to honor its contracts-even if that meant selling parts which eventually ended up in China (an acceptable destination to the French). Not only did Fruehauf lose money, but the company became the unwanted center of a highly charged public debate in France concerning the role of the United States and its firms in France. At that point, it was clearly a no-win situation that took years to overcome.

It is absolutely critical to remember that what is legal in one country may not be legal in another. This important lesson applies to many aspects of business, including patent protection of industrial property rights. Many firms have falsely assumed that more protection existed in a foreign country than proved to be the case. If companies are not careful, highly valued trade secrets can be lost, with no legal recourse.

Companies may experience troubles by being unaware of a country's regulations and preferences concerning products and packages. The wording on a package or label may create difficulties. Countries expect foreign marketers to adhere to rules, and their failure to do so may prove costly. Coca-Cola, for instance, aroused the anger of the Italians when it printed the mandatory list of ingredients on its bottle cap. Local courts ruled that the cap was easily tossed away and, therefore, did not serve as an acceptable location for this list. Coca-Cola, of course, quickly modified its package and listed the ingredients on the bottles themselves, but the incident had its costs.

Many companies have encountered legal problems trying to sell various diet foods because, in several countries, a product name containing the word "diet" can be sold only in pharmacies. Thus, these lighter-in-calories products can now be found on store shelves in some countries with "Lite" used in their names.

In Australia, the manufacturer of "Aim" toothpaste was taken to court by one of its competitors because of an Australian law that prohibits the sale of competitive products in similar packages. A very strict interpretation and enforcement of this law forced Unilever to change its Aim package even though it had spent $5 million on Aim's promotion. The error was costly, but it was correctable with the appropriate alterations.

FINANCE

Small overseas firms are sometimes so impressed with the size and growth of U.S. markets that they forget about the possible risk of a U.S. economic downturn. The U.S. economy may be comparatively wealthy to many people, but it still experiences recessions and these need to be taken into consideration by the investing firms. Many foreign-owned firms in the United States have reportedly sunk because they failed to plan for worst case scenarios.

Since most foreign investors in the United States do not have their stock listed on U.S. markets, they seldom make an acquisition through stock swaps. This means that they are usually forced to borrow money. If the timing is poor or if they do not prepare for market downturns, they can be squeezed unexpectedly. For example, Agache-Willot (French) purchased Korvettes but was not prepared to invest another $28 million when a subsequent recession was experienced. By the time the firm finally agreed to infuse the additional needed capital, it was really too late. Korvettes went bankrupt a year later. U.S. firms have also fallen into the temptation of having a very high debt to equity ratio. This highly leveraged position works well when times are good, but it is risky and can lead to disasters in bad times. The USM subsidiary in Portugal reportedly became unnecessarily leveraged and then needed the parent company's help to insure its survival. Many others have found themselves in this same situation. (It might be noted that in England the U.S. term "highly leveraged" is nonsensical. Rather, they use the phrase "highly geared." These different wordings have confused people on both sides of the Atlantic!) A U.S. auto manufacturer in Europe encountered problems of a different nature. The company reportedly failed to consider long-run profit margins. As a result, its Spanish division began experiencing a profit squeeze. The managers tried to cut costs by changing labor workloads, sales commission, and even production schedules-all to no avail. In fact, labor resisted and costs actually increased.

Misinterpretations can sometimes cause major financial losses. One company, for example, decided to spend $2 million for a Brazilian plant it seems was not needed. The company's decision to invest the money was based upon an incorrect interpretation of data. The reported sales figures (stated in Brazilian cruzeiros) appeared very promising, but they had not been adjusted for high inflation. Only the number of cruzeiros had grown, not the number of products sold. It is often more prudent to evaluate sales levels employing physical measures (such as weight, volume, number of units, etc.) rather than financial ones. Then inflation and currency value fluctuations are less likely to cause such errors.

MARKET RESEARCH

One of the worst errors a company can make is failing to determine if a market exists for its products or services prior to market entry. Unfortunately, many firms have fallen prey to this mistake and blindly assumed that their products would be desired. At times, they have been "right" (perhaps "lucky" might be the more appropriate word). Other times, however, they have not been so fortunate. Often the market simply was not as promising as anticipated. Several firms have discovered only after initial entry attempts that no market ever existed. Sound and thorough market research would have revealed these and other avoidable problems companies have encountered in international business.

INSUFFICIENT MARKET

Companies exporting food products seem to have been especially prone to experiencing difficulty in foreign markets. A U.S. manufacturer of cornflakes, for example, tried to introduce its product in Japan, but the attempt failed miserably. Since the Japanese were not interested in the general concept of breakfast cereals, how could the manufacturer expect them to purchase cornflakes?

A well-known U.S. soft drink company predicted the existence of a large Indonesian market for its product, but the prediction was based on a faulty market research study. The study was conducted in large Indonesian cities and the results were projected to be representative of the entire population. Unfortunately, major differences existed between rural and urban areas of Indonesia. In this case, the cities housed many foreign visitors who purchased the soft drink during the study. When the company concluded that a major market existed, it set up large bottling and distribution facilities but realized only limited sales to city tourists. In conducting market research tests, it is important to determine who is purchasing the product and how representative they are of the entire population.

After learning that ketchup was not available in Japan, a U.S. company is reported to have shipped the Japanese a large quantity of its popular brand-name ketchup. Unfortunately, the firm did not first determine why ketchup was not already marketed in Japan. The large, affluent Japanese market was so tempting that the company feared that any delay would permit its competition to spot the "opportunity" and capture the market. A market test would have revealed the reason behind the lack of availability of ketchup: soy sauce was the preferred condiment there. The company involved, however, was able to purchase Japanese soy sauce for profitable resale in the United States (a possible variation of the old saying, "if you can't beat them, join them"). Kentucky Fried Chicken reportedly found itself in a similar situation when it attempted to enter the Brazilian market. Hoping to eventually open 100 stores, the company began operations in São Paulo. Sales, though, were unexpectedly low. Why? The firm had not thoroughly researched the possible competition. A local variety of low-priced charcoal broiled chicken was available on almost every corner of the city. Because the locals considered this chicken tastier than the Colonel's recipe, Kentucky Fried Chicken hastily revised its plans and began offering hamburgers, Mexican tacos and enchiladas. The company's troubles were not over, however, for these food products were practically unknown in Brazil and met with little customer interest.

Unilever was forced to temporarily withdraw from one of its foreign markets when it learned the hard way that the French were not interested in frozen foods. Happily, the company was able to re-enter the market at a later date offering products more appealing to the French.

CPC International met some resistance when it first tried to sell its dry Knorr soups in the United States. The company had test-marketed the product by serving passersby a small portion of its already prepared warm soup. After the taste test, the individuals were questioned about buying the product. The research revealed U.S. interest, but sales were very low once the packages were placed on grocery store shelves. Further investigation uncovered that the market tests had not taken into account the U.S. tendency to avoid dry soups. During the testing, those individuals interviewed were unaware that they were tasting dried soup. Finding the taste quite acceptable, the interviewees indicated they would be willing to buy the product. Had they known that the soup was sold in a dry form and that the preparation required 15-20 minutes of occasional stirring, they would have shown less interest in the product. In this particular case, the soup's method of preparation was extremely important to the consumer, and the company's failure to test for this unique product difference resulted in a sluggish market.

Clever marketers often analyze product differences and try to use them to the company's advantage. Based on a research study conducted in the United States, one U.S. firm introduced a new cake mix in England. Believing that the housewife would enjoy feeling as if she were participating in the preparation of the cake mix, the U.S. marketers devised the scheme to "add an egg." Thinking they had developed a universal approach, they tried to sell the mix in England. The mix failed, though; the English simply do not like fancy U.S. cakes. They prefer tough and spongy cakes suitable for accom-panying their afternoon tea.

Numerous companies have also experienced diffi-culties when trying to market certain "tasty" products. Tastes desirable to some are often unacceptable to others. Occasionally, a flavor can be successfully modified, but many times it is just totally inappropriate. Warner encountered difficulties when it tried to sell a cinnamon-flavored "Freshen-up" gum in Chile. Because the gum's taste was unacceptable there, the product fared poorly in the marketplace. Coca-Cola also tried to market a product in Chile with little success. When the company attempted to introduce a new grape-flavored drink, it soon discovered that the Chileans were not interested. Apparently, the Chileans prefer wine as their grape drink. These examples exemplify why market research can be so important.

Chase & Sanborn met resistance when it tried to introduce its instant coffee in France. In the French home, the consumption of coffee plays a more significant role than in the English home. Since the preparation of "real" coffee is a touchstone in the life of the French housewife, she will generally reject instant coffee because of its casual characteristics.

A poorly located sales outlet can also contribute to an insufficient market. A classic example involves one of the oldest U.S. fast food companies. This firm, having gained a great deal of domestic experience, decided to open overseas outlets. The management employed sophisticated techniques, and the possible location sites were narrowed down to three addresses in Hamburg, Germany. Careful "traffic counts" were undertaken to determine the best location, and the most frequently passed site was then purchased. A store was built, but sales were surprisingly slow. Was the traffic count in error? No! In this case, while it was true that great numbers of people were passing by the location, hamburgers were not foremost on their minds-they went by the hamburger site only because a major bordello was located next door!

McDonald's also chose an inappropriate location when it first expanded into Europe. The company opened an outlet in a suburb of

Amsterdam but soon learned that to attract adequate local traffic, the store should have been downtown. Once the company moved into town, sales immediately improved.

A well-known franchised health club based in New York quickly discovered that what sells in the United States may not sell overseas. Building on its previous success, the firm decided to open a club in Singapore but soon learned that the club did not appeal to the local population. The small expatriate community was delighted with the club, but its numbers were too small to make the club a profitable venture.

Another company tried to market aerosol spray furniture polish in one of the less developed countries. Analysis of the local average income levels suggested that the local population could afford the product. This type of data, though, can be misleading when most of the wealth is concentrated and owned by a few. Therefore, average income levels can erroneously indicate that many people in a population can afford a product. In this particular case, only the few individuals who enjoyed the highest incomes could afford the "luxury" of an aerosol spray furniture polish. Even they, however, were not very interested in the product; they did not believe that such labor saving devices were needed for their servants.

Sometimes the relevant factor determining a product's success involves the technological advancement of the potential customer. A sophisticated product may elicit interest during market testing, but it may fail in the marketplace because it receives a predictably erroneous reputation of undependability. Companies have discovered this fact all too frequently. For example, one company manufactured a product far superior to any similar product being used in a particular African nation. Since market tests indicated strong consumer interest, the firm introduced the product.

Shortly thereafter, word spread among the locals that the product was not reliable. This was not true, however. The product broke because the new owners did not understand its maintenance requirements. They refused to oil it even though they were instructed to do so. Because this type of maintenance was atypical of their lifestyle, they soon returned to their earlier, more primitive tools that required no special care. In effect, no market existed for such advanced products.

In some cases, it becomes necessary for a firm to develop a totally new product, one that is completely stripped of frills or complex features. General Motors successfully used this process during the development of its Basic Transportation Vehicle. Singer too profited from its introduction of a basic hand-powered sewing machine.

Although the United States consists of 50 states, the country is usually considered one market. Naturally, subtle cultural differences exist among the states. Neighboring districts in other parts of the world, however, often represent vastly different cultures even though they may be as geographically close as neighboring states. This concept is hard for many U.S. managers to fully understand.

The Sunbeam company, for example, assumed that since Germans consumed substantial amounts of toast, the Italians would also. To the company's misfortune, it soon discovered that this did not prove to be the case. The firm encountered additional problems in Italy when it tried to introduce a ladies' electric shaver. Although sales had been fairly strong in some parts of Europe, they remained poor in Italy. Apparently Italian men preferred women with unshaved legs.

People speaking similar languages do not necessar-ily represent totally similar cultures, either. One U.S. company, assuming that a similar language must indicate similar tastes, tried to sell a U.S. after-shave lotion in England. An expensive advertising campaign was launched but failed. Why? The average British male saw no functional value in the use of after-shave lotion and even believed the use of scents to be effeminate.

Numerous governments have tried to send aid to developing countries. Sometimes, however, their well-intended gifts have been of little use. At one time, for example, great quantities of milk powder were distributed in South America. Claiming that the milk made them ill, the people used it instead to whitewash their houses. Research revealed that the local people were indeed correct. North Americans and Europeans retain an enzyme necessary for the breakdown of milk throughout their lives. Many South Americans, on the other hand, retain the enzyme only while of nursing age. Therefore, the older children and adults were unable to digest the milk. No demand for this product existed even though it was free!

INADEQUATE FEASIBILITY STUDIES

It should now be obvious that a firm needs to conduct research to determine if an adequate market for its products exists. This research must be performed carefully since an inadequate feasibility study may prove more disastrous for the company than none at all.

For instance, one company that chose to cut costs and save time opted to use a feasibility study that a competitor had conducted earlier. At the time the study was originally undertaken, the investment was regarded favorably by the Asian government and the opportunity seemed encouraging. However, the political atmosphere changed during the time that had elapsed. As a result, the firm built its plant but immediately experienced difficulties. The company's use of an outdated feasibility study caused it to overestimate positive results and underestimate probable problems.

Many firms have created headaches for themselves by acting before sufficient data had been gathered. Consider, for example, a well-known U.S. manufacturer of nondurable consumer goods that formed a partnership with a local Japanese company. The Japanese firm supplied encouraging data so, after a one-week investigation by the assistant to the president, the U.S. manufacturer quickly agreed to the arrangement. Not too surprisingly, the venture fell short of expectations. Even with a complete change of top management, the investment stagnated. The company's hasty entry decision had been based upon an inadequate market analysis and the belief that the market would welcome the entry of prestigious U.S. brands. The firm had assumed that it could easily win the confidence of the marketplace and take over a sizable percentage of it.

After a research team verified the existence of an adequate market, one Swiss pharmaceutical firm built an $8 million manufacturing plant in Southeast Asia. The researchers, though, had overlooked an extremely important feature of the market-the local black market. Because of this added competition, the firm experienced lower earnings than expected and found itself with excess production capacity.

Sometimes what appears to be a thorough feasibility study simply is not. After conducting what was believed to be an intensive study, one firm discovered that a number of factors that should have been considered prior to its entrance abroad had been overlooked. Initial research confirmed the desirability of erecting an iron and steel mill, but the mill was forced to close its doors within one year. All equipment was removed and the building was stripped. Those involved in the feasibility study had correctly determined the availability of labor. They had failed, however, to report that the country under consideration was one in which private ownership was inconsistent with the policies of social reform supported by the government. Almost all manufacturing was publicly owned and operated. The laborers, many of whom had been exploited on farms, were encouraged to believe in "capitalistic exploitation." Consequently, they constantly demanded higher wages and increased benefits. Labor unrest, low output, and poor quality resulted. The feasibility study should have revealed the existence of this popular "public ownership" ideology. Since another firm had failed earlier in a similar investment for similar reasons, the investors should have been tipped off that a recurrence of the problem was likely.

As a final example, consider the experience of the Rheem company in the Italian market. The firm's initial strategy of buying raw materials from a local firm, ISI, also included selling the finished product, welded pipe, locally. The plan was put into operation, but Rheem soon learned that not only did ISI produce the same welded pipe, it also maintained insider contracts with the major buyer of the pipe-the government. Because Rheem was buying its raw material from ISI, it was unable to undercut ISI's price and, as a foreign-owned firm, it was not able to secure the Italian government contracts. Unfortunately, it had not developed any export plans. Thorough research should have uncovered these problems and thus Rheem would have known to consider alternative plans.

As evidenced, a firm's reliance on outdated or incomplete feasibility studies can cause it to blunder. Improperly conducted studies can also create difficulties. This is easily illustrated by a classic story that involves the market research conducted some years ago by Reader's Digest. The researchers concluded from their findings that the Germans and the French consumed more spaghetti than Italians. Further analysis revealed that this false finding surfaced as a result of the questions asked. The survey questions dealt with the purchases of branded and packaged spaghetti. Many Italians, however, buy spaghetti in bulk. By qualifying the way in which the product was purchased, the researchers arrived at a false conclusion about spaghetti consumption. To conduct sound market research, one must pay strict attention to both method and content.

SUMMARY

This chapter has focused on the importance of paying attention to detail. Seemingly minor points of law can create major problems for companies. Financial strategies, market research, and feasibility studies must all be undertaken and conducted with great care. In fact, the significance of meticulous research has been stressed throughout this book.

19

Lessons Learned

As discussed in the previous chapters, international businesses can indeed encounter a variety of unexpected developments. Occasionally, some of these surprises benefit the companies involved. Unfortunately, in numerous other instances, the surprises prove to be undesirable and often costly. Many of the troubles encountered by firms in the past actually could have been avoided.

Venturing overseas can be extremely tricky. A company may employ sophisticated management techniques but still blunder if any detail is overlooked. Even failing to ask the right question can cause a blunder. Unfortunately, there are hundreds of reported cases of companies blundering overseas. These errors are indeed regrettable, but we can learn from them. There is no need to repeat the mistakes others have made.

ADAPTATION

Numerous headaches have resulted when firms have failed to correctly adapt their products or packages to local environments. Sometimes it is only the color of the package that needs to be altered to enhance a product's sales. Since color preferences and symbols vary from country to country, it is wise to seek local advice as locals are aware of such "bad" colors.

A lesser-known variable worthy of consideration is "number." Packages that prominently display a specific number increase the risk of consumer avoidance. Since many people believe in lucky and unlucky numbers, even the number of products pictured on a label can prove troublesome. Sometimes it is neither the number displayed on the package nor the color that creates a problem, but rather the picture on the label.

In many other instances the product itself requires alteration. Food, beverages, and tobacco products often need to be modified in order to accommodate the tastes of local consumers. Cigarette manufacturers learned long ago that U.S. brands sell well overseas-if the tobacco is carefully blended to suit local preferences. Products that are not modified to meet local needs, of course, face a high risk of failing in the marketplac:

Sometimes the company or product name may require modification. A domestically successful name may be inappropriate or ineffective in a foreign market. Names have created many a humorous, obscene, offensive or unexpected situation.

NATIONALISM

Many avoidable problems have occurred because managers have been insensitive to the nationalistic feelings of the natives of the host country. It is usually best for companies to maintain low profiles in overseas ventures. There is seldom any need for a firm to try to turn an overseas manufacturing plant into an exact duplicate of its home plant. Companies that have tried to do this have often met stiff resistance from both employees and local customers.

Foreign manufacturers in the United States learned this lesson long ago. Many U.S. laborers are now working for foreign-owned firms but are unaware of their company's origins. Managers should avoid any unnecessary comparisons that might reflect the home country management's belief that the host country might be inferior in some way to the home country. It is often possible- sometimes even desirable- to compare products, but it is not prudent to publicly compare governments, labor, or technology.

It may be wise to hire most, if not all, top-level managers of the foreign subsidiary from the available host country management pool. Not only will these individuals project a more local image, but also they usually understand local problems well and can often help the company avoid blunders.

If an expatriate is to be hired, extra care must be taken. Effective expatriate managers must possess special abilities and traits if they are to avoid blundering. Among the most important characteristics are:

- o An ability to get along well with people.
- o An awareness of cultural differences.
- o Open mindedness.
- o Tolerance of foreign cultures.
- o Adaptability to new cultures, ideas, and challenges.
- o An ability to adjust quickly to new conditions.
- o An interest in facts, not blind assumptions.
- o Previous business experience.
- o Previous experience with foreign cultures.
- o An ability to learn foreign languages.

PROMOTION

Many companies have encountered serious problems trying to coordinate their sales efforts. All plans should be in writing, and it is advisable to charge someone with the responsibility of central coordination. Thus, risks are lessened and money-saving opportunities may arise.

Coca-Cola, for instance, requires that all overseas marketing plans be submitted to the central office well before they are instituted. This allows the company time to examine the concepts. The firm's experience with similar plans can be reviewed and necessary changes can be made. Sometimes central company managers discover that similar plans have failed in other overseas ventures or sometimes they determine that similar plans have succeeded.

There is no need to reinvent the wheel. Coordination not only reduces the possibility of errors, it also provides a company with the opportunity to fine-tune its promotions.

Another company well known for its successful marketing campaigns is Anheuser-Busch. It uses some of the same themes in many countries (its ants ads were especially popular in China) and ties in with major sports events around the world, but only after careful evaluation of each market. As Steve Burrows, President and CEO of Anheuser-Busch International reports, most marketing initiatives are modified to fit the local markets.

Dozens of blunders have been made by firms that failed to carefully investigate the local customs and preferences of their potential customers. Since social norms vary so greatly from country to country, it is extremely difficult for any outsider to be knowledgeable of them all. As pointed out previously, local input can be vital. Many promotional errors could have been averted had this warning been heeded.

TRANSLATION

Advertising is a tricky business. More mistakes seem to have been made in advertising than in any other business task, and these errors have most often been caused by faulty translations. It is usually recommended that the translation of an advertisement stress the ad's general theme and concept rather than precisely duplicate the original slogan.

There are several methods known which can help a company avert potential translation disasters. Certainly a company may hire an exceptionally brilliant translator, but certain types of errors can still surface.

The translator may enjoy an extraordinary gift for the language or have studied in the foreign country but may be unfamiliar with many idiomatic expressions and slang. Therefore, in many cases it is wise to also hire a second translator, one familiar with the local slang and unusual idioms, to "backtranslate."

Backtranslation is one of the best techniques available to reduce translation errors. Backtranslation requires that one individual translate the message into the desired foreign language and that another party translate the foreign version "back" into the original language. Thus, a company can determine if its intended message is actually being presented.

An Australian soft drink company discovered the value of backtranslation during the planning stages of its entry into the Hong Kong market. The company had hoped to employ its successful slogan

"Baby, it's cold inside," but before using the translated version of the slogan, the firm had it translated back into English. This proved to be a wise move. The message backtranslated to "Small mosquito, on the inside it is very cold." "Small mosquito," a local colloquial expression for a small child, simply did not convey the same thing as the friendly English slang word "baby" for "woman." The intended message would have been lost had the original translated version been used.

The use of backtranslation uncovers many translation errors but can be frustrating if performed by mediocre translators. Naturally, the better the translator is, the fewer the problems encountered. The difficulty, therefore, lies in determining the ability of a potential translator. One slow and expensive method is to allow the translator a trial run. This method will expose any problems, but it then becomes necessary to determine if the errors were committed by the original translator or by the person translating back to the first language.

Firms requiring major or important translation work should thoroughly investigate any potential translator. The following points should be covered during the candidate's interview.

- Does the translator maintain or have access to a library or reference books dealing with the appropriate subject and industry?
- Does the translator understand the required technical terms? Does the translator know the foreign words for these specialized terms? If not, how are they to be learned? Does the translator have a staff or access to experts in various fields (e.g., law)?
- Will someone check the work? If so, what are the credentials of the assistant? (It is often advisable to request references and copies of material translated for other clients.)
- How recently has the translator been to the country involved? (Sometimes it is necessary to determine how current the translator's knowledge is. Because languages do change (especially slang), it is not enough to hire someone familiar with the foreign language and culture. Even a native tends to lose track of slang and idioms after being away from home for a few years.)

Once a translator has been chosen, there are several things that a company can do to facilitate the job. For instance, since it has often taken the company many months to develop the promotional materials, a translator should not be asked to translate the material hurriedly. Given adequate time, a much better translation is likely to result. A simple literal translation is not generally appropriate, so a translator may need time to be creative.

Of course, this is not to say that the translator should not be given a deadline. It is important to tell the person when the material must be finished and the timing of its expected use.

On occasion, a manager has failed to inform the translator of the season in which the ad is to run, and the translator has assumed an inappropriate time period. A company does little to enhance its image when it runs a winter advertisement in the summer. (A few companies have also blundered by promoting advertisements during ill-suited seasons when they simply forgot that the southern hemisphere has the opposite seasons of the northern hemisphere.)

Naturally, it is important for the translator to understand the type of media to be used and the general characteristics of the audience. This allows the person to determine the proper level of formality and the correct tone. A translator must be given the freedom to modify original wording. As discussed previously, literal translations can prove disastrous. Also, because the translated version of a message may require more words than the original, it is not wise to limit the translator to a particular amount of time or space. Doing so may seriously jeopardize the effectiveness of the message.

If possible, firms are advised to reduce the use of overly technical terms and to avoid industry jargon in their promotional materials. It is also advisable to limit the use of large numbers. Any number over 10,000 may be easily mistranslated. The number "billion," for example, is numerically written with nine zeroes in the United States but with 12 zeroes in Europe.

Since humor is also almost impossible to translate, it is best to avoid using jokes in advertising. What is regarded as funny by some is often not considered so by others.

Finally, a translator should be provided with as much relevant information as possible and should be informed of the message's objectives and what is essential to the theme.

By allowing the translator to examine previous company translations as well as translated slogans of competing companies, the individual can not only assure that any key phrase associated with the company is included but can avoid accidentally using any competitors' phrases.

To reduce translation needs and overcome com-munication difficulties in countries that experience high levels of illiteracy, visual methods of communication are sometimes used. Libby, for instance, has successfully promoted its products through inexpensive commercials that feature a clown enjoying Libby products. In these ads, no words are spoken.

USING ENGLISH IN NON-ENGLISH-SPEAKING COUNTRIES

Sometimes companies have found that the best solution to the translation problem is simply to not translate the material. If the locals can understand English, or if they simply do not need to comprehend the message, then it may be safer for a firm from an English-speaking country to stick with its English copy. The use of translators is always risky, because they are putting words into the company's mouth. A firm does not need them to put a foot in there also!

To reduce the problems which may occur when English is used in a non-English-speaking country:

- Keep the entire message short and simple, including words and sentences.
- Avoid jargon or slang.
- Avoid idioms.
- Avoid humor if possible.
- Use appropriate currencies and measurements.
- Cite examples if feasible.
- Repeat important points.

If a company decides to go ahead with an English message through a verbal advertisement directed to an audience whose native language is not English, the speaker should speak slowly, carefully and correctly pronounce all words, pausing between sentences.

As it is very likely that during some part of the overseas planning or management someone from the company will engage in a conversation with an individual who has some difficulty understanding English, the following guidelines should be followed:

- o Time should be allowed for questions and discussions.
- o Patience is important-permit the individual to find the words to respond.
- o Questions should be asked to determine if the message has been comprehended.
- o The individual should be complimented and reassured of his or her ability to speak English.
- o Express gratefulness that the individual is speaking English.
- o Express regret that the conversation could not have been spoken in the other person's language. (It should be noted, however, that a few polite social words spoken in the foreign language are appreciated and highly recommended.)

Ideally, company literature and material should be provided prior to the conversation. This allows the other individual a chance to prepare and should greatly increase the person's comprehension. After the discussion, the person should be sent a summary of the conversation. This also will increase the likelihood that the conversation was correctly understood.

During World War II, the phrase "loose lips sink ships" was used to discourage people from talking about military matters when they were within the hearing range of strangers. For international businesses the phrase might be appropriately modified to "misunderstood lips sink companies." Multinational firms will encounter enough unavoidable and unpredictable problems to be tried and tested. They need not make avoidable blunders as well.

MARKET RESEARCH

The use of properly conducted market research could have reduced or eliminated most international business blunders. Market researchers have the ability to uncover adaptation needs, potential name problems, promotional requirements, and proper market strategies. Even many of the translation blunders could have been avoided if sound research techniques had been used.

A number of the cited blunders occurred because firms tried to use the same product, name, promotional material or strategy overseas that they used at home. They were hoping that what worked well at home would also work well abroad. Although this is understandable, it is nevertheless often unrealistic. Although standardization promotes certain efficiencies, in many instances it is not a worthwhile strategy to pursue. Limitations do exist, and it is important for firms to recognize and understand this.

The use of market research enables a firm to determine its limits of standardization. The research serves two major functions: it can help a company identify what the firm can hope to accomplish and it can help a company realize what the firm should not do. Neither dimension should be overlooked.

This might best be illustrated with the experience of one European vehicle manufacturer. It tried to sell its standard line of trucks in Saudi Arabia, but sales were far below expectations. After several frustrating years, it conducted market research to understand the problems.

The results were a shock. Not only did it firmly establish that the Saudi drivers had a strong brand loyalty for a competitor's product, the research also revealed that the Saudis did not like the flat-front style of the trucks being offered (preferring the more rounded front on competing trucks), the larger service facilities introduced (seeming too impersonal and inflexible), and even the size of the truck's front seat (too small).

It turns out, Saudi drivers typically carry many passengers in their trucks and did not want to change their habits.

Few would question the value of marketing research as part of international business planning. Unfortunately, it is not an easy undertaking and is extremely complicated. Even the smallest of details must not be ignored during analysis. The data required varies with the firm, its products, and the decisions being made. Research helps a company determine whether or not to go abroad, which countries to enter, how to enter the foreign markets, and which marketing strategies to use.

CONCLUSION

This collection of international business blunders was not gathered with the intention of using it to poke fun at multinational companies or to make them appear inept. Rather, it was assembled to provide valuable, vicarious examples of business practices that should be avoided. The blunders others have experienced provide us with interesting lessons-ones surely preferable to learning through experience.

In reality, companies are generally quite competent. Considering the many ways a firm can blunder, it must be doing most things correctly just to survive. This thought was best expressed by a senior executive from General Motors when he was asked to verify one of the problems reported in this book.

He replied that although GM may have made a few errors overseas, when that very small number is compared with the many decisions made by GM, it is "a good batting average." This is true. Most firms make few serious mistakes and even fewer avoidable blunders. If they did make many blunders, they simply would not be in business long. Although numerous errors have been committed, one must realize that the mistakes have been made by many different companies over a number of years.

The fact that firms make these mistakes should not be all that surprising anyway. After all, it is not really a company that blunders, but its employees. Employees are only human, and we all make mistakes. Sometimes our errors are personal, but sometimes they are made on behalf of corporations.

It should also be noted that the blunders reported may not be totally accurate. Although most of the anecdotes have been reported in the media and efforts were made to verify them, verification has not been easy. Many corporations have been reluctant to respond to inquiries. Several firms have replied with a version of "we are sorry but we cannot provide you with the information about that possible event. The person who had been responsible for that area is no longer with the company." These statements possibly bear an added message: if one wants to remain with a firm, avoid making blunders.

Since firms do not appreciate appearing foolish, they sometimes deny a witnessed event. But as the public becomes more and more aware that all firms have made some mistakes, these denials become less necessary. There are cases, however, where reports of company blunders have proven to be false. The wrong companies have been identified or the entire story has been fictionalized. This author discovered an excellent example of a false report when trying to verify a story regarding Exxon's ventures in Thailand. The report stated that Exxon's ad "Put a tiger in your tank" failed in Thailand because the tiger does not represent power and strength there. However, a series of letters and investigations in both Asia and the United States revealed what had really happened. Overzealous competitors had deliberately planted the false story, hoping the U.S. media would pick it up. In fact, not only is the tiger a symbol of strength in Thailand, Exxon continued to use the ad effectively and was able to capture a large share of the local market.

Unfortunately, this book may also contain a few errors. Naturally, any error is greatly regretted. There certainly have been errors of omission, as this book does not cite or report every blunder ever committed.

Bibliography

Baran, Paul A.: *The Political Economy of Growth*, New York, Modern Reader Paperbacks, 1975.

Benería, Lourdes. *Gender, Development, and Globalization, Economics as if All People Mattered,* New York and London, Routledge, 2003.

Burke, Frank M., *Valuation and Valuation Planning for Closely Held Businesses*, Englewood Cliffs, NJ, Prentice Hall, 1981.

C P Mahajan: *Commerce and Business Management in Modern World*, ABD Pub, Delhi, 2008.

Commons, J. R., *Institutional Economics-Its Place in Political Economy*, The University of Wisconsin Press, Madison, Wisconsin, 1934.

Desmond, Glenn, and John A, Marcell, *Handbook of Small Business Valuation Formulas and Rules of Thumb,* Valuation Press, 1993.

G A Desmond: *International Business*, Arise, 2007.

G.S. Batra and R.C. Dangwal: *Liberalisation, Globalisation and International Business*, Deep and Deep, Delhi, 2005.

Harrigan, K. R.: *Strategies for Declining Businesses.* Lexington, MA: Heath, 1980

Howard, P.: *Business Finance*, Roseville, 1990

J N Jain and P P Singh: *Modern International Business : Theory and Practice*, Regal Pub, Delhi, 2007.

Kasper, Larry J.: *Business Valuations, Advanced Topics*, Westport, CT, Quorum Books, 1997.

Knapp, C. L.: *Commercial Damages, A Guide to Remedies in Business Litigation*, Matthew Bender, 1993.

Loomes, G.: *Current Issues in Microeconomics*, New York: St. Martin's Press, 1989.

Ranbir Singh Rana: *International Business : Contemporary Issues in Cultural Environment*, Jyoti Enterprises, New Delhi, 2008.

Index

❑❑❑